School Climate

School Climate: Measuring, Improving and Sustaining Healthy Learning Environments

Edited by

H. Jerome Freiberg

RoutledgeFalmer
Taylor & Francis Group

LONDON AND NEW YORK

First published in 1999
by Falmer Press
Reprinted 2003
by RoutledgeFalmer
11 New Fetter Lane, London, EC4P 4EE

Transferred to Digital Printing 2003

RoutledgeFalmer is an imprint of the Taylor & Francis Group

A catalogue record for this book is available from the British Library

ISBN 0 7507 0641 4 cased
ISBN 0 7507 0642 2 paper

Library of Congress Cataloging-in-Publication Data are available on request

Jacket design by Caroline Archer

Typeset in 10/12pt Times by
Graphicraft Limited, Hong Kong

Printed in Great Britain by Biddles Ltd., Guildford and King's Lynn on paper which has a specified pH value on final paper manufacture of not less than 7.5 and is therefore 'acid free'.

Contents

List of Figures and Tables

Climate instruments used in measuring school climate environments

Chapter	*Title*	*Author*	*Measures*
1	Measuring, Improving and Sustaining Healthy Learning Environments	H. Jerome Freiberg T A. Stein	1. Student drawings 2. Journal narratives
2	The Role of School and Classroom Climate in Elementary School Learning Environments	Bert P.M. Creemers Gerry J. Reezigt	3. Dutch Climate check list
3	Using Informal and Formal Measures to Create Classroom Profiles	Charles Teddlie James Meza, Jr.	
4	Using Learning Environment Assessments to Improve Classroom and School Climates	Barry Fraser	4. Individualized Classroom Environment Questionnaire Science (ICEQ) 5. Laboratory Environment Inventory (SLEI) 6. Questionnaire on Teacher Interaction (QTI) 7. Constructivist Learning Environment Survey (CLES) 8. School Level Environment Questionnaire (SLEQ)
5	Organizational Health Profiles for High Schools	Wayne K. Hoy John A. Feldman	9. OHI-Organizational Health Inventory (44-item Likert questionnaire)
6	Organizational Climate and Teacher Professionalism: Identifying Teacher Work Environment Dimensions	Sharon Conley Donna E. Muncey	10. Questionnaire items measuring work environment dimensions
7	Perceptions of Parents and Community Members as a Measure of School Climate	Carla J. Stevens Kathryn S. Sanchez	11. Houston Independent School District student/parent/community surveys
8	The Teachers' Lounge and its Role in Improving Learning Environments in Schools	Miriam Ben-Peretz Shifra Schonmann Haggai Kupermintz	Questionnaire 12. Part A: characteristics of teachers' lounges 13. Part B: Domains of impact of teachers' lounges
9	The Impact of Principal Change Facilitator Style on School and Classroom Culture	Gene E. Hall Archie A. George	14. The Change Facilitator Style Questionnaire (CFSQ)
10	The Phoenix Rises From its Ashes . . . Doesn't it?	Sam Stringfield	15. The Phoenix Academic Climate Differential
11	Three Creative Ways to Measure School Climate and Next Steps	H. Jerome Freiberg	16. Elementary to middle school transition concerns 17. High school entrance and exit surveys 18. Ambient noise effect surveys 19. 10 variables for change

Acknowledgments

I am indebted to many people for their assistance in creating this book, including Ms Ruth Silva for her able organization and her keen eye for wayward syntax and to Saundra McNeese for her administrative support in completing this book.

This text would not be possible without the expertise, assistance and support of Malcolm Clarkson who met me at Heathrow airport on the weekend to discuss the book project, Anna Clarkson, who carried the ideas forward to a complete book, and to Fiona Drysdale, and Sarah Daniels, for their diligence in effective communication and copyediting.

This book is dedicated to the work of James L. Ketelsen, former CEO of Tenneco Oil and Gas and current founder and director of Project GRAD (Graduation Really Achieves Dreams), a program that gives hope and a future to thousands of youths in the inner-cities of the United States.

Introduction

H. Jerome Freiberg

> Moving forward requires some sign posts along the way and measuring climate must be one of the beacons of educational reform. (Jerome Freiberg, 1998)

School climate is much like the air we breathe — it tends to go unnoticed until something is seriously wrong. The concern for the climate or atmosphere of the school and its effect on the student and the learning environment, has been a concern of the educational community for more than a century. School administrators at the turn of the twentieth century wrote about these concerns. Arthur Perry, principal of school No. 85 in Brooklyn, New York, wrote a book in 1908 for other school administrators entitled: *The Management of a City School*. He underlined the importance of the school surroundings to support the learner:

> Although it is quite impossible to reduce to any mathematical ratio the extent to which pupils are affected by the quality of their material environment, nevertheless it must be admitted that they are distinctly influenced by their surroundings, and that it becomes a duty of the school to provide something more than mere "housing". (p. 303)

Perry continues his discussion of the school environment with what he feels is "One of the most potent ideals . . . in school is that of *esprit de corps* . . ." He explains further by stating:

> This *esprit de corps*, school atmosphere, pride in the school and thought for its name and honor, is not to be gained in a day. It must become a matter of tradition and, once established, be handed down from one set of pupils to another. The influence of the older pupils upon the younger; of the graduates of the school upon their younger brothers and sisters, and their friends; of the parents and other citizens in the community — all this is of immense and direct value in its effect upon the conduct of pupils. It counts for much if the parents advise their friends, "Get your boy into No. 100 if you can; it is a great school"; if the alumni think that it is a special honor to graduate from the school; and if the older pupils correct the young offenders in the name of the school. (p. 304)

Perry recognizes that many agents are involved in the development of the *esprit de corps* including the teacher, parents, older students, principal, outside speakers, and enthusiastic alumni. He also describes in the section of his book devoted to *esprit de corps* the effective use of assemblies, student exhibitions, discussion forums, celebrations of special days including birthdays, student organizations, school journals, and athletic programs that all add to common spirit of the school.

Nearly a century later, formal education is still a powerful tool and with all the new twenty-first century technologies, school remains the primary vehicle for a youth's transition into adult society. Education may occur in many places — home, family, friends, television, internet, and computers — but school is the one place that provides a common meeting place for future generations across the society. School is a place where adults outside the family can interact with youth and help shape their futures through positive role modeling and on-going interactions. Schooling influences society in subtle but far reaching ways. According to United Nations data reported in *Progress of Nations* (UNICEF, 1996), the level of schooling (e.g., education) of women, particularly in developing countries, is the best predictor for birth rates, increase in family income, and better child health and nutrition. Dictatorships and totalitarian regimes usually focus on schools to control the populace. In a democracy, school becomes the great socializer and preparer for entry into the citizenship of a country.

It is predicted by economists, that education will be the next great global battle ground. The ability of a country to create and disseminate new knowledge and utilize existing knowledge and intellectual resources will determine the economic and social well-being of a country. A nation's ability to enhance its education systems and schools will be the pathway to this well-being. Knowing how this place called school enables or inhibits the learning process is an important factor in the success of any educational organization and the future success of a country. Keeping a pulse on the wrist of the school enables those responsible for the well-being of our youth to respond to changes in the greater society. Checking the learning rhythm of a school and the conditions that support it, enable schools to be a protective and resilient factor in the lives of children and youth rather than another barrier (Freiberg, 1994).

The 1950s saw a revived interest in the issue of school environment. Halpin and Croft (1963) called it — the organizational climate of school. They developed an instrument called the Organizational Climate Descriptive Questionnaire (OCDQ). This questionnare began the process of looking at the school climate and organization with an emphasis on teacher and principal behaviors as seen from the teachers' perspective.

Halpin and Croft identified four characteristics of teacher behavior including, (i) Disengagement (uncommitted to the task); (ii) Hindrance (teachers perceive they are burdened by paper work and other non-instructional activites); (iii) Esprit (satisfaction with social and professional needs and accomplishments); and (iv) Intimacy (positive relations with colleagues). The four characteristics of principal behavior including, (i) Aloofness (principal keeps social distance from faculty and staff); (ii) Production Emphasis (principal does not incorporate faculty feedback and uses, gives little latitude); (iii) Trust (acts as a role model for the type of behavior expected in the school); and (iv) Consideration (relates well to faculty and responds to their needs). Hoy, Tarter and Kottkamp (1991) revised the original eight dimensions into six including supportive principal behavior, directive principal behavior, and restrictive principal behavior. Teacher factors included, Collegial Teacher Beahvior, Intimate Teacher Behavior, and Disengaged Teacher Behavior.

The OCDQ and their later revisions, OCDQ-RE (Revision Elementary) and OCDQ-SE (Revision Secondary) were developed to measure changes in the organizational climate as perceived by teachers and establish a school climate profile which followed the continuum from an open to closed organization.

Since Halpin and Croft's original work, researchers have greatly expanded the notion of climate through measures used to identify the disparate elements that make up the learning environment. School climate has multiple dimensions encompassing organizational, environmental, social emotional, structural and linguistic elements. The sources of data collection in schools have expanded from exclusive use of surveys (mostly with teachers) to surveys and interviews with student focus groups; to video taped discussions; to town meetings with students, parents teachers and others; and from fixed category to open ended observations measures in a move to triangulate and verify findings. A recent case in point is an inner-city high school in the mid-west where student climate data was collected from 541 9th–12th grader students. It showed several areas of school climate improvement from the previous year but one significant area of decline. The student survey indicated a decline in teacher support of students. In focus group meetings with small groups of students conducted by the administrative team, the third-party survey findings were confirmed. The students articulated their feelings that teachers were not providing the additional help they needed in their content areas to enable them to achieve success. Both sets of findings were shared with the faculty, staff and administration. A discussion among the faculty and administration of the climate issues as perceived by students resulted in action plans to provide tutorials before school and during school time. It is interesting to note that after-school tutorials were not possible due to safety concerns for students who had to walk home after dark.

School: The Societal Meeting Place

With all its problems and challenges, school remains the most universal connector in the rites of passage between childhood and adulthood. With only slight variations, schools around the world are remarkably similar. The organizational structures of schooling vary only slightly from one country to the next. Schools tend to have a set group of students with one teacher, fixed times for instruction, set times for starting and stopping the school day, physical facilities that are factory-like in appearance, recognizable from one country to another, and administrative structures that are mostly hierarchical. Teacher certification is normally established by outside professional organizations or state governmental agencies and once certified, teachers are prescribed curriculum to deliver to their learners. The commonalties continue with the ways in which schools judge the learning of their charges, usually through measures that focus on grades and tests. Many schools are required to give state or national tests that are used to sort and place students on potential career tracks (e.g., college-bound, academic, to trade-bound, vocational). Since the early 1990s, international measures have been developed by countries to compare the achievement of their students against those of other nations. In the United States, state by state comparisons are also made on national standardized tests and within local schools, district administrators compare the achievement results of students from school to school. The problems of schooling are also universal: student apathy as evident by lack of attendance (truancy); leaving school before reaching a specified age (dropping out); use of stimulants that diminish participation (drugs, drinking alcohol and tobacco abuse); and the notion that too many students are "tourists" passing through rather than "citizens", active learners in the classroom (Freiberg, 1996).

Multiple Measures of Climate in Schools

Given this universality of the organization and role of schools and schooling across the globe, *School Climate: Measuring, Improving and Sustaining Healthy Learning Environments* has drawn from the international community to broaden the scope of the book. Authors from four nations are represented in this book, including Australia, Israel, The Netherlands and the United States. *School Climate* provides 18 climate instruments and approaches to measure climate from multiple perspectives including, student, teacher, parent, community and administrator perspectives. The table on page ix displays the types of instruments found in each chapter of the book. The measures also include viewpoints that recognize and validate the complexity of school organizations and look at places, in and out of school, where people congregate, all of which frame the health of the learning environment. This book is designed to meet the needs of school and district administrators, teachers, school board and community members who want answers to the questions: *How Are We Doing? How Healthy Is Our Learning Environment?*

Using the Climate Instruments

School Climate is the result of national and international efforts to improve the quality of life in school for students and educators. Each of the instruments may be used by individuals, schools or districts for *non-commercial* use. The authors of this book have given their permission for their measures to be used by educators in their local environment. However, any publication in print or electronic forms of the measures would require written permission by the appropriate authors.

Measuring climate from a variety of perspectives was a goal in the original design of the book and has been realized with the inclusion of multiple instruments and with the permission to allow educators to use the instruments in their local settings. Before change and a responsive action plan can be formulated, some evidence of what is occurring within the school and classroom settings needs to be determined. *School Climate* focuses on the health of the learning environment and identifies areas that need to be improved, as well as areas that need continued support or significant rethinking. The measures should provide the necessary tools to determine the level of health of a school. The climate instruments in *School Climate*, measure elements of school and classroom life from the teachers' lounge to the cafeteria, from hallways and playgrounds to bathrooms, from the traditional classroom to constructivists classroom. These measures are intended to be used as benchmarks for growth rather than hammers for change. The book provides strategies for teacher, parent, student and administrator teams to use the ideas and instruments as a basis for dialogue about what is important for each shareholder in the learning process.

There is a renewed interest in creating healthy learning environments — we trust *School Climate: Measuring, Improving and Sustaining Healthy Learning Environments* will add to the understanding of climate and the effects it has on those who call school a place to learn, work, share ideas and interact with others. The following is a synopsis of each of the chapters in the book.

Chapter Overviews

Chapter 1: Measuring, Improving and Sustaining Healthy Learning Environments, H. Jerome Freiberg, University of Houston and T.A. Stein, SUNY, Plattsburg.

This chapter provides a conceptual overview of the issues related to measuring, improving and sustaining healthy learning environments. It looks at why school climate is so important to the people who work, teach and learn in schools. It describes the differences between direct and indirect climate measures and gives uncommon examples from student drawings, and teacher and student journals that may be incorporated to assess the climate of a school or classroom. The chapter sets the framework for the multiplicity of climate factors and measures that are needed to develop a school climate profile and the strategies educators may use to improve or sustain healthy learning environments.

Chapter 2: The Role of School and Classroom Climate in Elementary School Learning Environments, Bert P.M. Creemers and Gerry J. Reezigt, Rijsuniversiteit, Groningen, The Netherlands.

In this chapter the authors focus on the role of and the relationship between climate factors and the effectiveness factors viewed within the framework of a School Effectiveness Plan. They propose that school climate factors need to be separated from school effectiveness factors in exploring their influence on educational outcomes. They need to be viewed as complimentary, but not similar. Although they influence educational outcomes when they are complementary, each group maintains its internal conceptual consistency. Creemers and Reezigt review the theories and research in school climate studies and present a synthesis of effectivenes research. They conclude by providing a model of a check list used in Dutch schools, which can be used by schools to begin the conversation of change.

> *Chapter 3: Using Informal and Formal Measures to Create Classroom Profiles*, Charles Teddlie, Louisana State University and James Meza Jr., University of New Orleans, Louisana.

The authors provide examples in this chapter of operationalizing an integrated approach which studies school climate and school effectiveness factors together. They provide guidelines for creating profiles of a schools' learning environment on various dimensions; management, instructional, and social psychological climate, based on teacher observation. The methodology used merges the principles of both teacher effectiveness research and school effectiveness research, using formal and informal measures to provide an overall picture. They present research results from two schools involved in a national reform program. Only one of the two schools is successful in restructuring efforts. The success or failure is measured against observed benchmark data from effective and ineffective schools. They conclude by providing research results from a different school district, currently using profiling as a means of beginning the restructuring process.

> *Chapter 4: Using Learning Environment Assessments to Improve Classroom and School Climates*, Barry Fraser, Curtin University of Technology, Australia.

The author focuses on issues of "perception", ideal and preferred, of the main participants in the educational process — the teacher and the students. Fraser concentrates on exploring the differing perspectives of the same situation, i.e. teacher and students' perceptions of the classroom environment. Fraser uses multiple teacher and student perspectives to enhance instructional outcome achievement by integrating varied components to achieve congruence of approach. He provides five instruments for use in assessing perspectives, four from the student perspective and one from a teacher perspective. The process of ensuring instrument validity, reliability and replicability is described. The chapter also provides results from research studies conducted in Australia and the United Kingdom.

> *Chapter 5: Organizational Health Profiles for High Schools,* Wayne Hoy, Ohio State University and John Feldman, Cranford Public Schools, New Jersey.

The authors of this chapter use health as a metaphor for examining school climate. School climate is in turn related to achieving three identified school outcomes:

student achievement, teacher commitment and faculty trust. They distinguish between school culture and school climate and explain their reasons for choosing to concentrate on climate as it allows for mapping and measurement, whereas culture tends to be too abstract. In order to view school climate in terms of its health, the authors devised the Organizational Health Inventory. They describe and explain the process they used in constructing the Inventory. A brief but succinct review is provided of the various perspectives on organizational health, and an explanation of their choice (Parsons, 1953) to develop theoretical underpinnings and conceptualizing of the Inventory.

Hoy and Feldman present a 44-item Likert questionnaire, resulting from an initial pilot study and a re-testing in 78 secondary schools. The Inventory provides data to place the health of the school along a continuum from "Very Healthy" to "Unhealthy" schools. The authors conclude by recommending the instrument to practitioners and researchers as a reliable, systematic and simple diagnostic tool to provide baseline data which can then be used to implement site-specific strategies.

> *Chapter 6: Organizational Climate and Teacher Professionalism: Identifying Teacher Work Environment Dimensions*, Sharon Conley, University of California, Santa Barbara and Donna E. Muncey, St. Mary's College of Maryland.

Conley and Muncy discuss the issue of teacher perception in a different context from that of classroom immediacy — the overall teaching work environment context, which includes the classroom, but also other areas that impact on the working life of the teacher. They explore the issue of "teacher as professional" and identify the variables in the work environment that may enhance or detract from their professional status. They conclude by providing an illustrative, quantitative case study profile of one school. The study is based on work environment variables they have identified as "prominent dimensions" of the school work environment. Alongside this case study, they also provide data from four other schools in the same district to round out the analytic options.

> *Chapter 7: Perceptions of Parents and Community Members as a Measure of School Climate*, Carla J. Stevens and Kathryn S. Sanchez, Houston Independent School District.

This chapter turns to parent and community perspectives and perceptions of school climate as an important issue in exploring the achievement of school outcomes. The study was conducted as part of the Houston Independent School District (HISD) efforts to evaluate and improve effectiveness of the HISD public schools. Survey results were to be used to base planning and operational decisions to improve school climate. The survey was developed by the HISD and administered to students, parents, and community and business members within the Houston ISD.

The survey was based on dimensions considered to enhance students' school experience — for example, student achievement; decision making processes; parent involvement in the educational program; safe school environment and school as a community member. The conceptual framework was taken from a review of effective schools research, specifically research on school climate. The results from the parent and community survey administered during the 1991–92; 1992–93; 1993–94 school years are reported and discussed in their chapter.

> *Chapter 8: The Teachers' Lounge and Its Role in Improving the Learning Environment in Schools*, Miriam Ben-Peretz, Shifra Schonmann and Haggai Kupermintz, Israel.

This chapter explores what the authors call "uncharted terrritory" — the Teachers' Lounge. The authors question its place as part of the workplace environment for teachers, and whether it is a part of the school or, merely, a transitional place to have coffee between classes? If a part of the workplace environment — does it affect the school climate and in turn affect student learning outcomes? Does it have its own climate? The authors detail the research project carried out in 19 schools in Israel. They developed and administered a two-part questionnaire (based on social, political and work dimensions) — which incorporated teacher perceptions of the climate in the teachers' lounge and their discernment of the influence of the lounge on school life. A total of 409 elementary school teachers (95 per cent female) responded. Of the respondents, 84 per cent of the teachers from urban schools had a mean of 12 years teaching experience. On average they reported a five-day work week and visited the lounges more than twice a day. To gauge the relationship between teachers' lounge climate and student achievement, data on students' academic achievement in two standardized tests, one in math and one in reading comprehension was collected for the 19 schools in the study. The authors concluded that while they could not offer a conclusive causal interpretation for their findings, they conjectured that the relationship between teachers' perceptions of lounges and student achievement is reciprocal. Positive perception facilitates professionalism and leads to high achievement and, in turn, strengthens the social function of the lounge.

> *Chapter 9: The Impact of Principal Change Facilitator Style on School and Classroom Culture*, Gene E. Hall, University of Northern Colorado, Greeley and Archie A. George, University of Idaho.

This chapter presents a conceptual framework for exploring and analyzing principal leadership — specifically as a change facilitator. The authors maintain that leaders make a difference regardless of what they do or do not do in setting climate in the school. Teachers' perception and interpretation of principal activities lead to the construction of school culture and, to a certain extent, classroom culture. They review the concept of "leader", "leadership" and "change facilitator style" in the literature. The concept of "change facilitator style" is examined in detail and its praxis implications are discussed. This led them to the development of the "Change Facilitator Style Questionnaire" instrument based on the change facilitator style dimensions identified. The conceptual framework, the scales used, and its practical application are explained in the chapter. They conclude by reiterating the power of the role of the principal in influencing the direction of implementation of innovations by teachers, and stress the caution necessary in the use of the questionnaire. The process is a people process, hence respect, responsibility and confidentiality are crucial in the administration and interpretation of such surveys.

Chapter 10: The Phoenix Rises From Its Ashes . . . Doesn't it? Sam Stringfield, Johns Hopkins University.

Sam Stringfield describes a change situation involving administrators and teachers attempting to change student outcomes for the better. His account of an inner-city school's seven-year effort to revitalize itself involves the principal as leader, directing and influencing the direction of instructional change — leading to the decision to use a private school instructional program with proven credentials. He describes the nature of the collaboration process between the two schools — one private and successful and the other attempting to emulate that success. The reasons for the initial success in the collaboration are explicated through examining the roles of the various participants. Then comes the watershed mark — the sustaining of success. Stringfield concludes by discussing why the "success" was not maintained. However, this conclusion may not be the final word — as another change cycle amongst the staff at the client school seemed to be in process.

Chapter 11: Three Creative Ways to Measure School Climate and Next Steps, H. Jerome Freiberg, University of Houston.

Feedback about individual and organizational health of a school learning community is a necessary component for school reform and improvement efforts. The quality of teaching and learning is a reflection of many complex factors but without continuous and varied sources of feedback, improvement efforts are eroded by a lack of history of accomplishments and a sense of direction. In practice, few climate measures tap students as a source of feedback. However, by third grade, most students could tell you if they like or hate school, which teachers are caring and if they are learning. Most third graders have spent more than 5,000 hours in classrooms (pre-k through 3rd grade). They represent a critical basis upon which to measure the health of a school and the effects of school reform efforts, in addition to other more traditional voices in the school (teachers, and administrators). Student climate transitional concerns from elementary (grades 5 or 6) students moving to middle school, and middle school students (grade 8) moving to high school, based on interviews and survey results, were analyzed and provided to school personnel to create plans to respond to the needs of the learners. The chapter and book close with *10 Variables for Change*. Accompanying each variable are indicators that help define the variable. The variables and indicators for change are designed to guide the reader in planning the use of the climate measures presented throughout the book.

Conclusions

Any one factor will not in itself determine a school's climate and its influence on the learning of students. However, it is the interaction of school and classroom climate factors that create a fabric of support that enable members of the school community to teach and learn at their optimum levels. While climate is mostly an affective or feeling element of learning, it has clear implications for achievement and academic well being. Lasting change comes from the little things in schools and classrooms. There are many ways to measure change in school climate but without some sense of what was, it will be very difficult to conclude what is and what should be. Moving forward requires some sign posts along the way and measuring climate must be one of the beacons of educational change (Freiberg, 1998).

References

FREIBERG, H.J. (1994) 'Understanding resilience: Implications for inner-city schools and their near and far communities,' in Wang M.C. and Gordon, E.W. *Educational Resilience in Inner-city America: Challenges and Prospects*, Hillsdale: Lawrence Erlbaum.

FREIBERG, H.J. (1996) 'From tourists to citizens in the classroom', *Educational Leadership*, **51**, 1, pp. 32–7.

FREIBERG, H.J. (1998) 'Three creative ways to measure school climate', *Educational Leadership*, **56**, 1, pp. 22–6.

HALPIN, A.W. and CROFT, D. (1963) *The Organizational Climate of Schools*, Chicago, Illinois: Midwest Administrative Center, University of Chicago.

HOY, W., TARTER, J.C. and KOTTKAMP, B. (1991) *Open School/Heathy Schools: Measuring Organizational Climate*, London: Sage.

PERRY, A. (1908) *The Management of a City School*, New York: Macmillan.

UNICEF (1996) *The Progress of Nations: The Nations of the World Ranked According to their Achievements in Child Health, Nutrition, Education, Family Planning and Progress for Woman*, New York, NY: United Nations.

Chapter 1

Measuring, Improving and Sustaining Healthy Learning Environments

H. Jerome Freiberg and T.A. Stein

Why is Climate so Important to Learning?

School climate is the heart and soul of a school. It is about that essence of a school that leads a child, a teacher, an administrator, a staff member to love the school and to look forward to being there each school day. *School Climate* is about that quality of a school that helps each individual feel personal worth, dignity and importance, while simultaneously helping create a sense of belonging to something beyond ourselves. The climate of a school can foster resilience or become a risk factor in the lives of people who work and learn in a place called school.

A school's climate can define the quality of a school that creates healthy learning places; nurtures children's and parents' dreams and aspirations; stimulates teachers' creativity and enthusiasm, and elevates all of its members. It is about the special quality of a school that the voices of the children and youth (described in *Freedom to Learn*, Rogers and Freiberg, 1994) speak to when they explain why they love their schools:

> "All my teachers show respect to all of the students in the classes, and so we show respect to them".

> "They treat you like family".

> "If I was you, I would come to this school because, well, it's like family".

> "This is just really our home. . . ."

> "On a personal basis, they [the teachers] go to each individual and ask how you are doing. . . . It's hard. You can tell by their faces at the end of the day. . . . Like they're real tired, but they are still willing to help you out".

> "You have to start with the students. If you can somehow make them feel like they have a place in the world, then they would want to learn more about how to live in that world".

"I think our freedom is more freedom of expression than just being wild and having no self-control. It's like we have a purpose, and so our freedom is freedom to express ourselves".

"Most of the teachers here really care about me. They help not just with the subjects they teach, but with other subjects and personal things. It is different than other schools where they tell you to get your mind off anything that is not their subject".

"Most of the teachers want us to study and do well in school so that we can do well in life. If I dropped out of school, my teachers would be disappointed".

"The teachers care about your grades; they care about the whole class. They help you out a lot. . . . You can go up to them, they listen to you, they support you. They do things out of the ordinary that teachers don't have to do. . . . They just don't teach you math, they find out how you are doing. If they have an off period, you're welcome to come talk with them. Even, I mean, problems with your schoolwork or just problems like at home, they try to help".

"She'll give you a chance. When you do something wrong, she'll let you do it over again until you get it right . . . [In] other schools you don't get a chance, they would be yelling at you. They just tell you that you are suspended. They won't even talk to you. You know, Ms. Jones, she'll never let you give up".

"When you are at regular school, you do something wrong, they'd either say, 'You got detention,' or 'You have suspension,' but at this school, they try to help you out with your problems. This is a school of opportunity". (pp. 3–16)

It is also about a seventh grade class, in an inner-city middle school, who feel the responsibility for their learning that they don't need a teacher to supervise their actions. This is put to the test when their teacher is absent and the substitute did not show. A student journal reflects that day:

"I feel lucky today because the day has just started and we have already been trusted in something we have never been trusted on, being alone. It is 8:15 and everything is cool. Nothing is even wrong. . . ."

When students become citizens of the school, they take responsibility for their actions and those of others. On the October day that Sergio wrote about, a student sent the attendance to the office, while another student reviewed the homework with the class and started classroom presentations scheduled for the day. When the substitute teacher finally arrived, the students were engaged in learning. They had been taking responsibility for the classroom operations since September and, in a sense, were being prepared for this experience. What occurred in the school or classroom before the event to create a climate that said it was all right to take the initiative to learn without an adult being present? What factors support the students' decision to embrace a norm that encourages order rather than chaos, quality of work rather than the prevailing norm for doing the minimum? A program entitled Consistency Management and Cooperative Discipline (CMCD) (see Freiberg, Stein and Huang, 1995; Freiberg, 1996, 1999 for additional explanation of the program) had been in place for two years at the middle school. The CMCD program supported students being citizens of the learning environment rather than tourists — taking responsibility for their actions and the actions of others. The program changed the existing climate that was controlling and untrusting to one that was supportive and gave students opportunities for experiencing the skills necessary for self-discipline.

Climate as Metaphor

If I say "School climate, what is the first word that comes to your mind?" the usual word association from educators is "feel", "well-being", "health", "learning environment", "safety", (both physical and psychological) "openness", and "caring" within schools and classrooms. On the Internet searching the term "school climate" brings over five million matches. Narrowing those down with greater detail in the search will provide more than 145 sites that relate directly to the topics presented in this book. The number of sites has tripled in the last few years. When defining the climate of a school we tend to use metaphors similar to the descriptions listed above. A school is not an organic being in the biological sense but it does have the qualities of a living organism in the organizational and cultural sense. The physical structure of schools can have direct influences on the health of individuals who work and learn there. The amount of light, noise, chemicals, and air quality are part of most work environments — schools are no different. Beyond the physical nature of schools there are other elements that reflect the way people interact and this interaction produces a social fabric that permeates the working and learning condition.

Climate: Organizational or Cultural?

School Climate: Measuring, Improving and Sustaining Healthy Learning Environments, takes both an organizational climate and cultural view of schools with the former more predominant in the book. Hoy, Tarter and Kottkamp (1991) distinguish between climate and culture in how schools are viewed, with school or organizational climate being viewed from a psychological perspective and school culture viewed from an anthropological perspective. *School Climate* derives its knowledge from both fields of inquiry. Some authors within the book provide perspective and climate measures that can quantify elements of school organization through validated survey instruments, while other authors examine the school culture and use stories, discussions, cases, student drawings, teacher and student journals, interviews, video and ambient noise check lists to describe what is occurring in schools and classrooms.

This book provides more than one pathway to help those most directly involved in schools to determine the health of the learning environment. If one believes in continuous improvement, then a healthy climate for learning is best determined by those in the environment who can draw from multiple sources of data and feedback, using measures or approaches that reflect the values and norms of the near and far school community and respond to pressing issues and questions.

National School Climate Report Cards

The issue of school climate has been catapulted to national educational prominence. As the world moves into the information age, then knowledge more than manufacturing becomes the driving force behind educational policies. The chairman of the State Board of Education in Texas described how a two fold increase in oil prices would bring an additional 26 billion dollars into the state. However, if every high school graduate in the state added four years more of education, they would also bring 26 billion dollars into the state. The learning environment of students emerges as a much more significant economic as well as social and educational issue for the new millennium. Moving beyond high school to higher education requires a different learning environment and needs to start very early in a child's schooling experience. Figure 1.1 shows the ratings and rankings by *Education Week* (1997) of the schools in each state in the United States. They used *class size, ratio of pupils to teachers in secondary schools, school organization and school safety* as criteria for giving a grade from A to F on how positive the climate was. Of the larger states, Texas with a score of **78** was ranked in the top six of all states, with California being ranked near the bottom with a score of **62**. The state with schools with the best climate was Vermont (**87**) and the worst was Utah (**61**). *Teacher Magazine* (1998) reported another climate "report card" using class size and student engagement (student absenteeism, tardiness, and classroom misbehavior) criteria. Maine scored at the top of this list with a score of **81**, Vermont was fifth with a score of **77**. Texas was given a score of **75** and California a "failing" grade of **51**. No state received a score of **90** or better in either report card.

State Policy and School Climate

Many of the factors identified by the two report cards (class size and teacher/student ratios) are beyond the control of many local schools as they are determined by state policy based on per pupil funding. Policy and funding issues at the state level can influence the climate of schools at the local level. Texas in the late 1980s, for example, began to "roll-out" reductions in class size to 22:1, beginning at the kindergarten and first grade levels (5–6 year olds) and expanded this reduction in

Figure 1.1 State by state: School climate grades

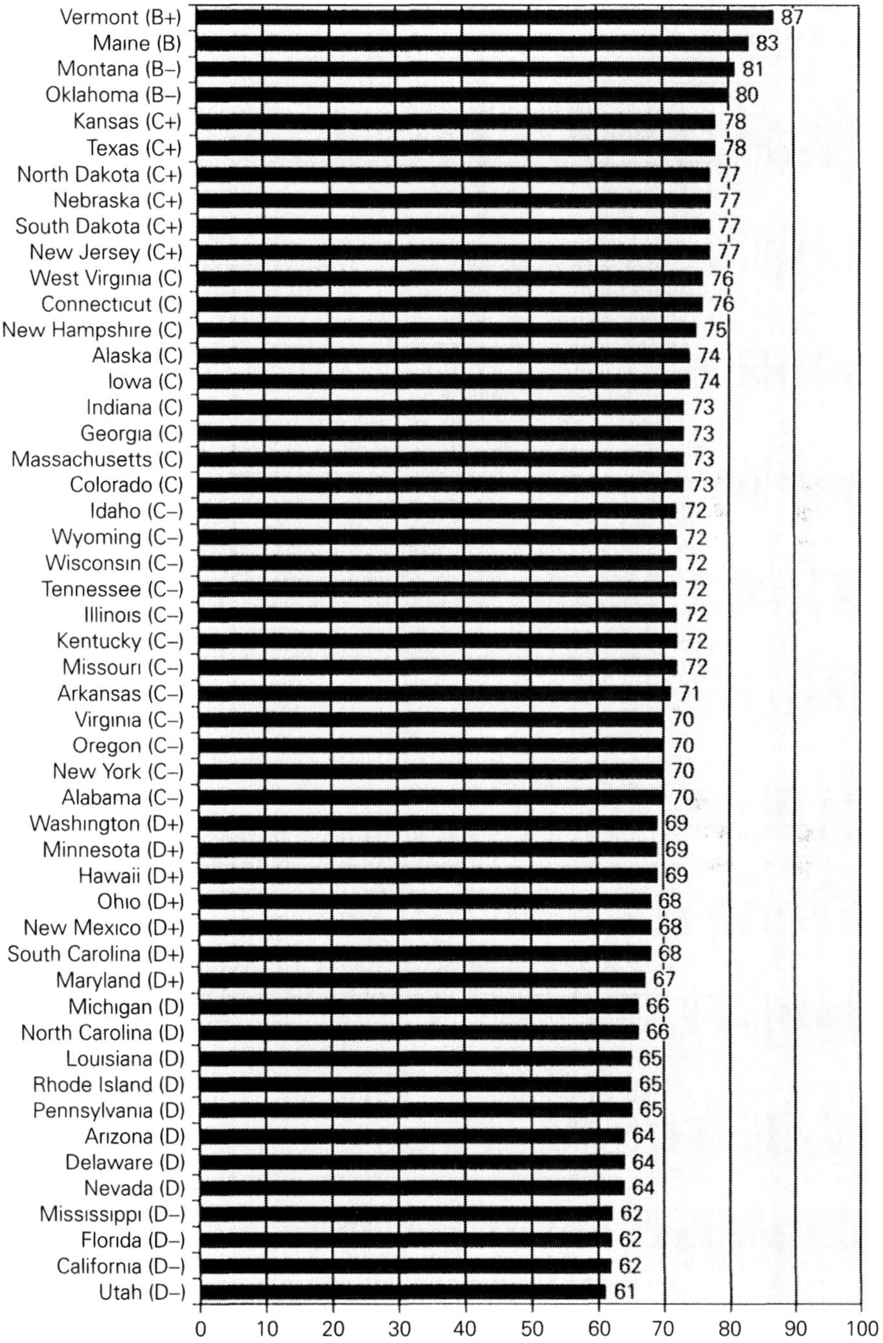

State (grade)	Score
Vermont (B+)	87
Maine (B)	83
Montana (B–)	81
Oklahoma (B–)	80
Kansas (C+)	78
Texas (C+)	78
North Dakota (C+)	77
Nebraska (C+)	77
South Dakota (C+)	77
New Jersey (C+)	77
West Virginia (C)	76
Connecticut (C)	76
New Hampshire (C)	75
Alaska (C)	74
Iowa (C)	74
Indiana (C)	73
Georgia (C)	73
Massachusetts (C)	73
Colorado (C)	73
Idaho (C–)	72
Wyoming (C–)	72
Wisconsin (C–)	72
Tennessee (C–)	72
Illinois (C–)	72
Kentucky (C–)	72
Missouri (C–)	72
Arkansas (C–)	71
Virginia (C–)	70
Oregon (C–)	70
New York (C–)	70
Alabama (C–)	70
Washington (D+)	69
Minnesota (D+)	69
Hawaii (D+)	69
Ohio (D+)	68
New Mexico (D+)	68
South Carolina (D+)	68
Maryland (D+)	67
Michigan (D)	66
North Carolina (D)	66
Louisiana (D)	65
Rhode Island (D)	65
Pennsylvania (D)	65
Arizona (D)	64
Delaware (D)	64
Nevada (D)	64
Mississippi (D–)	62
Florida (D–)	62
California (D–)	62
Utah (D–)	61

Axis: 0 10 20 30 40 50 60 70 80 90 100

Source: 'Quality counts'. A supplement to *Education Week*. Jan. 22, 1997 Vol. XVI

class size each year until grade four (10–11 year olds). After a decade of smaller classes, changes in class size which occurred over several years, allowed for the orderly hiring of teachers and building of additional classrooms. In 1998, California which has suffered under nominal support for schools owing to taxing limitations, mandated a reduction in class size in one year. It will take several years to make the transition in construction and hiring from large classes (35–40 students) to smaller, 22 students per class. The change in California also comes at a time when demographics of an ageing teaching profession are resulting in higher levels of retirements, resulting in shortages of teachers. This problem will only grow, as it is estimated by the US Department of Education that nearly two million new teachers will be needed in the United States during the next fifteen years. This problem is not unique to the United States. The ageing teaching population throughout Europe and Japan will result in a transformation of the teaching profession. The climate of a school may be affected by many factors.

Given the trend in the United States and other nations to quantify everything, one has to be somewhat cautious that these "report cards" do not become another source of stress for school-based educators. However, with some persistence and care, these state-by-state comparison reports cards could become a positive source for improving some climate factors in states that need significant reductions in school and classroom size and teacher to student ratios. There is a tendency for those in education and the larger community, to seek one solution, one definition and one approach to a problem. School climate is a multifaceted endeavor and how one sees a problem also shapes its definition.

Research on School Climate

During the last twenty years there has been extensive research on identifying the factors that comprise the quality of a school (see Brookover, Beady, Flood, Schweitzer and Weisenbaker, 1979; Rutter, Maughan, Mortimore, Ouston and Smith, 1979; Lightfoot, 1983; Hoy, Tarter and Kottkamp, 1991; Teddlie and Stringfield, 1993; Rogers and Freiberg, 1994; Fashola and Slavin, 1998). The research has been guided by many different voices. These range from talking about schools as if they were akin to factories, identifying the characteristics of the inputs necessary to obtain the desired outputs, to talking about schools as if they were akin to families, stressing the dynamics of caring which ground the kind of positive familial relationships which lead to healthy growth.

If stories and student and teacher perceptions form the spirit of climate, then research methodology known as meta-analysis, in which findings of many research studies are aggregated, can produce another perspective on the framework of school climate. A meta-analysis reported by Wang, Haertel and Walberg (1997) found that "When averaged together the different kinds of instruction and climate had nearly as much impact in learning as the student aptitude categories" (p. 205). They created a database consisting of 11,000 statistical findings from which they determined the most significant influences on learning. They found 28 categories of learning influences with *classroom management*, the most significant influence, followed by metacognitive and cognitive processes, home environment and parental support and student teacher social interactions. Social behavior attributes, motivational affective attributes, peer group, quality of instruction, school culture and classroom climate rounded out the top learning influences. State and school level policies, school organization and demographics had the least influence on learning. The implications are significant in that this meta-analysis, combined with stories and learner perceptions derived from other sources, triangulate to support the idea that climate is a real factor in the lives of learners and that it is measurable, malleable and material to those that work and learn in schools.

Multiple Perspectives of Climate

The last twenty years has seen an extended argument as to whose voice is really the true voice. What has been lost amid these debates is the capacity to glean truth from among the diversity of voices. Let us use art as an example. As one stands viewing a painting or a sculpture, one rarely views the artistic piece merely from one position, we move about it, looking at it from different lighting and physical perspectives in order to realize its complete value. So it must be with our study of schools. One perspective is simply not enough to see the breadth of the whole process. It is precisely through a dialogue of many different voices that we can come to a fuller understanding of the complex dynamics that play out in the kinds of schools the students and teachers spoke of earlier. This book offers just such a dialogue. Each of the authors in this book talk about different aspects of what it takes to develop, maintain and measure the health of a school. Each author's voice resonates with past voices, carrying on particular traditions or perspectives about schooling. Just as viewing a painting or a sculpture from various perspectives adds to a richer appreciation of the artistic quality of the piece, so does viewing schooling from each of these varying traditions add to a richer understanding and appreciation of the essence of a healthy school.

In 1670, the Dutch artist, Jan Steen, who was known for his accurate depiction of everyday life in The Netherlands, presented the heart of school climate in a painting entitled: "A School for Boys and Girls". Steen depicts a serene headmaster seated at a table and an engaged headmistress writing in a book surrounded by students in various stages of chaos. One child is standing on a table and singing, two others are fighting, three girls are reading one book on the floor, two boys are engaged in writing, other children are playing, one child is sleeping, and one child is standing behind the teacher making faces. This picture of classroom school climate is in contrast to Issack van Ostade's painting, "The Classroom" (1664). Ostade depicts all the students engaged in writing and reading individually or in small groups and the headmaster reading a paper presented to him by one of the children.

Interest and concern for the environment of schools and classrooms was not lost on educators in the late 1800s and early 1900s. In 1892, Larkin Dunton wrote:

> it is quite possible for a school to be too quiet. . . . But a sharp distinction is to be made between the necessary noise of earnest industry and the wilful confusion resulting from unrestrained mischief. (p. 324)

Perry (1908), a school principal at Public School No. 85 in Brooklyn, New York, described in *The Management of a City School*, the importance of the school's physical environment. He talks about the need to provide "something more than mere housing", the need for *esprit de corps* which is taken from French, it literally means "spirit of the body". A modern working definition from Webster's dictionary for *esprit de corps* is, "A common spirit of enthusiasm, a liveliness of mind and expression among the members of the group". How does one begin to measure school climate let alone improve or sustain it?

Measuring Climate: Directly and Indirectly

Many measures of school climate are presented in this book and you will see there are two distinct categories — direct and indirect. Direct measures refer to the fact that someone must go forward and interact with others to collect climate data. The use of climate surveys, classroom observations, interviews, video taping, journal narratives, student drawings, focus groups and the like, require interactions that in some ways insert the data collector into the daily lives of those whose working conditions we are seeking to be informed. There are degrees of directness and intervention based on the level of interactions needed to solicit a response.

Direct Measures

Two unique, less invasive, examples of direct measures are student drawings and journal narratives by teachers and/or students. They can provide a rich source of data but are seldom used to determine school or classroom climate. Young children present a particular problem in finding age-appropriate sources to solicit accurate information about how they feel about school. Reading and comprehension levels on questionnaires are too difficult for most children below third grade and interviews with a stranger may result in the student providing answers they think the data collector wants. Student drawings enable young children to depict how they feel about their environment. While someone needs to solicit the students to draw a picture, the request and their response is usually open-ended. The three drawings presented in Figure 1.2, show distinct differences in how students see their classroom. I collected drawings 1.2a and 1.2c in the mid 1970s and 1.2b in the 90s. In Drawing 1.2a, a second grader creates a picture with a great distance between the class and the teacher. This is in contrast to Drawing 1.2b where the student draws all the students surrounding their teacher Mrs. Grant. Drawing 1.2c shows a class in which corporal punishment is used. The student draws an area for "spanking" located in the right side of the drawing. The use of drawings with children has been

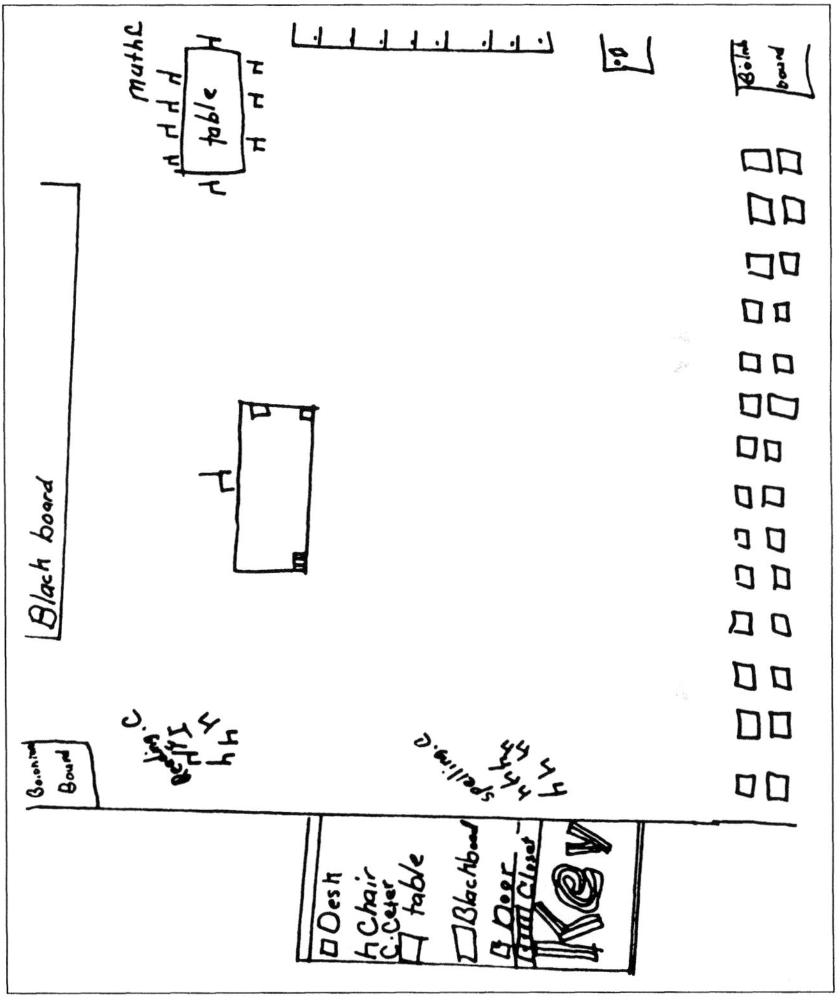

Figure 1.2a Student drawing illustrating how they see their classroom

Figure 1.2b Student drawing illustrating how they see their classroom

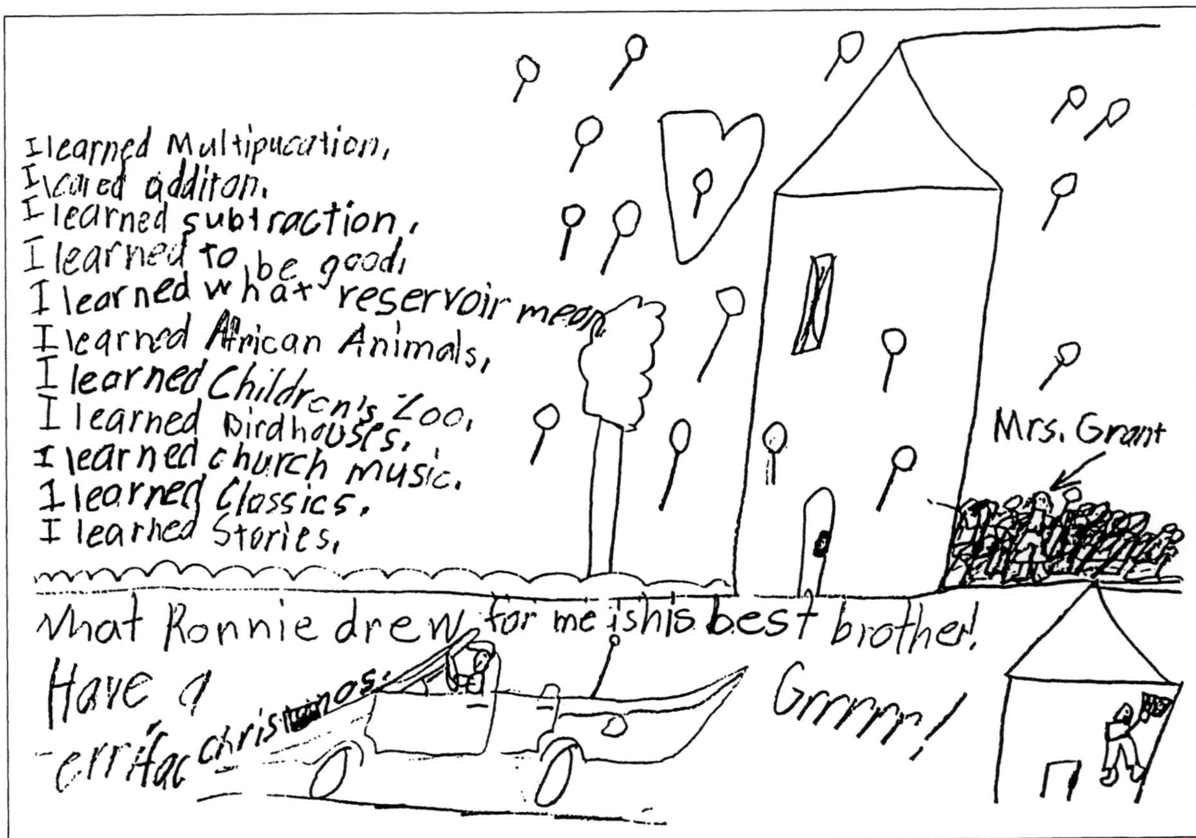

Figure 1.2c Student drawing illustrating how they see their classroom

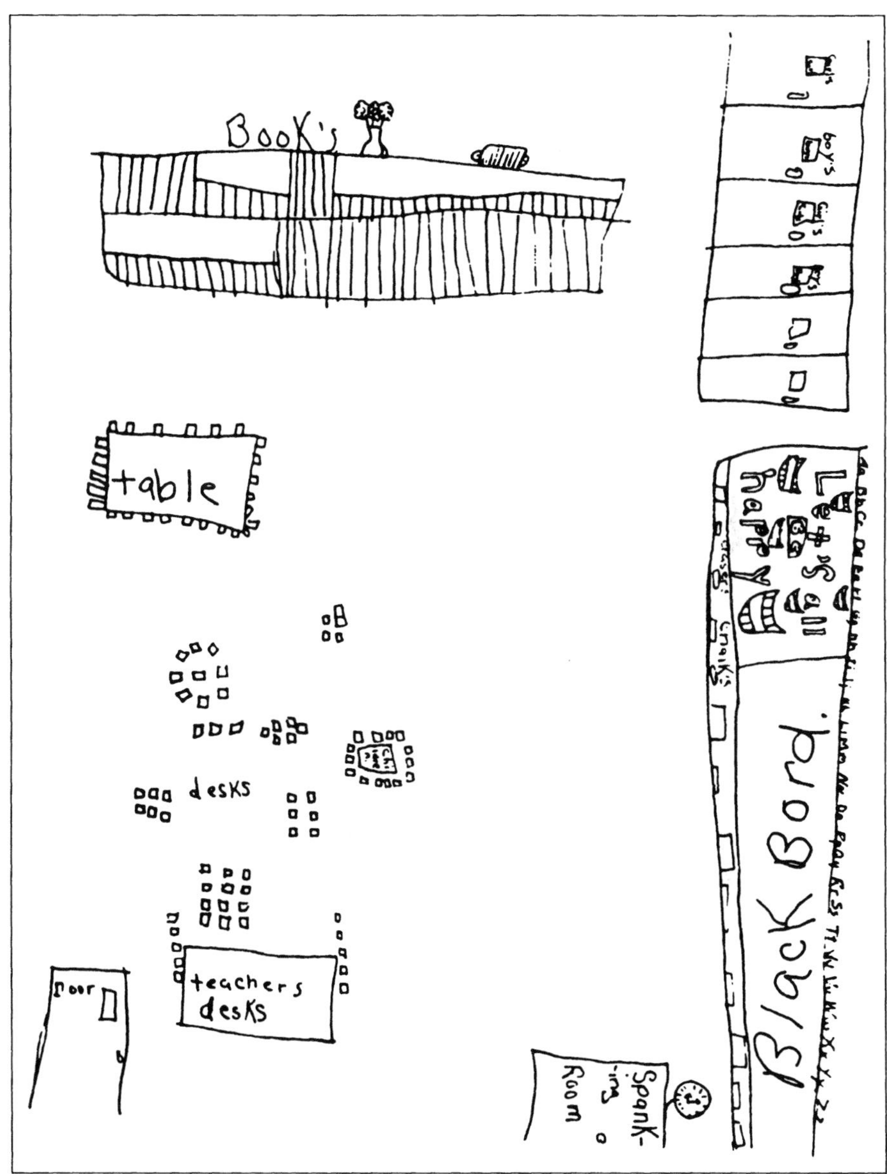

a tool for psychotherapy for many years but is an untapped source of information about classroom or school climate. More recent assessments of climate are beginning to draw from many fields to determine the health of learning environments.

Teacher or student journals present another source of data about the climate of a school or, in the example of Table 1.1, the impact of an innovation on a middle

Table 1.1 Extract from Consistency Management Journal

August 1996
Patricia Garvey
Prior to the beginning of school, I listed problems of management, which I had encountered during the 1995–1996 school year. Some of the problems included limited time-on-task due to the magnitude of the particular manager's job, unclear paper flow, difficulty following directions, and interruptions during the lessons.

The time-on-task problem has been addressed by appointing two paper distribution managers and paper return managers per class The paper return managers are also responsible for filing completed paperwork by class period.

The paper flow problem has been improved as a result of labeling trays with "Class work-in" and "Class work-out" and labeling folders with tags such as "First Period-In" and "First Period-Out".

The directions have been written in a skeleton outline format. This has improved the student's knowledge of the course objectives, warm up, assignment agenda, homework, and up-coming test dates. Samples of the homework worksheets are taped to the board as an additional visual reminder for students as they leave the room.

An orientation manager was added to the list of managers in order to decrease the number of interruptions during class. The secretary was helpful in completing detention and/or parent conference letters.

Students were given a syllabus and a scope and sequence for the first two six weeks. The list of tests was included in the scope and sequence.

November 1996
The students have started to "easeup" in their study skills. Therefore, the students study skills are going to be emphasized during the third six weeks.

We started the six weeks by completing a self-evaluation of the second six weeks. Students also wrote a list of goals for the third six weeks.

The next objective was to reorganize the student's notebooks. We reviewed the importance of writing the heading and labeling handouts as "classwork", "homework", "notes", "vocabulary", etc. Students placed samples of their work from the second six weeks in their portfolio.

The (Consistency Management) Learning Tool requirements will be reinforced more consistently. The students will be given rewards if, on random binder checks, they have all of their learning tools and the dividers are being used effectively. Students who write in ink and do not use a pencil for math will lose 20 points per assignment. This has been very effective . . . and improves haphazard writing skills on assignments.

Since I talked with the students about their grades and improving the quality of their work, I have received more homework assignments than I had been receiving during October.

Students seem to like having time limits and they seem to enjoy complaining about this more regimented approach to teaching. Nevertheless, they have increased productivity since I began this different CM approach.

I have given students practice using skeleton outlines for note taking. They are also learning to summarize the lessons writing the main idea/concept and then copying several examples of the concept or rule.

Students are learning to use test failure to build future successes. I am emphasizing corrections and asking questions as learning tools that will help the students improve their productivity

school mathematics teacher. Her journal which was requested of all participants in the classroom management innovation (see Freiberg, 1996; 1999) is a personal reflection of her own well-being in her inner-city middle school mathematics classroom and thoughts about implementing a new classroom management program (CMCD). It becomes clear in her journal she has decided to improve communications and expectations with the students about the quality and quantity of work and the building of study skills. She is also seeking a more productive work environment with her students. You may also see in her narrative the struggle to solve problems that interfere with her teaching and student learning. Too often in urban schools teachers have given up on changing their environments. It becomes evident from this journal that the need for continuous improvement is still part of her professional work ethic.

Also, Sergio's comments (discussed on page 12) which were drawn from his daily journal about his feelings when his teacher was absent, reflect another important source of information about school health through the eyes of the most important source — the learner. Since the journal was not designed as a specific climate measure and was part of the normal learning process in the seventh grade reading classroom, the data is actually more *indirect* than direct. This reflects a second type of data source.

Indirect Measures

The second category of climate measures are those that are indirect, in that the data collection does not require direct interactions with individuals and minimizes or eliminates the need to insert the data collector into the daily lives of teachers and students. Indirect measures encompass existing data sources, usually records that are kept by the teacher, school or local education authority, including attendance records of students and teachers; visits to the nurse's office (these are effective measures of student stress levels); discipline referrals to the office; suspensions and expulsions; teacher and administrator turnover rates; student achievement; student mobility rates and the like. There are other types of indirect measures including an analysis of the physical presentation of the building, hallways, and classrooms. For example, the range of colors, levels of lighting, and the existence of plants throughout the building can create a light or dark mood in the school. The type of work displayed in the classrooms or hallways may reflect the level of involvement by students in selecting their own work or the lack of participation of students in this selection. Barren hallways, commercially bought posters, bulletin boards, and spartan furnishings may be observed without disrupting or influencing the lives of children or teachers. The level of noise in the hallways, cafeteria or other common areas for example is measurable (see Chapter 11 for discussion of the Ambient Noise Check List) and may provide specific indications of the stress levels placed on the teachers and students created by extraneous sources within the school building. A combination of direct and indirect measures should provide a balanced profile of a school.

Improving Learning Environments

It is not enough to collect data, something must be done with it. Other professions, including law, medicine, engineering, and accounting, have changed greatly in recent decades to meet modern conditions. Schools, by and large, have shown a unique resilience for the *status quo*. The technological revolution has only slightly changed day-to-day school operations and the way decisions are made. Despite the rapid pace of the information age, it seems most schools function much as they did one hundred years ago. Why is this? We believe the main reason for this monolithic reluctance to change can be traced to a lack of "Feedback"! Those that work on schools have an almost complete lack of timely evidence as to the eventual effect of their work or the necessary conditions for improvement. When data are available, school culture is such, that it is rarely used to make instructional or organizational decisions. Surely, test scores are reported at the end of each school year but that has little or no effect on improving the conditions of the learner for nine months prior to the test. These test results reflect the past rather than the present or the future. Few decisions seem to be made based on up-to-date data regarding any school climate factors. School climate should be measured from multiple perspectives, and throughout the school year, so that each person responsible for the education of youth can see how healthy the learning environment is and what needs to be changed or sustained. *Continuous improvement requires continuous information about the learner and the learning environment.*

Five Questions for Improving School Climate

Where do you start if your climate is not very healthy. One new administrator described the start of school at a middle school with the following:

> There are more kids in the halls than in the classroom. The third floor is the worst. The walls are made of sheet-rock and a student who starts by kicking a small hole in the morning, becomes a gaping hole large enough to hide a student by the afternoon. There are multiple fights each day on every floor and the cafeteria is abyss of noise, stress and more fights. On a good day for student discipline the APs and I only see a hundred students.

Clearly this school has a need to improve its climate but where do you start when there are so many areas that need to be improved?

School climate strategies need a quick start and should be visible to all the faculty and staff and be able to be completed in a few weeks rather than months. An unusual but successful school climate strategy used by administrators and teachers at one school reflected the need to have a highly visible change that would let all the faculty members know that change is possible. After a series of school climate meetings that included initially faculty and then staff, they decided to improve the "faculty-staff" *restrooms*. Since all the faculty would be influenced by this strategy it would meet the criteria of high visibility and could be completed in a few weeks. They added real paper products rather than those purchased through the school district's lowest bidding process. Each grade level would be responsible for a three month period. Second, they added air freshener, new paint, pictures, mirrors, and a bulletin board with the latest information from the school climate committee. Once the restrooms were improved more faculty and staff were willing to participate in the more extensive changes that focused on creating small unit organizations where teams of teachers worked with a set group of students to improve the quality of interactions between and among faculty and students.

An outgrowth of a Student Cadre group at an inner-city middle school, called the "Ambassadors", decided that greeting students and faculty each morning at 7:00 a.m. at the front door would improve the climate at the school. It has become a trade-mark of the school and there are many more students interested in joining student groups to improve the climate or, as the students say, the "friendliness" of the school. The Cadre students were recommended by teachers and selected by grade level teams of teachers. The Student Cadre includes at least 80 per cent of the students that would normally never be selected for such a group.

Improving school climate requires a consistent effort and reflection upon the issues that have led to current conditions. Where does an administrator or school climate team begin?

(i) Start with your senses and ask yourself: How does the school look, smell, feel and, yes, taste — would I eat in the student cafeteria?
(ii) What direct and indirect climate measures can be used to help document and create a base-line for change?
(iii) What initial climate changes can we make that would have the highest visibility and be accomplished in the shortest period of time (e.g. a few weeks)?
(iv) What groups or individuals should be involved to encourage and create an environment for sustainable school climate improvements?
(v) What long-term changes are needed to create a healthy environment for all members of the learning community?

Once the climate of the school moves from the unhealthy toward the healthy part of the continuum, how does one sustain and keep the teaching and learning environment healthy? Or if a school climate is currently healthy, how do you keep it going?

Sustaining Healthy Learning Environments

"Our school climate is great" affirmed the principal of a specialized high school. "We have high test scores, great attendance, the staff like each other and socialize after schools hours, so why am I so worried?" Perhaps it is because school climate is much like tending a garden, it takes continuous effort. Carl Rogers, known as one of the founders of humanistic psychology, spoke to me about this type of on-going support during a discussion we had several years ago.

> I work every day in my garden. The roses, flowers, and plants do well in southern California climate if you water, provide natural food and till the soil to allow oxygen to reach the roots. I am aware that weeds are always present. It is the

> constant caring that prevents the weeds from taking over the garden. Person-centered education is much like my rose garden — it needs a caring environment to sustain its beauty. (Carl Rogers Personal Communication with Jerome Freiberg 1984)

Sustaining a healthy learning environment may take as much effort and care as improving an unhealthy one. While some measures for example give an overall view of the climate of a school there may be some climate elements that are masked by the norming process. By looking only at the means, some key areas may be missed. For example, student survey data collected by subject areas for 30 inner-city schools K–12 has shown that students perceive the climate in mathematics classrooms to be significantly lower than the climate in reading classrooms. This is consistent for grade levels 3–12 (Freiberg, Connell and Lorentz, 1997; Freiberg, Stein and Van Veen, 1998; Van Veen, 1998; and Freiberg, 1999). It is also a given, both in the United States and in other countries (Chiari, 1997), that student perceptions of climate are less favorable the higher the grade level. As students move from the elementary grades through the middle grades and onto high school, students perceive school climate to be more negative, teacher support to be less and classroom environments to be less healthy. This may be a function of school organization in which students experience smaller more personalized elementary schools of 400–700 students for six years and then are thrust into larger middle (1,200+) and high schools (2,000+) where they become disconnected with the education process (See a review by Cotton, K., 1998, http://www.nrel.org for research on the effects of school size on student achievement and well-being).

One would expect that school climate under normal conditions would improve each year, but with the entry of new groups of students and, at times, new teachers, the need to both sustain and improve school climate is a *continuous process* and requires a *continuous effort*. It may be more the little things linked together over time that sustain a healthy climate for learning compared to larger one-time organizational changes. A case in point is the need for school members to celebrate collective success and accomplishments rather than just individual efforts.

Celebrating Success

Sustaining climate efforts is a constant in the schooling process. A large middle school (1,200) in the inner-city moved from being on the state and district lists for low academic performance to being at the mean for the district and off the state "watch list" for low performing schools. They have sustained their improvement efforts with yearly retreats, celebrations of successes, and a focus on problem prevention rather than problem solving. The retreats are open to all faculty, administration and staff members. From the algebra teacher to the cafeteria workers, each member of the school community has a opportunity to reaffirm their commitment to the learner and each other. It has become an important focal point for the school. The need for reaffirmation of goals and dreams is a common thread in schools that sustain quality.

Three Questions for Sustaining Climate

When it is evident that a school's climate is in need of improvement the five questions listed on page 25 would be good starting point. However, where does a school administrator or school improvement team begin to reflect on sustaining a healthy learning environment? Perhaps a few additional questions will serve as a basis for this next phase of climate self-assessment. There are three universal questions each member of the school community should ask:

(i) What factors enabled us to create a healthy learning environment?
(ii) Have there been any changes that would require adjustments in order to sustain the environment?
(iii) What is my personal commitment to sustaining a healthy learning and working environment?

Each of these questions reflect the need to determine (i) How did we get here? (ii) What changes have occurred since and what adjustments are needed? and (iii) What is my role in sustaining a healthy learning environment? There are many more questions to be asked for sure but a starting point is necessary to determine where we have started, where are we now and where are we going?

The Global Nature of School Climate

School climate is not unique to the United States as you will see in reading the chapters in this book. Interest in measuring, improving and sustaining school climate is global in nature. Youth and teachers around the world face similar concerns and issues in the organizational and cultural milieu of schools. The international nature of youth problems is reflected in its schools. Problems faced by youth in information age societies require a level of support that provides resilience when they face personal and educational challenges. School can be an important source of building resilience or one more barrier to a productive life. Schools play an important role in creating the necessary conditions for learning.

My work in Europe during the last decade has brought me into contact with many educators whose concerns about youth parallel those of American educators. For example, teachers in northern Italy are concerned about the lack of student motivation to learn and parental involvement, and their students are concerned about the lack of involvement in their classrooms. Educators in Austria are concerned about the rising levels of youth violence with a doubling of youth crime in the last decade. In England, educators are concerned with the level of rowdyism and break-down of social order in schools (Slee, 1999). In 1997, in The Netherlands, one third of boys whose origin is Morocco, have been in trouble with the police and attendance levels of many lower achieving schools in Amsterdam can be less than 50 per cent on any given day (Van Veen, 1998). While the United States is enjoying a reduction in overall crime, including youth crime, those declines may be short-lived as the children of the "baby boom" generation enter adolescence and adulthood. Statistical averages, demographic reports and future projections of youth poverty, crime and violence can be daunting to many of us who care about children. These data should be placed, however, in the context that one caring adult can provide the resilience needed to overcome adversity. Caring adults who work together in schools and bring members of the community to support children can create an oasis for children and youth.

Conclusion

The concept of climate has both history and geographic universality. Defining school climate needs to take into account the depth and multiplicity of its roots and the speed and capacity of schools to change. The definition should evolve in your readings from the following chapters. Rather than trying to estabish a static definition, we hope after reading *School Climate: Measuring, Improving and Sustaining Healthy Learning Environments*, that you will have a much broader view of what are the elements that foster positive climate of a school and how to measure, improve and sustain healthy learning environments. Throughout this book you will be provided with numerous examples of instruments and procedures to measure the climate from the teachers' workroom to the constructivist classroom. It is our hope that you will use these tools as magnifying glasses to enlarge the scope of your work and provide an on-going source for continuous improvement. Future generations of children depend on our ability to make a difference in how we initially structure their learning environments. Use the instruments to find out what is needed and then use the information derived from multiple sources to be vigilant to the changing needs around you, including your own.

References

Brookover, W.B., Beady, C., Flood, P., Schweitzer, J. and Wisenbaker, J. (1979) *School Social Systems and Student Achievement: Schools Can Make a Difference*, New York: Praeger.

Chiari, G. (1997) *Climi di classe e apprendimento*, Milano, Italy: FrancoAngeli.

Cotton, K. (1998) http://www.nrel.org

Dunton, L. (1892) *Education*, February, p. 324 cited in Perry, A. (1908) *The Management of a City School*, New York: Macmillan, p. 212.

Edmonds, R.R. (1979) 'Effective schools for the urban poor', *Educational Leadership*, **37**, pp. 15–24.

Freiberg, H.J. (1989) 'Multidimensional view of school effectiveness', *Educational Research Quarterly*. **13**, 2, pp. 35–46.

Freiberg, H.J. (1994) 'Understanding resilience: Implications for inner-city schools and their near and far communities', in Wang, M.C. and Gordon, E.W., *Educational Resilience in Inner-city America: Challenges and Prospects*, Hillsdale: Lawrence Erlbaum.

Freiberg, H.J. (1996) 'From tourists to citizens in the classroom', *Educational Leadership*, **51**, 1, pp. 32–7.

Freiberg, H.J. (ed.) (1999) *Beyond Behaviorism: Changing the Classroom Management Paradigm*, Needham Heights: Allyn and Bacon.

Freiberg, H.J., Connell, M. and Lorentz, J. (1997) 'The effects of socially constructed classroom management on mathematics achievement', paper presented in March at the national meeting of the American Education Research Association, Chicago, IL.

Freiberg, H.J., Stein, T. and Huang, S. (1995) 'The effects of classroom management intervention on student achievement in inner-city elementary schools', *Educational Research and Evaluation*, **1**, 1, pp. 33–66.

Freiberg, H.J., Stein, T.A. and Van Veen, D. (1998) 'An international comparison of classroom climate from learner perspectives', poster session in April at the national meeting of the American Education Research Association, San Diego, CA.

Fashola, O. and Slavin, R. (1998) 'Schoolwide reform models: What works?' *Phi Delta Kappan*, **79**, 5, pp. 370–79.

Hoy, W., Tarter, J.C. and Kottkamp, B. (1991) *Open School/Healthy Schools: Measuring Organizational Climate*, London: Sage.

Lightfoot, S.L. (1983) *The Good High Schools: Portraits of Character and Culture*, New York: Basic Books.

Perry, A. (1908) *The Management of a City School*, New York: Macmillan.

'Quality Counts': A supplement to *Education Week*, January 22, 1997 Vol. xvi.

'Quality Counts '98', *Teacher Magazine*, January, 1998.

Rogers, C.R. and Freiberg, H.J. (1994) *Freedom to Learn*, 3rd ed., Columbus: Merrill.

Rutter, M., Maughan, B., Mortimore, P., Ouston, J. and Smith, A. (1979) *Fifteen Thousand Hours: Secondary Schools and Their Effects on Children*, Cambridge: Harvard University Press.

Slee, R. (1999) 'Theorizing discipline: Practical implications for schools', in Freiberg, H.J. (ed.) *Beyond Behaviorism: Changing The Classroom Management Paradigm*, Needham Heights: Allyn and Bacon.

Teddlie, C. and Stringfield, S. (1993) *Schools Make a Difference*, New York, NY: Teachers College.

Van Veen, D. (1998) 'Building arks for stormy weather', paper presented in February at the 50th Annual Conference of the American Association of Colleges for Teacher Education (AACTE), New Orleans, LA.

Wang, M.C., Haertel, G.D. and Walberg, H.J. (1997) 'Learning Influences' in Walberg, H.J. and Haertel, G.D. (eds) *Psychology and Educational Practice*, McCuthan: Berkley, CA, pp. 199–211.

Chapter 2

The Role of School and Classroom Climate in Elementary School Learning Environments

Bert P.M. Creemers and Gerry J. Reezigt

Introduction

In this chapter, we will discuss school and classroom climate from an educational effectiveness point of view by focusing on the meaning of climate for student outcomes. Mortimore et al. (1988) and Levine and Lezotte (1990) refer to climates which enhance student outcomes as "positive" or "productive" climates. But what place do climate factors have in effectiveness theories and how are climate concepts related to effectiveness characteristics? We will explicitly incorporate climate factors in a model of educational effectiveness; we will compare our views with other theories; discuss the implications for school improvement; present a Dutch climate checklist; and, finally, draw our conclusions.

Climate and Effectiveness Factors

Recently, climate factors have been incorporated in effectiveness models (Creemers, 1994; Stringfield, 1994). Stringfield defines the school climate very broadly as the total environment of the school, including the parents and the community. This makes it difficult to study specific climate factors and their unique effects on students. Creemers (1994) defines climate factors more narrowly and expects them to exert influence on student outcomes in the same way as the effectiveness factors do.

In our model, based on Creemers (1994), climate factors have their own place next to the effectiveness factors. We will discuss our views along the lines of this model, starting at the bottom of the model and then going upwards (see Figure 2.1).

Educational Outcomes

A school should pursue outcomes in the cognitive domain, simply because children go to school to learn things that they cannot learn anywhere else. But this does not

Figure 2.1 Climate factors in educational effectiveness

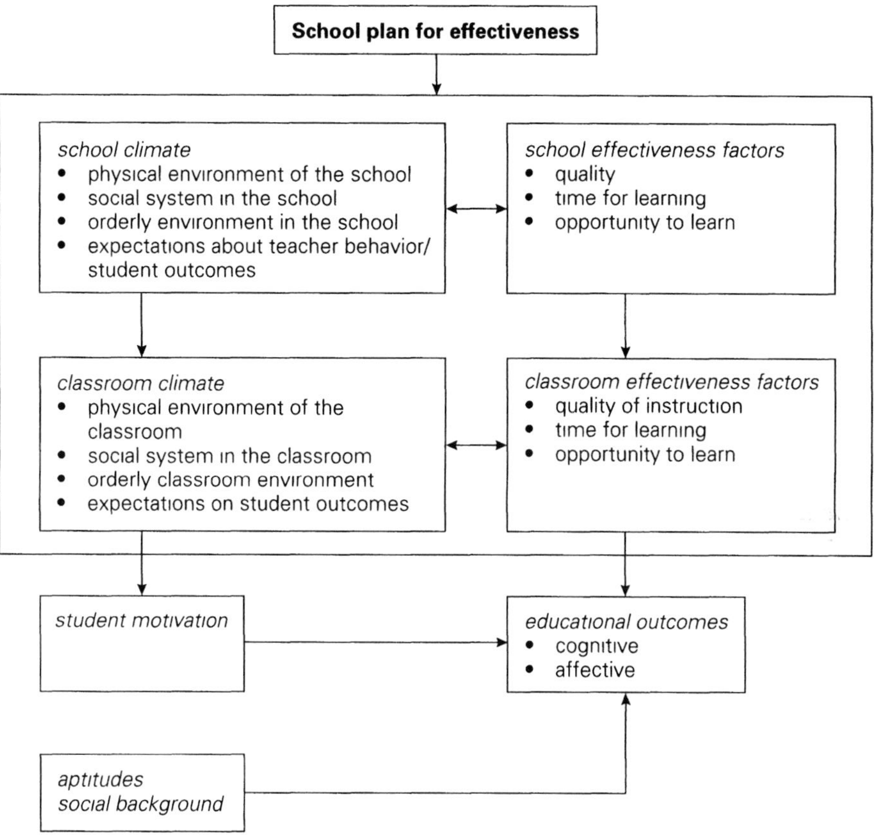

mean that affective outcomes are not important. Schools hope, for example, that students will achieve adequate self-concepts and positive attitudes towards learning. Schools want their students to acquire social skills. Affective outcomes are not only important in their own right, but they are also thought to influence cognitive outcomes positively. For that reason, we have included both types of outcomes in our model.

Outcomes are determined by student aptitudes and social background. The influence of schools and classrooms can only be estimated correctly after controlling for these factors (the "value-added" concept of effectiveness, Mortimore et al., 1988; Van der Werf, 1995). Aptitudes and social background are especially important for the cognitive domain, but their influence on affective outcomes is not yet clear (Grosin, 1993). We have included student motivation as a factor which may influence the cognitive as well as the affective outcomes. Motivation itself may be influenced by school and classroom factors, while aptitude and social background are not. Therefore, motivation stands apart in our model.

Effectiveness Factors

Outcomes are most strongly influenced by classroom effectiveness factors. Without classroom instruction, learning will not occur (Creemers, 1994; Wang et al., 1993). We have, therefore, drawn a strong line between these factors and the outcomes. The classroom level is now firmly included in effectiveness theory, although it has been focusing on the school level for a long time (Fraser, 1991; Teddlie, 1994).

At both levels, we have categorized effectiveness factors in three key concepts of quality, time and opportunity (Creemers, 1994). Quality should lead to enough time and opportunity to learn so that students achieve good results. The quality of instruction at the classroom level is determined by three components: the curriculum, the grouping procedures which are applied, and the behavior of the teacher. On the basis of theory and research findings, the following factors are supposed to constitute these components (see Figure 2.2).

Figure 2.2 Classroom effectiveness factors

Quality of instruction	
Curriculum	• explicitness and ordering of goals and contents
	• structure and clarity of content
	• advance organizers
	• evaluation, feedback and corrective instruction
Grouping procedures	• mastery learning
	• ability grouping
	• cooperative learning (dependent on differentiated material, evaluation, feedback and corrective instruction)
Teacher behavior	• classroom management
	• homework
	• clear goal setting (restricted set of goals, emphasis on basic skills, emphasis on cognitive learning and transfer)
	• structuring the content (ordering of goals and content, advance organizers, prior knowledge)
	• clarity of presentation
	• questioning
	• immediate exercises
	• evaluation, feedback and corrective instruction
Time for learning	
Opportunity to learn	

Source: Creemers, 1994

When the components are in line with each other, their effects will be reinforced. This is called the *consistency* principle (Creemers, 1994). When teachers show high quality behavior, use good materials and are able to select grouping procedures which fit their behavior and the curricular demands, the effects on achievement will be much higher than when teachers show high quality behavior but use curricula or grouping procedures which do not correspond with their behavior.

In our model, the school level is considered conditional for the classroom level. Its influence on outcomes is mediated by the classroom factors. Therefore, only those factors conditional for the quality of instruction, time and opportunity to learn are seen as important at the school level (see Figure 2.3).

Figure 2.3 *School effectiveness factors*

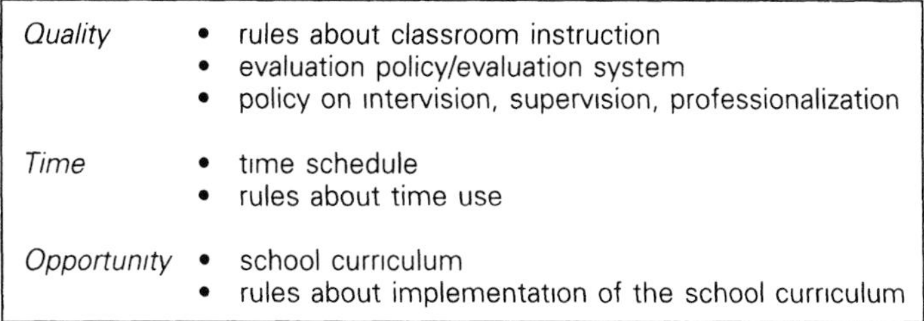

Quality	• rules about classroom instruction • evaluation policy/evaluation system • policy on intervision, supervision, professionalization
Time	• time schedule • rules about time use
Opportunity	• school curriculum • rules about implementation of the school curriculum

Source: Creemers, 1994

The *consistency* principle also holds for the school level. At this level we also discern the principles of *cohesion*, *constancy* and *mutual responsibility*. When all members of the school team achieve *consistency*, they create *cohesion* in the team. *Constancy* refers to the importance of continuity. Schools should not change policies and rules every other year because this may damage their effectiveness. *Mutual responsibility* means that schools should not evaluate only students, but also their own functioning. Teachers hold themselves and their colleagues responsible for the effectiveness of the school.

Climate Factors

Effectiveness factors (the right side of the model) cannot explain all educational outcomes. Even after controlling for background factors, part of the variance in student outcomes remains unaccounted for. There must be another group of factors influencing outcomes. Moreover, the effectiveness of schools is not stable (Freiberg, 1989). Schools with high outcomes in one year are not automatically the same schools with high outcomes the next year. Also, schools do not automatically achieve high outcomes across different subjects (Luyten, 1994). Finally, effectiveness factors do not exist in a vacuum. Schools and classrooms are more than the sum of their effectiveness factors. They have personalities of their own (Hoy, 1990). Therefore, climate factors complete our picture. We see climate factors, like effectiveness factors, as alterable by students, teachers and schools. The climate factors at the school and classroom level regard similar key concepts, but have different meanings dependent on the level, just as do the effectiveness concepts of quality, time and opportunity. We think the principles of *consistency*, *cohesion*, *constancy* and *mutual responsibility* are also applicable to the climate factors.

We think the classroom climate factors will exert a direct influence on outcomes while the effects of school climate are mediated by the classroom level. In addition, classroom climate will have a direct influence on the motivation of students for learning. So the classroom climate will influence outcomes directly and indirectly, mediated by the students' motivation.

In broad definitions, "climate may include anything from environmental aspects of the school to the personalities of the students and educators, as well as academic performance, levels of physical activity, and the processes and materials used throughout instructional procedures" (Johnson and Johnson, 1993). We think that such a broad definition is not appropriate, because it does not clearly separate climate factors from effectiveness factors and not even from the educational outcomes. Instead, we have taken the four groups of climate factors of Anderson (1982) as a point of departure:

- ecology (physical and material aspects);
- milieu (the composition of the population of a school);
- social system (relationships between persons); and
- culture (belief systems, values).

First, we decided to leave out milieu, because it does not fit our ideas of climate factors as easily alterable factors. Although private schools and public schools (magnet schools) can influence their milieux to some extent, this is not so easy as deciding about a new curriculum. Moreover, according to Anderson (1982) and Kreft (1993), milieu does not seem to exert any influence of its own when it is analyzed together with other climate factors. Second, we split the physical aspects into the actual aspects of the environment (the size of a classroom, the age of a school building) and the way in which people in the school are dealing with the physical aspects. A classroom may be small, but it can be well kept or messy. A school building may be old, but it can be well-maintained or be in a deplorable state. Third, we have defined the social system as the relationships which are appropriate at either the classroom or the school level. Finally, we have defined the culture category of Anderson as the expectations people may have about the educational outcomes.

We have included the following set of classroom climate factors in our model:

- the physical environment of the classroom (for example, its size, its location within the school);
- the social system (relationships and interactions between students and relationships and interactions between students and their teachers);
- an orderly classroom environment (arrangement of the classroom, cosiness, functionality);
- teacher expectations about student outcomes (positive expectations, feelings of self-efficacy, professional attitude).

At the school level, we have included the following set:

- the physical environment of the school (school building, corridors and canteens, school yard and playgrounds);
- the social system (relationships and interactions between teachers and among the teaching staff and the school staff, rules and agreements concerning behavior toward each other and toward students, between the school and the parents, between the school and external agencies);
- an orderly school environment;
- the expectations about teacher behavior and student outcomes.

A Plan for Effectiveness

Our final issue is the relationship between the climate and effectiveness factors. We think that schools should relate both types of factors by a plan for effectiveness. In such a plan, schools must make clear which student output they want to achieve: Which outcomes are pursued? Which outcomes are excluded? Should all students achieve the outcomes? Furthermore, schools should know how they want to achieve these outcomes. First, they have to decide on the effectiveness factors. What kind of instruction are teachers supposed to give, what kind of books will be used, what kind of agreements have to be made on the school level? Second, schools have to decide on the climate factors. What should the physical environment look like, how are teachers and students supposed to relate to each other, what should teachers expect of their students?

We have put the climate and the effectiveness factors in the perspective of the school's plan for effectiveness, because we see them as means that can help schools to achieve high outcomes. They should not be seen as goals in their own right. A plan for effectiveness is necessary to decide on the best combination of climate and effectiveness factors. Ideally, these should reinforce each other's beneficial effects. For example, teachers may want to teach in a rather strict manner, in which they are the central force in the classroom. This puts constraints on the classroom climate: students cannot be allowed as much freedom as when teachers want their students to learn from each other too.

Theories and Research on School and Classroom Climate

School and classroom climate have been studied separately in four research traditions. Anderson (1982) described school climate research as the stepchild of organizational climate research and school effects research. Classroom climate research might be described as the stepchild of psychological and classroom research.

The organizational studies discuss the difference between school climate and school culture. Sometimes the climate is seen as behavior, while culture is seen as values and norms (Hoy, 1990; Heck and Marcoulides, 1996). Sometimes the school culture is considered as a dimension of the school climate. Hoy, 1990; Hoy et al., 1990; Hoy and Woolfolk, 1993 has suggested a health metaphor for the concept of climate, which links climate with outcomes. A healthy organization, according to Hoy, deals effectively with outside forces while directing its energies toward its goals, i.e. educational outcomes. It is characterized by high performance standards, high teacher expectations, and an orderly learning environment with good relationships between teachers.

The school effects research tradition (Brookover et al., 1979; Edmonds, 1979) included school climate factors such as orderliness (Scheerens, 1992). Effective and ineffective schools were found to have different climates. The effects of climate factors on achievement were mostly positive. For that reason climate factors were regarded as one of the main sources for the change and improvement of schools. The school effects studies neglected the classroom level and the classroom climate was not considered a research topic at all.

The classroom effects research tradition initially focused on climate factors defined as managerial techniques (see Doyle, 1986). Later, the discussion focused on the question as to where climate factors end and effectiveness factors begin. Management is necessary to create conditions for learning and instruction, but management itself is not sufficient for student results (Creemers, 1994). This research tradition did not study the school level.

The psychological tradition of classroom environment research paid a lot of attention to instruments for the measuring of student perceptions of climate. Many studies report on their psychometric characteristics (Fraser, 1991; Houtveen et al., 1993). When studies link student perception of the classroom climate to cognitive and affective outcomes, the most common finding is a positive correlation. Climate factors (such as the way a teacher behaves towards the students; Wubbels et al., 1991) and their effects are studied as isolated constructs (Johnson and Johnson, 1993). It is relatively new to look at effective teaching (that is, teaching aimed at high cognitive outcomes) and methods for classroom interactions (that is, teacher behavior aimed at student wellbeing) at the same time (Oser et al., 1992).

Effectiveness research now has taken the first steps to integrate elements of the four research traditions. This integration is a complex process which yields variables at three levels (school, classroom, and student), two types of independent variables (climate and effectiveness factors), two types of dependent variables (cognitive and affective outcomes) and possibly two types of covariates at the student level (regular student background variables such as socio-economic status, and background variables explicitly meant as controls for the affective outcomes).

Methods for School Improvement

We have stressed the importance of an integrated approach which studies climate and effectiveness factors together. As a consequence, we think that school improvement which enhances student outcomes in the cognitive and affective domains necessarily concerns climate and effectiveness factors together. We will illustrate this by giving examples of projects which addressed one group of factors and projects which dealt with both groups at the same time.

European governments have been pushing schools to improve their school climates. Sweden mentions the climate in the School Regulations: "the school shall through its atmosphere and environment develop the pupils' self-reliance and independent judgement" (Ekholm and Kull, 1996). In a longitudinal climate study over 25 years, Ekholm and Kull see few changes in schools, even though teachers have received training to pursue the goals mentioned in the School Regulations. The only change is that teacher-student relations and interactions have become less formal. Still, this change could have occurred because of changes in society in general and not because of the Regulations. Ekholm and Kull suggest that for climate changes to occur, changes in the effectiveness factors should also be stressed.

The Dutch educational policy became interested in climate factors recently because people began to worry about the loss of values in society. They thought the school should teach students how to behave as responsible citizens (Klaassen, 1994). The effective schools movement is sometimes seen as damaging for the pedagogical tasks of schools: schools, the suggestion is, are so involved in effective teaching that they forget about climate. According to Klaassen, effective teaching and a positive climate are not opposed, but may reinforce each other's effects. Mooy and De Vries (1993) have similar views. They think a good school climate, characterized by a set of behavioral rules and sanctions, succeeds in committing teachers and students to the school, with the aim of achieving high student outcomes. To actually achieve these high outcomes, however, a good climate alone is not sufficient. Instruction must be adequate, too.

On a smaller scale, Hertz-Lazarowitz and Cohen (1992) report on a program aimed at improving the social climate in schools. The intervention consisted of student discussions in small groups. Topics were acquaintance, trust building, acquisition of listening skills, roleplay, and self-presentations. After the intervention, students and teachers perceived more communication, a greater openness, and more cooperation during the school day and beyond. A similar project is described by Fraser (1991). Although these projects show that the classroom climate can be changed, it is not clear what the interventions mean for the effectiveness factors and for the cognitive and affective outcomes of students.

For many years, school improvement projects used to introduce effectiveness factors by means of a top down approach. Research findings, for example the famous five-factor model of Edmonds (1979), were merely dropped into schools. It soon became clear that changes either did not occur or disappeared after the end of the project. The improvement attempts may have been too strongly related to the content of improvement and too weakly to the environmental context (Scheerens, 1992), i.e. the climate factors in schools. Successful changes in effectiveness factors should be accompanied by changes in the climate factors.

The difference between recent effectiveness projects and the older top-down projects is their attention to the situation of the teachers and the schools which are to implement an innovation. An example is the Barclay-Calvert project in the United States (Stringfield and Herman, 1996). In this small scale project (two schools), the curricular and instructional program of a highly effective school (Calvert) is to be implemented by an ineffective school (Barclay). The Barclay staff were trained in the Calvert philosophy. They were not asked to change without knowing why. Also, the Barclay school implemented the Calvert program slowly, with one additional classroom changing each school year. The school team was not forced to change overnight. Finally, the Barclay teachers became convinced that the Calvert program could help them to overcome their problems (Stoll et al., 1996). The first results in terms of student outcomes seem promising (Stringfield and Herman, 1996).

The Success for All project (Slavin, 1996) provides teaching routines, grouping procedures, and materials. Several factors in the project structure refer to climate factors and help teachers to change more easily (Ross and Smith, 1996). Teachers are constantly supported by a project facilitator who helps them to use the program materials, and they are supported by their principal and colleagues. The project achieves positive student effects, but also changes in the school and classroom climate.

Recent projects sometimes explicitly pay attention to the climate factors and their role in achieving high outcomes. The ATLAS communities (Orrell, 1996) use the school climate survey to find out how teachers, students and parents think about climate factors. Such a survey shows strong and weak points in the school, which may have to be addressed before any other innovatory activities can take place.

Measuring School Climate and Classroom Climate

First we will discuss problems in the measurement of climate and formal and informal ways to assess climate. Then we will present a Dutch climate instrument.

Problems in Measuring Climate Factors

Climate factors have often been operationalized as perceptions of people (Anderson, 1982). Perceptions lack objectivity but in the field of climate factors objective indicators are hard to use. Researchers have used objective proxies such as the school size, or the composition of the student body, but they are rather meaningless. Perceptions of climate factors may be more realistic even though they are more subjective.

Hoy et al. (1990) think that perceptions may differ from one person to another in the same organization. The school climate perceived by the principal may differ from the climate perceived by the teachers. This causes interpretative trouble for researchers looking for just one climate indicator, but no trouble at all for researchers using a definition of climate in which different perceptions can coexist. In our view, perceptions can adequately operationalize climate factors.

Schools or teachers can use formal and informal methods to assess the quality of the climate factors. Questionnaires, checklists and rating scales are formal methods. These are useful to analyze the discrepancy between what schools want to achieve and their actual situation. They give a picture of their strong and weak points and show the way to improvement. A formal method is rational when a school has already decided to change and knows the direction to take. We think that schools can use informal methods in the stages when it is not yet clear which changes will have to occur, when discussion between the staff and the teacher can not yet be strongly focused on clearly delineated topics for change. In this sense, informal methods may be sometimes necessary before a formal method can be used. For example, schools may use the concepts in our model as a starting point for informal and rather broad discussions about school policies, classroom practices and outcomes at the student level. Schools may need such a phase before actually starting to study their climate factors as such and before they use formal methods to assess their climate factors. Broad conceptual discussions are needed to put the climate in the perspective of the school's effectiveness. The concepts of the model and the way they are related in the model may give schools an opportunity to develop their own plan for effectiveness, to define the important climate factors and effectiveness factors and their expected effects on student outcomes. As a consequence, the school can decide what will have to be improved: climate factors, effectiveness factors, or both, and the school may further use formal methods to focus on the selected factors.

Measuring the Climate Factors: A Dutch Checklist for the Assessment of the Quality of Classroom and School Climate

We will present a checklist of climate topics which is derived from a set of four instruments designed to measure school and classroom climate in Dutch elementary schools (Brandsma and Bos, 1994; Inspectie, 1995). The instruments were originally developed for representatives of the Inspectorate (see Appendix 2.1 for further information). We took the main concepts and items from the set and restated them as topics for schools and teachers to consider when they want to discuss their climate factors. The checklist measures four dimensions, each of which is important for a good climate:

- school plan for effectiveness;
- physical environment;
- teacher behavior; and
- school's system.

By answering the topics, schools can find out what their strong and weak points are. Each item, indicated by an asterisk, can be answered with "yes" or "no". The more positive answers a school can give, the healthier the school is. With many negative answers on one or more dimensions, a school should start worrying about its climate. In short, according to this checklist, a healthy school is a school that pursues a multitude of cognitive and affective outcomes; provides a pleasant atmosphere in classrooms, in the school building and in the lessons; and that has well-stated written agreements about major aspects of teacher behavior and student behavior. An unhealthy school is a school that falls short in one or more of the dimensions of the checklist. In the following, the items of the checklist are presented for the four dimensions.

Checklist for the assessment of the quality of classroom and school climate in Dutch elementary schools

Dimension A: School plan for effectiveness

Does your school pursue the following cognitive student outcomes?

• curiosity and willingness to learn	yes	no
• dedication to learning	yes	no
• a positive, critical attitude	yes	no
• taking initiative	yes	no
• independent studying	yes	no
• concentration	yes	no
• a high achievement motivation	yes	no

Does your school pursue the following affective student outcomes?

• student responsibility for own learning, social behavior, fellow students, the environment	yes	no
• social functioning: showing solidarity, being interested in others, being able to play and work together, showing respect and tolerance, social skills	yes	no
• values: development of an individual set of values, accepting the values of society, ability to change values in a rational way, show courtesy and being friendly	yes	no
• the acceptance of one's own and others' feelings	yes	no
• the acceptance of one's own restrictions	yes	no
• a feeling of safety	yes	no

Dimension B: Physical environment: classroom and school

Do your classrooms meet the following criteria?

• student work displayed on classroom walls	yes	no
• furniture that is clean, intact, and well adapted to the size of students	yes	no
• pleasant temperature	yes	no
• no unnecessary materials on student tables	yes	no
• tidy classroom, learning materials, and teacher's table	yes	no
• learning materials looked after by the teacher	yes	no

Does your school meet the following criteria?

- schoolyard divided for younger and older students yes no
- proper supervision before school, during breaks and after school yes no
- waste-paper baskets emptied regularly yes no
- no trash in the schoolyard yes no
- schoolyard separated from the street yes no
- playing materials safe for children and lawns, sandboxes etc. well kept yes no
- tidy corridors and canteen yes no
- individual lockers for students yes no
- school sufficiently illuminated yes no
- student work on walls yes no
- students assisting in the maintenance of the school yes no

Dimension C: Teacher behavior

Do the teachers create a relaxed classroom climate?

- showing a relaxed attitude and not acting superior yes no
- creating a safe atmosphere yes no
- making students feel free to ask and answer questions yes no
- encouraging students to engage in discussions yes no
- fostering a positive attitude in the class and student-teacher cooperation yes no

Do the teachers show interest in all students and provide positive feedback?

- not showing sympathy or antipathy for individual students yes no
- involving all students in the learning processes and valuing student participation positively yes no
- not stigmatizing students when they answer questions incorrectly yes no
- handling incorrect answers in a positive way and valuing student effort yes no

Do the teachers guard discipline and structuring?

- students know the classroom rules and sanctions after breaking rules yes no
- the teacher acts according to rules when students break the rules yes no
- when given assignments students know what they are expected to do yes no
- student absence is registered yes no
- achievement, progress, and socio-emotional development is registered yes no

Do the teachers stimulate self-discovered learning?

- the teacher is not impatient when students do not answer immediately — yes no
- the teacher provides a rich learning environment and stimulates learning by discovery — yes no
- the teacher stimulates group discussions and guards the participation of all students — yes no
- the teacher is not constantly talking — yes no

Do teachers model what they expect their students to do?

- the teacher shows respect for all students — yes no
- the teacher creates an atmosphere of community — yes no

Dimension D: The school's system

Does your school have clear agreements about pedagogical behavior of teachers and behavioral rules for students?

- there are written school agreements about the pedagogical behavior of teachers — yes no
- agreements concern the way teachers interact with students, the way students interact, discipline, interpretation of rules, punishment, reinforcement, feedback to students — yes no
- the timetable sets some time aside for social-affective outcomes — yes no
- behavioral rules for students are written statements, known to students and parents — yes no
- there are sanctions when students break the rules and parents are informed about these — yes no
- sanctions are used whenever necessary — yes no
- the school is alert to problem behavior of students and has a policy (for bullying, discrimination, truancy, criminal behavior, breaking classroom rules) — yes no

Does your school enhance affective outcomes?

- teachers have sufficient knowledge about the social-emotional development of students, behavioral problems, learning problems, gifted students — yes no
- the school is alert to the training of pedagogical skills of students — yes no
- the school pays extra attention to minority students — yes no
- the school pays attention to pedagogical contents in materials — yes no
- the school uses grouping procedures to enhance affective development — yes no

Does your school evaluate pedagogical behavior?

• the school evaluates pedagogical behavior of teachers	yes	no
• there is a policy on the pedagogical climate in the school	yes	no
• the social-emotional development of students is registered frequently and systematically	yes	no

Does your school have essential internal and external contacts?

• the principal actively supports the pedagogical behavior of teachers	yes	no
• the principal pays attention to the communication between teachers	yes	no
• the parents are informed about the pedagogical policy of the school	yes	no
• the school pays attention to the home situation of students	yes	no
• parents are content about the school and the way the school acts towards the students	yes	no
• the school has contacts with relevant institutions such as support services, special education, health services, police, social services	yes	no

Conclusion

In this chapter, we have tried to give climate factors their own place in a model for educational effectiveness. We think that climate factors need to be separated from effectiveness factors such as quality of instruction. They have their own, unique influence on student outcomes. Ideally, climate and effectiveness factors should be tuned to each other. Schools should draw up a plan for effectiveness, i.e. decide which outcomes they want to pursue, and then define their climate and effectiveness factors as instruments to achieve their intended outcomes.

Although there is a lot of research about climate factors, some of which we have discussed, research which integrates climate and effectiveness factors and studies their separate effects on outcomes is still very rare. Such research, however, is necessary to give schools an idea about the relative importance of the factors and their effects on student outcomes.

The need for an integrated approach is also felt in school improvement. We have shown some examples of projects which either strived for changes in climate factors or for changes in effectiveness factors, and some examples of projects who try to integrate both. We think that the integrated projects are much more likely to be successful and we have given some empirical evidence for this view. Still, similar to the research studies, many improvement projects do not yet systematically integrate climate and effectiveness factors.

Finally we have presented a Dutch checklist for the assessment of the quality of classroom and school climate factors. Schools can use this instrument when they want to get a clearer picture of their own strong and weak points of the school and classroom climate. We think that the checklist can be a good starting point for the self-assessment of schools and improvement in the climate domain. Whenever possible, schools should also use instruments to assess the quality of their effectiveness factors and they should try to analyze the climate and effectiveness factors in terms of our model: as means to achieve certain student outcomes which have been outlined in the school's plan for effectiveness. In this way, schools will show the integrated approach that we have also strongly advocated for research and improvement.

Appendix 2.1: Background information about the checklist

Our checklist was derived from a set of four instruments developed for the Dutch Inspectorate (Brandsma and Bos, 1994). The instrument is based on the dimensions derived from Arter (1987):

- the school's plan for effectiveness (screening and analysis of school documents);
- the physical environment (observation);
- teacher behavior (minimum 30 minute observation during lessons); and
- the school's system (interview with the school principal).

The instrument covers most of our concepts of school and classroom climate and does not mingle climate and effectiveness factors. There are, however, some differences between our views and the set of instruments. The instruments include the school's plan for effectiveness as a climate dimension, while we have separated this from the climate factors. We have made a distinction between the physical environment and the orderliness of the environment, but the instruments put these together. Finally, the instruments are a bit short on the school climate factor "social system" and it does not contain items about expectations, our fourth category of climate factors. Still, at this moment, in our opinion this set of instruments is the best one available.

In a try out, 30 randomly selected Inspectors visited 118 schools each for one day after analyzing school documents first. They observed classes and interviewed school principals. In addition, they met the school team and members of the school board. Finally, they sent a written report to the school which described the current status and outlined plans for the future. Brandsma and Bos (1994) report that the set of instruments is easy to use, yields reliable data and leads to high interpreter reliabilities. The following conclusions about the four dimensions were drawn.

- In general, schools do not make detailed statements about pedagogical aims and affective outcomes in their school policy documents.
- The physical school and classroom environment is rated positively in most schools.
- Teacher behavior toward students is judged positively with the exception of modeling of the teacher.
- Most schools do not achieve high scores on the dimension of the school's system. Schools have not developed a policy on climate factors.

The main conclusion is that the climate factors most prominent in Dutch elementary schools are the quality of the physical environment and the quality of teacher behavior in classrooms. The climate factors at the school level (plans for effectiveness and aims and the school's system) are not as well developed.

The following information is available about the reliability and validity of the instruments (Brandsma and Bos, 1994):

- *first dimension (school plan for effectiveness)*
  interrater agreement: 81 per cent of statements
- *second dimension (physical environment)*
  coefficient alpha for classroom indicators: 0.79
  coefficient alpha for school indicators: 0.82
  interrater agreement: 94 per cent of statements
- *third dimension (teacher behavior)*
  coefficient alpha for relaxed classroom climate: 0.82
  coefficient alpha for interest and feedback: 0.80
  coefficient alpha for discipline: 0.48
  coefficient alpha for self-discovered learning: 0.72
  coefficient alpha for modeling: 0.71
  interrater agreement: varies from 70 to 90 per cent of statements per subscale
- *fourth dimension (school's system)*
  the data were gathered by means of interviews, no reliability or interrater agreement available.

A group of Inspectors and external experts judged the face validity of the instrument and found it satisfactory. It was decided not to weigh the dimensions but to let them stand next to each other, as important in their own right.

References

ANDERSON, C.S. (1982) 'The search for school climate: A review of the research', *Review of Educational Research*, **52**, 3, pp. 368–420.

ARTER, J.A. (1987) *Assessing School and Classroom Climate*, Portland: Northwest Regional Educational Lab.

BRANDSMA, H.P. and BOS, K.T. (1994) *Vaststelling en waardering van het pedagogisch klimaat in basisscholen [Assessment and evaluation of the pedagogical climate in elementary schools]*, Enschede: Universiteit Twente.

BROOKOVER, W., BEADY, C., FLOOD, P., SCHWEITZER, J. and WISENBAKER, J. (1979) *School Social Systems and Student Achievement: Schools Can Make a Difference*, New York: Bergin.

CREEMERS, B.P.M. (1994) *The Effective Classroom*, London: Cassell.

DOYLE, W. (1986) 'Classroom organization and management', in WITTROCK, M.C. (ed.) *Handbook of Research on Teaching*, New York: MacMillan, pp. 392–431.

EDMONDS, R.R. (1979) 'Effective schools for the urban poor', *Educational Leadership*, **37**, 1, pp. 15–27.

EKHOLM, M. and KULL, M. (1996) 'School climate and educational change', *EERA-Bulletin*, **2**, 2, pp. 3–11.

FRASER, B.J. (1991) 'Two decades of classroom environment research', in FRASER, B.J. and WALBERG, H.J. (eds) *Educational Environments: Evaluation, Antecedents and Consequences*, Oxford: Pergamon, pp. 3–29.

FREIBERG, H.J. (1989) 'A multidimensional view of school effectiveness', *Educational Research Quarterly*, **13**, 2, pp. 35–46.

GROSIN, L. (1993) 'School effectiveness research as a point of departure for school evaluation', *Scandinavian Journal of Educational Research*, **37**, 4, pp. 317–30.

HECK, R.H. and MARCOULIDES, G.A. (1996) 'School culture and performance: Testing the invariance of an organizational model', *School Effectiveness and School Improvement*, **7**, 1, pp. 76–96.

HERTZ-LAZAROWITZ, R. and COHEN, M. (1992) 'The school psychologist as a facilitator of a community-wide project to enhance positive learning climate in elementary schools', *Psychology in the schools*, **29**, 4, pp. 348–58.

HOUTVEEN, T., VERMEULEN, C. and GRIFT, W. VAN DER (1993) *Bouwstenen voor onderzoek naar de kwaliteit van scholen [Measuring the Quality of Schools]*, Utrecht: Universiteit van Utrecht/ISOR.

HOY, W.K. (1990) 'Organizational climate and culture: A conceptual analysis of the school workplace', *Journal of Educational and Psychological Consultation*, **1**, 2, pp. 149–68.

HOY, W.K., TARTER, C.J. and BLISS, J.R. (1990) 'Organizational climate, school health, and effectiveness: A comparative analysis', *Educational Administration Quarterly*, **26**, 3, pp. 260–79.

HOY, W.K. and WOOLFOLK, A.E. (1993) 'Teachers' sense of efficacy and the organizational health of schools', *Elementary School Journal*, **93**, 4, pp. 355–72.

INSPECTIE VAN HET ONDERWIJS (1996) *Onderwijsverslag over het jaar 1995 [Educational Report About the Year 1995]*, Den Haag: SDU.

JOHNSON, D.W. and JOHNSON, R.T. (1991) 'Cooperative learning and classroom and school climate', in FRASER, B.J. and WALBERG, H.J. (eds) *Educational Environments: Evaluation, Antecedents and Consequences*, Oxford: Pergamon, pp. 55–75.

JOHNSON, W.L. and JOHNSON, A.M. (1993) 'Validity of the quality of school life scale: A primary and second-order factor analysis', *Educational and Psychological Measurement*, **53**, 1, pp. 145–53.

KLAASSEN, C. (1994) 'Scholen en morele vorming in een postmoderne tijd: over de pedagogische opdracht van het onderwijs [Schools and moral development in the postmodern age]', *Meso*, **14**, 75, pp. 2–10.

KREFT, I.G.G. (1993) 'Using multilevel analysis to assess school effectiveness: A study of Dutch secondary schools', *Sociology of Education*, **66**, 2, pp. 104–29.

LEVINE, D.U. and LEZOTTE, L.W. (1990) *Unusually Effective Schools: A Review and Analysis of Research and Practice*, Madison: National Center for Effective Schools Research and Development.

LUYTEN, H. (1994) *The Stability and Malleability of School Effects*, Enschede: Universiteit Twente.

MOOY, T. and VRIES, G. DE (1993) 'Pesten op school [Bullying in schools]', *Vernieuwing*, **52**, 10, pp. 37–9.

MORTIMORE, P., SAMMONS, P., STOLL, L., LEWIS, D. and ECOB, R. (1988) *School Matters: The Junior Years*, Wells: Open Books.

ORRELL, C.J. (1996) 'ATLAS Communities: Authentic Teaching, Learning, and Assessment for All Students', in STRINGFIELD, S., ROSS, S. and SMITH, L. (eds) *Bold Plans for School Restructuring: The New American Schools Designs*, New Jersey: Lawrence Erlbaum, pp. 53–75.

OSER, F.K., DICK, A. and PATRY, J–L. (1992) 'Responsibility, effectiveness, and the domains of educational research', in OSER, F.K., DICK, A. and PATRY, J–L. (eds.) *Effective and Responsible Teaching: The New Synthesis*, San Francisco: Jossey Bass, pp. 3–14.

ROSS, S.M. and SMITH, L.J. (1994) 'Effects of the Success for All model on kindergarten through second-grade reading achievement, teachers' adjustment, and classroom-school climate at an inner-city school', *Elementary School Journal*, **95**, 2, pp. 121–38.

SCHEERENS, J. (1992) *Effective Schooling: Research, Theory and Practice*, London: Cassell.

SLAVIN, R.E. (1996) *Education for All.* Lisse: Swets and Zeitlinger.

STOLL, L., REYNOLDS, D., CREEMERS, B. and HOPKINS, D. (1996) 'Merging school effectiveness and school improvement: Practical examples', in REYNOLDS, D., CREEMERS, B., BOLLEN, R., HOPKINS, D., STOLL, L. and LAGERWEIJ, N. (eds) *Making Good Schools, Linking School Effectiveness and School Improvement*, London: Pergamon.

STRINGFIELD, S. (1994) 'A model of elementary school effects', in REYNOLDS, D. et al. (eds), *Advances in School Effectiveness Research and Practice*, Oxford: Pergamon, pp. 153–89.

STRINGFIELD, S. and HERMAN, R. (1996) 'Assessment of the state of school effectiveness research in the United States of America', *School Effectiveness and School Improvement*, 7, 2, pp. 159–81.

TEDDLIE, C. (1994) 'The integration of classroom and school process data in school effectiveness research', in REYNOLDS, D. et al. (eds) *Advances in School Effectiveness Research and Practice*, Oxford: Pergamon, pp. 111–33.

WANG, M.C., HAERTEL, G.D. and WALBERG, H.J. (1993) 'Toward a knowledge base for school learning', *Review of Educational Research*, **63**, 3, pp. 249–94.

WERF, M.P.C. VAN DER (1995) *The Educational Priority Policy in The Netherlands: Content, Implementation and Outcomes*, Den Haag: SVO.

WUBBELS, T., BREKELMANS, M. and HOOYMAYERS, H. (1991) 'Interpersonal teacher behavior in the classroom', in FRASER, B.J. and WALBERG, H.J. (eds) *Educational Environments: Evaluation, Antecedents and Consequences*, Oxford: Pergamon, pp. 141–61.

Chapter 3

Using Informal and Formal Measures to Create Classroom Profiles

Charles Teddlie and James Meza, Jr.

This chapter describes methods whereby principals and other administrators can create classroom, grade, and departmental profiles of their schools' learning environments. These profiles can then be used to generate improvement in the management, instruction, and climate of learning environments at multiple levels of schooling. The application of classroom observation techniques to teacher improvement has been discussed before (Stallings and Freiberg, 1991). This chapter extends the use of classroom observation techniques to school improvement. The baseline comparison information contained in this chapter comes from more than ten years work involving the study of teacher effectiveness variables within the context of school climate effectiveness research. Recent applications of the methodology used in these studies to schoolwide improvements efforts will be described in the last two sections of this chapter.

Why Do School Improvers Need Classroom, Grade and School Level Teaching Profiles?

The Lack of Meaningful Reform in Classrooms

School restructuring efforts have been widely attempted by school districts and individual schools during the 1990s. A major goal of these school restructuring models has been to transform classroom teaching practice, which in turn should lead to improvement in student learning. According to several authors (e.g., Blythe and Gardner, 1990; Carnegie Task Force on Teaching as a Profession, 1986; Elmore, 1995; Murphy, 1991). Taylor and Teddlie (1996) described these predicted changes as follows:

> Anticipated among these changes was a modification in classroom activities with roles for teachers and students redefined. Learning activities were expected to tap complex, problem-solving thought processes, while teachers were envisioned to be less directive and more similar to coaches. Concomitantly, students were predicted to shed their traditional passivity and become actively engaged as learner-workers . . . (p. 2)

There is evidence, however, that such changes in classroom behavior are hard to accomplish. For example, Fullan (1993) indicated that the school's "learning core", consisting of both instructional practices and faculty culture, is very difficult to change. Keller and Soler (1994) further contend that real changes in teacher behavior are rare and, when they occur, are the result of the internalization of specific practices and beliefs. David (1991) noted that restructuring efforts, such as school based decision making, will not result in meaningful change unless they are accompanied by access to new skills and knowledge, as well as explicit support or change.

Elmore (1995) called for further research into teaching practice in restructuring schools, suggesting that the relationship between structural school changes and changes in teaching are mediated by factors such as teachers' skills and knowledge. Taylor and Teddlie (1992, 1996) present such research in their analysis of data from a prominent restructuring district. Despite verbal support from top level district administrators, evidence indicated that restructuring had, in fact, not influenced the classrooms. Teachers in schools classified as "highly restructured" were no more likely to collaborate with their colleagues than were teachers from restructuring schools. Teacher-directed and whole-group approaches prevailed in classrooms of both school types (high or low participation in restructuring), with group work and team teaching occurring rarely. The authors concluded that:

> Neither teachers nor administrators in this district were schooled in alternative pedagogies, and deeply ingrained cultural norms and practices militated against collegiality and experimentation with new practices. (Taylor and Teddlie, 1996, p. 15)

The link between school restructuring efforts and classroom behaviors in this supposedly highly restructured district had not occurred, and evidence from other studies indicate that this is not an isolated phenomenon. In these failed efforts, the school level change has not had an impact on the "instructional core" of the school as evidenced in the classroom.

The Link Between Teacher and School Effectiveness

The failure to find evidence of reformed classroom teaching in some restructured schools stands in stark contrast to research that has linked effective teaching with effective schooling. While the teacher effectiveness research (TER) and school effectiveness research (SER) literatures evolved separately, several studies have fruitfully merged the methods from these two areas over the past decade (Teddlie, 1994).

Due to dissatisfaction with the explanatory power of extant economic and sociological models, and climate which rarely viewed classroom and school practices as significant factors in student learning, researchers conducting extensive school effectiveness research (Brookover et al., 1979; Mortimore et al., 1988; Rutter et al., 1979; Stringfield, Teddlie and Suarez, 1985) began exploring classroom processes during the 1970s and 1980s. They used informal observations and survey proxies for teacher effectiveness research variables in their studies, and were rewarded by being able to explore aspects of the schooling process that had not been previously examined in school effectiveness research.

The area of teacher effectiveness research was very active from the early 1970s through the mid-1980s, when a substantial body of literature concerning effective teaching characteristics was fully developed. These characteristics included: quantity and pacing of instruction, opportunity to learn, time allocation, classroom management, active teaching, whole-class versus small group versus individual instruction, redundancy/sequencing, clarity, proper use of praise, pacing/wait-time, questioning skills, and other instructional practices.

Starting in the mid-1980s, researchers working within the school effectiveness research paradigm borrowed these variables and the instruments to measure them from teacher effectiveness research. They began explicitly including classroom observations (and consequently teacher effectiveness variables) in their research (e.g., Creemers et al., 1996; Crone and Teddlie, 1995; Stringfield and Teddlie, 1990; 1991; Stringfield, Teddlie and Suarez, 1985; Teddlie, Kirby and Stringfield, 1989; Teddlie and Stringfield, 1993; Virgilio, Teddlie and Oescher, 1991). Teddlie, Stringfield and their colleagues used the Stallings Observation System (SOS) and an instrument composed of variables gleaned from Rosenshine's (1983; 1986) reviews of teacher effectiveness research in their school effectiveness research.

These studies of teacher effectiveness variables within the context of school effectiveness variables revealed *consistent mean and standard deviation differences in classroom teaching between schools classified as effective or ineffective.* For example, results from Teddlie, Kirby, and Stringfield (1989) indicated that teachers in effective schools were more successful in keeping students on task, spent more time presenting new material, provided more independent practice, demonstrated higher expectations for students, provided more positive reinforcement, than did their peers in matched ineffective schools.

In addition to these mean differences in teaching behaviors between effective /ineffective schools, differences in patterns of variation were also found. For instance, the standard deviations (sds) reported for teaching behavior were smaller in more effective as opposed to less effective schools. This result indicates that there are ongoing processes at more effective schools (e.g., informed selection of new teachers, effective socialization processes) that result in more homogenous behavior among teachers in which the "trailing edge" (ineffective teaching) is somehow eliminated. The consistency of these differential results between effective/typical/less effective schools provided researchers and educators with "benchmark" data for comparison and staff development recommendations in restructuring schools.

The Link Between Teacher Observation and School Improvement

A series of quasi-experiments conducted in teacher effectiveness research during the late 1970s through the mid-1980s demonstrated that the alteration of classroom processes could produce mean gains in student achievement (e.g., Anderson, Evertson and Brophy, 1979; Good and Grouws, 1979; Stallings, 1986; Tobin, 1980; Tobin and Capie, 1982). Stallings (1986) employed a staff development plan (the Effective Use of Time [EUOT] program) and trained teachers how to more effectively devote percentages of their classtime to certain activities. Students in EUOT classes gained more on reading achievement than did control students.

Stallings and Freiberg (1991) demonstrated how a profile could be developed for a teacher that included specific changes in that teacher's allocation of time to certain activities. This profile was based on established criteria and observation of the teacher's behavior. The profile included 12 specific activities together with recommendations for increasing, decreasing, or leaving as is the allocation of time to these activities.

This literature suggests a direct linkage from classroom observations through the establishment of meaningful programs for school improvement: (i) teacher effectiveness research indicates that there are effective teaching characteristics, which can be measured using a variety of instruments; (ii) teacher effectiveness research also indicates that changes in these effective teaching characteristics, are associated with changes in student learning; (iii) staff development programs can be used to change the ineffective practices of individual teachers based on observations of that teacher and established criteria; (iv) grade/department/school level profiles can be developed based on aggregated data from observations of individual teachers; (v) staff development programs can be established to change teacher behaviors at grade/department/school/levels; and (vi) these grade/department/school level staff development programs can then be used to generate positive changes in student learning at each of those levels, thus leading to more effective schooling.

Examples of Informal and Formal Teacher Observational Systems

Several types of teacher observational systems will be described based on two distinctions:

(i) whether the system consists of formal measures (quantitatively oriented instruments composed of items with fixed responses), or informal measures (qualitative instruments composed primarily of open-ended responses); and

(ii) whether the teacher observational system was designed for evaluating individual teachers (e.g. teacher assessment systems in Florida, Georgia, Louisiana) or for general research purposes (e.g. the Stallings Classroom Snapshot) (see Table 3.1).

Table 3.1 Examples of different types of formal and informal teacher observation systems

	Informal measures	*Formal measures*
Individual teacher evaluation	Principal or other assessor classroom notes	State mandated teacher assessment systems
Grade, department, school evaluation	Classroom observation instrument (COI)	Virgilio teacher behavior inventory (VTBI)

Informal Teacher Observation

Effective principals, or their surrogates, normally observe their teachers intuitively following the Deal and Peterson (1990) procedure: frequent, short, unannounced visits to classrooms. During these visits, the principals make mental notes regarding teachers' skills. In school effectiveness research conducted by Teddlie and Stringfield (1993), the authors noted that effective principals knew which of their teachers were delivering high, average, or poor quality instruction, and also knew when teachers were performing above or below their usual level, based primarily on longitudinal informal observations.

These type of *ad libitum* observations are the most informal of those denoted in Table 3.1; their target is the individual teacher, and they contribute to the Principal's global evaluation of that person. More formal field notes associated with state mandated evaluations also fit into this category. Assessors in the Louisiana Teacher Assessment Program for Interns (LTAP-I) "script" the classes they observe, and then use the scripted notes to complete formal close-ended ratings (Louisiana Department of Education (LDE), 1995).

Field notes can be aggregated to form impressions of the overall teaching ongoing at a grade/department/school. For example, during the third phase of the Louisiana School Effectiveness Study (LSES-III), the researchers used the Classroom Observation Instrument (COI), an instrument designed to provide high-inference classroom data in the form of field notes completed as behavior occurred in the classroom. The Classroom Observation Instrument was composed of 15 categories of effective teaching behavior gleaned from teacher effectiveness research reviews (e.g., Rosenshine and Stevens, 1986) and included: measures of time-on-task (TOT), initial student practice, presentation of new material, and positive reinforcement. During LSES-III, observers coded a large number of Classroom Observation Instruments; altogether over 25,000 units of information were recorded (700 classes × 15 observation items × an average of 2.5 observer comments). These field notes were then used to generate case studies that described ongoing processes at the school/grade/teacher levels for the 16 schools involved in the study.

Formal Teacher Observation

Formal teacher evaluation systems have been used in several states and districts (e.g., California, Connecticut, Florida, Georgia, Louisiana, South Carolina, Texas) over the past 20 years (e.g., Capie et al., 1980; Ellet et al., 1994; Florida Coalition for the Development of a Performance Measurement System, 1983; LDE, 1995; Smith, 1985). These mandated systems have proven controversial (e.g., Brandt, 1985; Ellet et al., 1994; Maxcy and Maxcy, 1993) with critics claiming that top-down efforts will not work and/or that the teacher is the wrong "unit of analysis".

State mandated systems assess a large number of specific attributes of effective instruction. The Florida Performance Measurement System consisted of six broad domains, 31 concepts, and 121 indicators (Smith, 1985). The LTAP-I includes a set of domains, which are composed of effective teaching components, which in turn are composed of specific teacher attributes (LDE, 1995). These domains include planning, management and instruction. Under instruction, there are five effective teaching "components". Under the presentation of appropriate content "component" are several "attributes".

Such mandated teacher evaluation systems provide information that could theoretically be aggregated up to provide indicators of teaching effectiveness at the grade/department/school level. This aggregation, however, seldom occurs given the political and legal nature of state and district mandated systems.

On the other hand, there are numerous other teacher effectiveness research systems, which produce data that can be aggregated to higher units of analysis. These teacher observation systems include: the Flanders' Interaction Analysis Categories (Flanders, 1970); the Classroom Snapshot (CS) from the SOS (Stallings and Kaskowitz, 1974; Stallings, 1980); the Learning Environment Inventory (e.g., Walberg, 1976); the Classroom Activity Record (Evertson and Burry, 1989); the IEA Classroom Environment Study instruments (Anderson, Ryan and Shapiro, 1989); the Virgilio Teacher Behavior Inventory (Teddlie, Virgilio and Oescher, 1990); the Special Strategies Observation System and the International Classroom Observation Survey (Schaffer, Nesselrodt and Stringfield, 1994).

Using Benchmark Data for Comparison Purposes with Classroom Profiles

In order to interpret results from classroom observation studies, analysts need comparison data; i.e. they need to know how well effective teachers, or teachers from effective schools, have performed on these observational systems. These criteria could come from a variety of sources: state/district mandated criteria levels, "benchmark" data generated from other schools in the state/district, or benchmark data generated from published studies conducted in differentially effective schools, whichever is available.

Benchmark classroom observation data (Virgilio Teacher Behavior Inventory and Classroom Snapshot) from research conducted in Louisiana over the past decade are presented in Table 3.2. These benchmark data were generated from a series of studies comparing the quality of classroom instruction in differentially effective schools.

In these studies, schools were classified on two (more or less effective) or three levels (more effective/typical/less effective). Schools were given these ratings based on their students' achievement after the effect of their families socioeconomic status had been taken into consideration. These studies have demonstrated that quality of classroom instruction is directly related to school effectiveness: schools rated as more effective have a greater evidence of effective teaching than schools rated as typical or less effective. Data from these studies indicate that classrooms in more effective schools average 51 per cent interactive time on task and 76 per cent total time on task. On the other hand, classrooms in less effective schools average 37 per cent interactive time on task and 52 per cent total time on task (see Table 3.2).

Table 3.2 Results of benchmark studies comparing across levels of effectiveness

Dimension of effective schooling	More effective schools	Typical schools	Less effective schools
Interactive time on task	51%	43%	37%
Total time on task	76%	64%	52%
Classroom management	4.05	3.15	3.07
Quality of instruction	3.73	3.39	2.89
Social psychological climate	3.75	3.61	3.48

Note: This table summarizes the results from several studies of differentially effective schools (e.g., Crone and Teddlie, 1995; Stringfield and Teddlie, 1990; 1991; Stringfield, Teddlie and Suarez, 1985; Teddlie, Kirby and Stringfield, 1989; Teddlie and Stringfield, 1993; Virgilio, Teddlie and Oescher, 1991).

Altogether some 1,200 classroom observations were conducted in these studies in approximately 125 schools and 500 different classrooms. Stallings' Classroom Snapshot was used as the measure of interactive and total TOT. Scores on this instrument could range from 0% to 100% TOT. The Virgilio Teacher Behavior Inventory was used as the measure of classroom management, quality of instruction, and social psychological climate. Scores on items on the VTBI range from 1 (poor) to 5 (excellent).

These studies also indicate that there are consistent differences in Virgilio Teacher Behavior Inventory ratings collected from classrooms in differentially effective schools, as was the case with time on task. Individual item scores on the Virgilio Teacher Behavior Inventory range from 1 (poor) to 5 (excellent). For the benchmark studies, scores for more effective schools averaged around 3.85 across three general areas of teaching (Classroom management, Quality of Instruction and Social Psychological Climate) while those for less effective schools averaged around 3.00, which is the mid-point on the scale (see Table 3.2).

Another important result from these studies concerns the variance of ratings across classrooms in differentially effective schools. Teachers in more effective schools demonstrated less variance, while those in less effective schools demonstrated more variance. The "trailing edge" of teaching was eliminated in more effective schools. You will find effective teachers in less effective schools, but you will not find ineffective teachers in more effective schools. Data from these studies have been used in recent school improvement research as "benchmarks" with which to compare the performance of teachers in schools currently under study (e.g., Meza and Teddlie, 1996; Teddlie, 1994; 1996). Comparisons were used to determine if the staffs at the observed schools were performing at the level usually found in more effective, typical, or less effective schools. Staff development recommendations were made for areas in which the teachers' classroom behaviors appeared to be deficient.

Examples of Creating Classroom Profiles for Schools

Several techniques can be used for developing classroom profiles for several levels of schooling. These data can be aggregated at the appropriate levels and compared with benchmark data to guide staff development procedures.

General Procedures for Creating Profiles

There are seven steps in the process:

(i) selecting the teacher observation system(s) to be used;
(ii) selecting the classrooms to be observed, based on whether a representative (random or stratified random) or purposive (non-random) sample is required;
(iii) developing a procedure for classroom observation;
(iv) coding and entering the data onto computerized databases
(v) analyzing the data at the appropriate level(s) of aggregation and comparing that information to benchmark data;
(vi) deriving recommendations for staff development; and
(vii) reporting the results to appropriate audiences.

The choice of teacher observation systems involves two very important considerations: (i) it is useful to have data from two different systems; and (ii) it is important to have benchmark data for the systems that are used. It is useful to take informal notes in addition to completing the formal measures. Researchers are encouraged to make notes on classroom contexts/processes that will then help generate case studies and staff development recommendations.

If educators want a general faculty "snapshot" representative of the school, then random or stratified random sampling procedures should be used in classroom selection. Conversely, if educators are interested in teacher behavior at specified departments/grades, then purposive or non-random samples should be drawn. In the examples discussed below, elementary school administrators wanted representative samples, so evaluators selected classes randomly within grades. Samples were limited to 18–24 classes, due to time and money constraints. This size sample allowed for 3–4 observations per grade level per year.

Observations should be conducted by trained observers, who have conducted similar studies and are familiar with the systems being used. If multiple raters are used, estimates of interrater reliability should be calculated in advance and assessed periodically during the study. In the school improvement studies to be described below, and in the school effectiveness research referenced above, each observation consisted of a 45 to 60 minute time period during which that class was scheduled to be involved in regular classroom instruction.

Teachers being observed should carry on with their usual activities and be informed that researchers will be coming at an appointed time. Teachers should be explicitly told that their individual performance is not being assessed, but rather the overall quality of teaching throughout the grade level and school. The intention is to create a more relaxed classroom atmosphere, so that observed behavior is representative of typical lessons, rather than the proverbial "dog and pony show" that occurs in many state mandated evaluation systems. Data may be analyzed using SAS, SPSS, or other statistical packaged programs. Descriptive statistics are computed at the school level and then broken down by grade and department. Typically, data are not analyzed at the individual teacher level, due to the large error variance associated with having only one or two observations per teacher, plus the fact that the teacher is *not* the unit of analysis in these programs.

In school improvement programs, emphasis is placed on change at the school level which can then have a pervasive effect on other units, but individual teachers are not singled out for solitary improvement efforts. Targeted individual teacher development is the change mode utilized in mandated state and district teacher evaluation systems, and it usually carries heavy political burdens (e.g., Ellet et al., 1996; Maxcy and Maxcy, 1993).

Results from these analyses are then compared with benchmark data such as those in Table 3.2. This allows researchers to compare specific types of behaviors for grade/department levels. For instance, the VTBI evaluates 38 specific behaviors spread out over five general areas. If analysts wanted to do so, they could compare average grade/department rating on all 38 items with benchmark data.

Separate reports may be prepared for the different educational audiences, or provide overall feedback to administrators, and grade/department specific information to teachers. Reporting comparisons across grades or departments can cause problems (e.g., lowered staff morale, loss of esteem), so these comparisons should only be given to those staff responsible to schoolwide change. Recommendations for staff development can be made by external analysts, the school improvement team, or the school administration team.

A Pair of "Restructured" Schools

The following example comes from a study in which two schools, involved in a national reform program, were compared with one another (Meza and Teddlie, 1996). The comparison information was not given to the schools. The comparisons indicated that there was evidence of very effective teaching at one school (Eastside) and of mediocre to poor teaching at the other (Westside) (All *names in this chapter are pseudonyms*). These two schools are similar demographically. Eastside had a K–6th grade configuration, served around 500 students, with a total faculty composed of 34 members. The majority of the students at the school were on free lunch. Westside had a similar configuration, serving around 600 students, with a total faculty composed of 36 members. The majority of students at Westside were also on free lunch.

Eastside Elementary School analyses

Data indicated that Eastside teachers conducted classes similar to those found in effective schools (see Table 3.2). Eastside ratings were higher than those for the more effective benchmark schools in three areas (interactive and total time on task, social psychological climate) and were about the same as those for the more effective schools in two areas (management, instruction) (see Table 3.3).

Table 3.3 Summary of classroom instructional indicator data for Eastside Elementary School

Dimension	School Mean	sd
Interactive time on task	0.68	0.27
Total time on task	0.82	0.16
Management	4.06	0.98
Instruction	3.79	0.80
A. Presentation and questioning	4.13	0.90
B. Instructional strategies	3.63	0.83
Social psychological climate	4.48	0.68

Note: Scores on items on the Virgilio Teacher Behavior Inventory range from 1 (poor) to 5 (excellent).

The standard deviations reported for Eastside were relatively small, indicating that teachers were similar to one another in terms of their classroom behavior. This is a characteristic of effective schools: the "trailing edge" of teacher performance (ineffective teaching) does not occur very often. Eastside results broken out by grade levels also indicated that teachers at most grade levels conducted classes that were similar to those found in more effective schools (Meza and Teddlie, 1996):

- teachers at grades 2 through to 6 had time on task ratings that were higher than that obtained by teachers in effective benchmark schools.
- some scattered Eastside ratings (e.g., kindergarten, 1st grade, 4th grade) were similar to those found in average or ineffective schools.
- the lowest time on task was recorded at the kindergarten and 1st grade levels, with the 1st grade interactive time on task being about the same as that recorded by the average benchmark schools.
- the first grade also scored the lowest on the Virgilio Teacher Behavior Inventory.
- the 4th grade Virgilio Teacher Behavior Inventory rating for instruction was about the same as that attained by average benchmark schools.

Westside Elementary School analyses

Results from observations of Westside teachers indicated that they conducted classrooms that were mixed in terms of effectiveness (see Table 3.4). Referring to Table 3.2 data, it can be concluded that Westside teachers:

- conducted classrooms similar to those found in typical schools on the time on task indices and the Virgilio Teacher Behavior Inventory measure of social psychological climate.
- conducted classrooms similar to those found in less effective schools on the Virgilio Teacher Behavior Inventory measures of quality of instructions and classroom management.
- the standard deviations reported from Westside are large, indicating a wide spread of teachers.

Table 3.4 Summary of classroom instructional indicator data for Westside Elementary School

Dimension	**School Mean**	**sd**
Interactive time on task	0.47	0.30
Total time on task	0.59	0.30
Management	3.10	1.28
Instruction	2.61	1.16
A. Presentation and questioning	2.86	1.40
B. Instructional strategies	2.45	1.14
Social psychological climate	3.65	0.89

Note: Scores on items on the Virgilio Teacher Behavior Inventory range from 1 (poor) to 5 (excellent).

There was a wide range in ratings on all measures of teacher effectiveness across the grade levels at Westside. This wide range in both time on task variables and on other measures of teacher effectiveness indicates that there was no quality control being exerted at the school level. Students in such schools experience healthy learning environments in a random fashion. The implications for school improvement in environments with a wide range of teacher behaviors is obvious: a schoolwide system for quality control must be implemented whereby the "trailing edge" of the range of behaviors is eliminated, through altering both selection and socialization processes.

General Conclusions from the Two Sets of School Profiles

The two schools described had different contexts and ongoing school processes. Both were engaged in similar, long-term restructuring efforts, yet differed greatly on quality of observed classroom instruction, with one school having much more effective teaching than the other. Furthermore the effectiveness of classroom teaching at both these schools varied considerably by grade level. The general differences between these schools' contexts and their staff development programs are as follows:

- Eastside — currently undergoing restructuring, with excellent teaching schoolwide. Proposed staff development plan emphasizing specific grade level activities.
- Westside — currently undergoing restructuring, with poor to average teaching schoolwide and large grade level differences. Proposed staff development plan emphasized both schoolwide and specific grade level activities.

Using Classroom Profiles to Generate Staff Development and School Improvement Plans

Information from classroom profiles aggregated at one or several levels, are a necessary part of determining the overall climate of a school. It has a direct effect on school improvement through its impact on the development of differential staff development plans at the grade, department and/or school levels.

Stedman (1987) described several elements involved in ongoing, practical staff development in unusually effective schools: the training is directed to the specific needs of staff members and students; demonstration lessons are given to inexperienced teachers; teachers are allowed to observe experienced, effective teachers; and videotapes of effective teaching practices are presented to teachers needing improvement. Some of Stedman's observations are relevant to the instructional problems at the schools discussed below and are included in the staff development plan for Westside.

Classroom profiles, as a tool for the generation and maintenance of overall school climate improvement plans, are particularly useful when used in conjunction with benchmark data from differentially effective schools. Even though overall Eastside ratings were either equal to or better than benchmark data for effective schools, the presence of some grade ratings being similar to typical and ineffective schools, should provide school administrators with guidelines for continued and specific improvement plans. On the other hand, the indications at Westside of overall ratings were similar to benchmark data for ineffective schools, indicators on some dimensions, and at some grade levels, were equal to that of effective schools. This points to the presence of isolated instances of a positive classroom climate, which needs to be replicated throughout the school.

Recommendations for Staff Development at Westside

Two major conclusions can be drawn from the Westside data analyses:

- there was evidence of overall ineffective teaching.
- the "trailing edge" teacher performance occurred frequently in several grades.

Recommendations included the following (Teddlie, 1996):

(i) A schoolwide staff development program is needed, due to very low overall ratings, especially in time on task, instructional presentation and questioning, and instructional strategies. Consultants could be brought in for inservices on how to increase time on task and to improve the overall quality of instruction.

(ii) Since there are some good teachers at the school, demonstration lessons on topics such as classroom management might be useful. Westside is already broken up into four "separate" schools: 3 kindergarten through 4th grade wings and a 5th and 6th grade wing. The distribution of more and less effective grades is such that those teachers needing assistance, could get it with their "own" school.

(iii) Given the proclivity to start multiple reforms at Westside and then not follow through, it would be beneficial to terminate other effective teaching programs at Westside, and focus on one program. In order to involve the principal and the administrative staff in an ongoing reform process, they should be required to observe in all classrooms, and to pinpoint specific deficits to be addressed through tailored inservice training to meet recurrent needs of the faculty.

(iv) There are some limits to external feedback. This suggestion focuses on providing the teacher with specific data at the classroom and individual level. Significant change can occur when individuals reflect on evidence of their teaching. This can be accomplished when teachers analyze original source data based on an audiotape of their classrooms and following a procedure called LISAM (Low Inference Self-Assessment Measure) developed by Freiberg (1987). Teachers analyze their own interaction patterns in the classroom (Flanders, 1970) by coding from the tape the types and frequency of interactions. The procedures are explained in detail in Chapter 15 of *Universal Teaching Strategies* (Freiberg and Driscoll, 1996).

Conclusion: The Importance of Classroom Profiles in the Development of School Improvement Programs

It may be inferred from the writings of several researcher/reformers that an increased emphasis on the use of classroom observation data in the development of school improvement plans is needed. Brookover et al. (1984) included three modules on classroom teaching (effective instruction, academic engaged time, classroom management) as part of their 1980s school improvement inservice program. In order to most effectively utilize these modules in school improvement efforts, profiles of classroom teaching currently ongoing in the schools under study would, of course, be very valuable.

Similarly, Slavin's school change model (e.g., Slavin, Madden, Dolan, Wasik, Ross, Smith and Dianda, 1996) emphasizes that change has to occur at the intersection of the student, the teacher and the curriculum. His strategy for classroom improvement emphasizes active learning and cooperative learning. Likewise, Levin and colleagues (e.g., Keller and Soler, 1994; Levin, 1996) have begun to more explicitly explore how "powerful" learning occurs in the classrooms of Accelerated Schools. In order to most efficiently utilize these special strategies for school improvement, an assessment of current teacher classroom behavior at targeted schools is essential.

Unfortunately, both generic and specially targeted schools improvement programs typically *do not include* the assessment of current classroom teaching practices, even though such assessment is essential to the development of a true picture of the overall school climate for learning. In the developmental phase of most school improvement programs, surveys are given to multiple audiences (e.g., students, teachers, administrators, parents) asking them to assess the overall educational climate in the school, but these paper-and-pencil measure are geared toward a global assessment of the overall school climate and are *not adequate* for determining the targeted staff development for teachers (e.g., Stedman, 1987) necessary to bring about true change in the learning core of the school.

Recent state and district school improvement programs in Louisiana (Teddlie and Kennedy, 1996; 1997) utilize a process in which classroom observations in less effective schools play a strategic role in the development of the change plans for those schools. A field test of the Louisiana School Effectiveness and Assistance Program was recently conducted (academic years 1996–7 and 1997–8) involving three distinct phases:

(i) The development of a composite school effectiveness indicator (SEI) system to measure individual school level effectiveness after taking into consideration the family backgrounds of student attending those schools.
(ii) The field testing of a consistent process for assessing and improving schools provides qualitative process information to the Louisiana Department of Education (LDE) and diagnostic information to the individual school in the form of customized schoolwide profiles (i.e., School Assessment and Improvement Profiles). These profiles include classroom information similar to that generated for Eastside and Westside Elementary schools. This phase of the 1996–8 field test occurred in 3–4 districts, each with 3–4 pilot schools (see Tables 3.3 and 3.4 for examples of aggregated profiles).
(iii) The co-ordination of LDE assistance targeted to the weaknesses identified through the School Assessment and Improvement Profiles of the pilot schools from the second phase of the field study. These school improvement plans will include specific staff development for addressing weaknesses in teaching behaviors uncovered during classroom observations.

The fruitful merger of teacher effectiveness research, school effectiveness research, and school indicator systems will go a long way toward the accomplishment of true systemic reform. Sustaining healthy learning environments requires measures that include classroom teaching practices. Classroom profiles for teachers and administrators can transform the learning environment, in that they generate data on teacher effectiveness variables for inclusion on school indicator profiles that can then be used to sustain school improvement.

References

Anderson, L., Evertson, C. and Brophy, J. (1979) 'An experimental study of effective teaching in first-grade reading groups', *Elementary School Journal*, **79**, pp. 198–223.

Anderson, L.W., Ryan, D.W. and Shapiro, B.J. (eds.) (1989) *The IEA Classroom Environment Study*, Oxford: Pergamon Press.

Blythe, T. and Gardner, H. (1990) 'A school for all intelligences', *Educational Leadership*, **47**, 7, pp. 33–7.

Brandt, R. (1985) 'Ramrodding reform in Texas', *Educational Leadership*, **42**, 3, p. 94.

BROOKOVER, W.B., BEADY, C.H., FLOOD, P.K., SCHWEITZER, J.H. and WISENBAKER, J.M. (1979) *School Social Systems and Student Achievement*, New York: Praeger.

CAPIE, W., JOHNSON, C.E., ANDERSON, S.J., ELLET, C. and OKEY, J.R. (1980) *Teacher Performance Assessment Instruments*, Athens, GA: Univ. of Georgia Teacher Assessment Project.

CARNEGIE TASK FORCE ON TEACHING AS A PROFESSION (1986) *A Nation Prepared: Teachers for the 21st Century*, Washington DC: Carnegie Forum on Education and the Economy.

CREEMERS, B.P.M., REYNOLDS, D., STRINGFIELD, S. and TEDDLIE, C. (1996, April) World class schools: Some further findings. Paper presented at the annual meeting of the American Educational Research Association, New York, NY.

CRONE, L. and TEDDLIE, C. (1995) 'Further examination of teacher behavior in differentially effective schools: Selection and socialization processes', *Journal of Classroom Interaction*, **30**, 1, pp. 1–9.

DAVID, J. (1991) 'What it takes to restructure education', *Educational Leadership*, **48**, 8, pp. 11–15.

DEAL, T.E. and PETERSON, K.D. (1990) *The Principal's Role in Shaping School Cultures*, Washington, DC: USDE.

ELLET, C.D., LOUP, K.S., NAIK, N., CHAUVIN, S.W. and CLAUDET, J. (1994) 'Issues in the application of a conjunctive/compensatory standards-setting model to a criterion-referenced, classroom-based teacher certification assessment system: A state case study', *Journal of Personnel Evaluation in Education*, **8**, pp. 349–75.

ELLET, C.D., WREN, C.Y., CALLENDAR, K.R., LOUP, K.S. and LIU, X. (1996) 'Looking backwards with the *Personnel Evaluations Standards*: An analysis of the development and implementation of a statewide teacher assessment system', *Studies in Educational Evaluation*, **22**, 1, pp. 79–113.

ELMORE, R. (1995) 'Structured reform and educational practice', *Educational Researcher*, **24**, 9, pp. 23–6.

EVERTSON, C. and BURRY, J. (1989) 'Capturing classroom context: The observation system as lens for assessment', *Journal of Personnel Evaluation in Education*, **2**, pp. 297–320.

FLANDERS, N. (1970) *Analyzing Teacher Behavior*, Reading, MA: Addison-Wesley.

FLORIDA COALITION FOR THE DEVELOPMENT OF A PERFORMANCE MEASUREMENT SYSTEM (1983) *Domains: Knowledge Base of the Florida Performance Measurement System*, Tallahassee, FL: Office of Teacher Education, Certification, and Inservice Staff Development.

FREIBERG, H.J. (1987) 'Teacher self-evaluation and principal supervision', *National Association of Secondary School Principals*, **71**, p. 498.

FREIBERG, H.J. and DRISCOLL, A. (1996) *Universal Teaching Strategies* (2nd Edition), Needham Heights: Allyn and Bacon.

FULLAN, M. (1993) *Change Forces: Probing the Depths of Educational Reforms*, London: Falmer Press.

GOOD, T.L. and GROUWS, D. (1979) 'The Missouri Mathematics Effectiveness Project: An experimental study in fourth grade classrooms', *Journal of Educational Psychology*, **71**, pp. 355–62.

KELLER, B.M. and SOLER, P. (1994) The influence of the Accelerated schools philosophy and process on classroom practices. Paper presented at the Annual Meeting of the American Educational Research Association.

LEVIN, H.M. (1996) 'Powerful learning in Accelerated schools', *Accelerated Schools*, **3**, 3, p. 2.

LOUISIANA DEPARTMENT OF EDUCATION (1995) *Louisiana Teacher Assessment Program, 1994–5 Implementation, Evaluation Reports*, Baton Rouge: LDE.

Maxcy, S.J. and Maxcy, D.O. (1993) 'Educational reform in Louisiana', *International Journal of Educational Reform*, **2**, 3, pp. 236–41.

Meza, J. Jr. and Teddlie, C. (1996) *An Examination of Differential Teacher Effectiveness in two Restructuring Schools*, New Orleans, LA: University of New Orleans Accelerated Schools Center.

Mortimore, P., Sammons, P., Stoll, L., Lewis, D. and Ecob, R. (1988) *School Matters: The Junior Years*, Somerset, England: Open Books.

Murphy, J. (1991) *Restructuring Schools: Capturing and Assessing the Phenomena*, New York: Teachers College Press.

Rosenshine, B. (1983) 'Teaching functions in instructional programs', *Elementary School Journal*, **83**, pp. 335–51.

Rosenshine, B. and Stevens, R. (1986) 'Teaching functions', in Wittrock, M. (ed.), *Third Handbook of Research on Teaching*, New York: Macmillan.

Rutter, M., Maugham, B., Mortimore, P. and Ouston, J. (1979) *Fifteen Thousand Hours: Secondary Schools and their Effect on Children*, Cambridge, MA: Harvard University Press.

Schaffer, E.C., Nesselrodt, P.S. and Stringfield, S. (1994) 'The contributions of classroom observations to school effectiveness research', in Reynolds, D., Creemers, B.P.M., Nesselrodt, P.S., Schaffer, E.C., Stringfield, S. and Teddlie, C. (eds) *Advances in School Effectiveness Research and Practice*, London: Pergamon, pp. 133–52.

Slavin, R., Madden, N., Dolan, L., Wasik, B., Ross, S., Smith, L. and Dianda, M. (1996) 'Success for all: A summary of research', *Journal for the Education of Children Placed At Risk*, **1**, 1, pp. 44–76.

Smith, B.O. (1985) 'Research bases for teacher education', *Phi Delta Kappan*, **66**, pp. 685–90.

Stallings, J.A. (1980) 'Allocated academic learning time revisited, or beyond time on task', *Educational Researcher*, **2**, 11, pp. 11–16.

Stallings, J.A. (1986) Effective Use of Time in Secondary Reading Programs, in *Effective Teaching of Reading: Research and Practice*, Newark, DE: International Reading Association.

Stallings, J.A. and Freiberg, H.J. (1991) 'Observation for the improvement of teaching', in Waxman, H.C. and Walberg, H.J. (eds) *Effective Teaching: Current Research*, Berkeley, CA: McCutchan Publishing Corporation, pp. 107–34.

Stallings, J.A. and Kaskowitz, D. (1974) *Follow through Classroom Observation Evaluation (1972–1973)*, Menlo Park, CA: SRI International.

Stedman, L. (1987) 'It's time we change the effective schools formula', *Phi Delta Kappan*, **69**, 3, pp. 31–7.

Stringfield, S. and Teddlie, C. (1990) 'School improvement efforts: Qualitative data from four naturally occurring experiments in phase III of the Louisiana school effectiveness study', *School Effectiveness and School Improvement*, **1**, 2, pp. 139–62.

Stringfield, S. and Teddlie, C. (1991) 'Schools as affectors of teacher effects', in Walberg, H. and Waxman, H. (eds) *Effective Teaching: Current Research*, Berkeley, CA: McCutchan Publishing.

Stringfield, S., Teddlie, C. and Suarez, S. (1985) 'Classroom interaction in effective and ineffective schools: Preliminary results from phase III of the Louisiana School Effectiveness Study', *Journal of Classroom Interaction*, **20**, 2, pp. 31–7.

Taylor, D. and Teddlie, C. (1992) 'Restructuring and the classroom: A view from a reform district', paper presented at the annual meeting of the American Educational Research Association, San Francisco, CA.

TAYLOR, D. and TEDDLIE, C. (1996) Restructuring without changing: Constancy in the classroom in a restructured district, Unpublished manuscript: Louisiana State University, College of Education.

TEDDLIE, C. (1994) 'Integrating classroom and school data in school effectiveness research', in REYNOLDS, D. et al., *Advances in School Effectiveness Research and Practice*, Oxford: Pergamon, pp. 111–32.

TEDDLIE, C. (1996) *A Comparison of the Classroom Indicators of Effective Teaching in two 'Reform' Schools*, Baton Rouge, LA: K.T. Associates.

TEDDLIE, C. and KENNEDY, E. (1996) *'A proposal to the Louisiana Department of Education concerning the school performance model, school review process document, and school assistance program'*, Baton Rouge, LA: School Assessment and Improvement Services.

TEDDLIE, C. and KENNEDY, E. (1997) *Profiles of Teaching Behaviour from Three Studies of Louisiana Schools: Their Potential Use in the School Improvement Process*, Baton Rouge, LA: School Assessment and Improvement Services.

TEDDLIE, C., KIRBY, P. and STRINGFIELD, S. (1989) 'Effective versus ineffective schools: Observable differences in the classroom', *American Journal of Education*, **97**, 3, pp. 221–36.

TEDDLIE, C. and STRINGFIELD, S. (1993) *Schools Make a Difference: Lessons Learned from a 10-year Study of School Effects*, New York: Teachers College Press.

TEDDLIE, C., VIRGILIO, I. and OESCHER, J. (1990) 'Development and validation of the Virgilio Teacher Behavior Inventory', *Educational and Psychological Measurement*, **50**, 2, pp. 421–30.

TOBIN, K. (1980) 'The effects of an extended teacher wait-time on student achievement', *Journal of Research in Science Teaching*, **17**, pp. 469–75.

TOBIN, K. and CAPIE, W. (1982) 'Relationships between classroom process variables and middle school achievement, *Journal of Educational Psychology*, **74**, pp. 441–54.

VIRGILIO, I., TEDDLIE, C. and OESCHER, J. (1991) 'Variance and context differences in teaching at differentially effective schools', *School Effectiveness and School Improvement*, **2**, 2, pp. 152–68.

WALBERG, H.J. (1976) 'Psychology of learning environments: Behavioral, structural, or perceptual?' in SHULMAN, L.S. (ed.) *Review of Research in Education* (Volume 4). Itasca, IL: F.E. Peacock, American Educational Research Association.

Chapter 4

Using Learning Environment Assessments to Improve Classroom and School Climates

Barry J. Fraser

The strongest tradition in past learning environment research involved investigation of associations between students' cognitive and affective learning outcomes and their perceptions of their classroom environments (Goh, Young and Fraser, 1995). Fraser (1994) reviewed 40 past studies of the effects of classroom environment on student outcomes involving various cognitive and affective outcome measures, various classroom environment instruments and various samples (ranging across numerous countries and grade levels). Learning environment was found to be consistently and strongly associated with achievement and affective outcomes; with better achievement on a variety of outcome measures occurring in classes perceived as having greater cohesiveness, satisfaction and goal direction; and less disorganization and friction. In McRobbie and Fraser's (1993) research in science laboratory classrooms, affective outcomes were superior in situations in which there was greater integration between the work covered in laboratory classes and theory classes.

A promising but neglected application of classroom environment instruments is their use as process criteria in evaluating new curricula. An evaluation of the Australian Science Education Project (ASEP) revealed that, in comparison with a control group, students in ASEP classes perceived their classrooms as being more satisfying and individualized and having a better material environment (Fraser, 1979). The significance of this evaluation is that the use of classroom environment variables revealed important differences between curricula, even when various outcome measures showed negligible differences.

Actual and preferred forms of classroom environment questions can be used in investigating differences between students and teachers in their perceptions of the same actual classroom environment and of differences between the perceived actual environment and the environment preferred by students or teachers. This research revealed that, first, students preferred a more positive classroom environment than was perceived to be present and, second, teachers perceived a more positive actual classroom environment than did their students in the same classrooms. This interesting pattern of results has been found in the USA, Israel, and Australia (Fisher and Fraser, 1983).

Actual and preferred forms of classroom environment instruments can be used together in exploring whether student achievement is better when there is a higher similarity between the student-perceived actual classroom environment and that preferred by students. A person-environment interaction framework was used in exploring whether student outcomes depend, not only on the nature of the classroom environment, but also on the match between students' preferences and the environment. Fraser and Fisher's (1983) study involved the prediction of achievement from the five actual individualization variables measured by the Individualized Classroom Environment Questionnaire (ICEQ) and five variables indicating actual-preferred interaction. The similarity between perceptions of actual and preferred environment was as important as individualization *per se* in predicting student achievement of important affective and cognitive aims. This research suggests that class achievement can be enhanced by changing the actual classroom environment in ways that make it more congruent with the environment preferred by the class. For example, if students agreed that they would prefer more teacher personalization, the teacher could attempt to raise the level of actual classroom personalization by moving around the class more to talk individually with students or by more often helping students who are experiencing difficulties with their class work.

One application of school environment instruments involves examination of differences in the climates of different types of schools. Docker, Fraser and Fisher (1989) reported the use of the Work Environment Scale (WES) with the sample of 599 teachers in investigating differences between the environments of various school types. There was fair agreement among teachers in different types of schools about what they would prefer their school environments to be like. In contrast, teachers' perceptions of their actual school environments varied markedly, with the climate in elementary schools emerging as more favorable than the environment of high schools on most of the WES scales. For example, elementary schools were viewed as having greater Involvement, Staff Support, Autonomy, Task Orientation, Clarity, Innovation, and Physical Comfort and less Work Pressure.

The School-Level Environment Questionnaire (SLEQ) was used in exploring differences between the climates of elementary and high schools among a sample of the 109 teachers in 10 schools in Tasmania. Some clear general patterns of differences were found in the favorableness of the school environments in the types of schools. The most striking pattern was that the climate in elementary schools was more favorable than the environment of high schools on most of the SLEQ scales. In particular, compared with high school teachers, elementary school teachers perceived their school climates considerably more favorably in terms of greater Affiliation, Professional Interest, Staff Freedom, Participatory Decision Making, Innovation, and Resource Adequacy. Differences were greater than one standard deviation for Affiliation, Participatory Decision Making, and Resource Adequacy.

Burden and Fraser (1993) note that, over the past decade, educators have been placing greater importance upon the process of learning and are moving away from "within-child" explanations for success and failure to "systems-oriented" approaches that focus on evaluating the total context in which learning occurs. Given these trends, it is not surprising that research on learning environments has escalated around the world (Fraser 1986, 1994; Fraser and Walberg, 1991; Wubbels and Levy, 1993). A classroom's or school's climate or environment not only is important in its own right, but it can also influence student achievement and attitudes (Haertel, Walberg and Haertel, 1981).

Although systematic observation and qualitative case studies are common approaches to studying the learning environment, another useful approach involves questionnaires which assess students' or teachers' perceptions of their classroom or school environment. These paper-and-pencil perceptual measures are economical, are based on experiences over an extended time, and involve the pooled judgments of numerous students or teachers. Also, students' and teachers' perceptions of learning environment explain variation in student learning (Fraser, 1994).

The main topics considered in the rest of this chapter are instruments for assessing learning environments and techniques for improving learning environments.

Instruments for Assessing Learning Environment

This section considers the following four instruments for assessing students' perceptions of classroom learning environment:

- Individualized Classroom Environment Questionnaire (ICEQ)
- Science Laboratory Environment Inventory (SLEI)
- Questionnaire on Teacher Interaction (QTI)
- Constructivist Learning Environment Survey (CLES).

In addition, an instrument for assessing teachers' perceptions of school environments, the School-Level Environment Questionnaire (SLEQ), is considered. Each instrument is suitable for convenient group administration, can be scored either by hand or computer, and has been extensively field tested and found to be valid and reliable (Fraser, 1994). Table 4.1 shows the name of each scale together with the level (elementary, secondary, higher education) for which each instrument is suited.

Moos (1973) proposed three basic types of dimension for classifying human environments. Relationship Dimensions identify the nature and intensity of personal relationships within the environment and assess the extent to which people are involved in the environment and support and help each other. Personal Development Dimensions assess basic directions along which personal growth and self-enhancement tend to occur. System Maintenance and System Change Dimensions involve the extent to which the environment is orderly, clear in expectations, maintains control, and is responsive to change. Table 4.1 shows the classification of each learning environment scale according to Moos's scheme.

Individualized Classroom Environment Questionnaire (ICEQ)

The ICEQ differs from other classroom environment scales in that it assesses dimensions (e.g., Personalization, Participation) which distinguish individualized

Table 4.1 *Overview of scales in five learning environment instruments (ICEQ, SLEI, QTI, CLES, and SLEQ)*

Instrument	Level/age group	Items per scale	*Scales classified according to Moos's Scheme*		
			Relationship dimensions	**Personal development dimensions**	**System maintenance and change dimensions**
Classroom Environment Instruments					
Individualized Classroom Environment Questionnaire (ICEQ)	Secondary (age 12–17)	10[a]	Personalization Participation	Independence Investigation	Differentiation
Science Laboratory Environment Inventory (SLEI)	Secondary (age 12–17) Higher Education	10	Student Cohesiveness	Open-endedness Integration	Rule Clarity Material Environment
Questionnaire on Teacher Interaction (QTI)	Secondary and (age 12–17) Elementary (age 7–11)	8–10[b]	Helpful/Friendly Understanding Dissatisfied Admonishing		Leadership Student Responsibility and Freedom Uncertain Strict
Constructivist Learning Environment Survey (CLES)	Secondary (age 12–17)	7	Personal Relevance Scientific Uncertainty	Critical Voice Shared Control	Student Negotiation
School Environment Instrument					
School-Level Environment Questionnaire (SLEQ)	Secondary and Elementary Teachers	7	Student Support Affiliation	Professional Interest	Staff Freedom Participary Decision Making Innovation Resource Adequacy Work Pressure

Notes: [a] The ICEQ has a short version containing 5 items per scale.
[b] The QTI has a short version containing 6 items per scale.

classrooms from conventional ones. The initial development of the long form ICEQ was guided by several criteria:

- Dimensions chosen characterized the classroom learning environment described in the literature of individualized and open education.
- Extensive interviewing of teachers and secondary school students ensured that the ICEQ's dimensions and individual items were considered salient by teachers and students.
- Items were written and subsequently modified after receiving reactions from selected experts, teachers, and junior high school students.
- Data collected during field testing were subjected to item analyses in order to identify items whose removal would enhance scale statistics.

The final version (Fraser, 1990) contains 50 items in the long version and 25 items in the short version, with an equal number of items belonging to each of the five scales. A five-point scale is used for responses, with the alternatives of Almost Never, Seldom, Sometimes, Often, and Very Often. The scoring direction is reversed for many of the items. Typical items in the ICEQ are "The teacher considers students' feelings" (Personalization) and "Different students do different work" (Differentiation).

Appendix 4.1 contains a complete copy of the short version of the ICEQ. Items in Appendix 4.1 without *R* in the Teacher Use column are scored 1, 2, 3, 4, and 5, respectively, for the responses, Almost Always, Often, Sometimes, Seldom, and Almost Never. Items with *R* in the Teacher Use column are scored in the reverse manner. Omitted or invalidly answered items are scored 3 (or, alternatively, assigned the mean of the other items in the same scale).

Science Laboratory Environment Inventory (SLEI)

Because of the importance and uniqueness of laboratory settings in science education, a new instrument specifically suited to assessing the environment of science laboratory classes at the senior high school or higher-education levels was developed in collaboration with colleagues from various countries (Fraser, Giddings and McRobbie, 1995). The SLEI has the five scales (each with seven items) and the five response alternative are Almost Never, Seldom, Sometimes, Often, and Very Often. Typical items are "The teacher is concerned about students' safety during laboratory sessions" (Teacher Supportiveness), and "We know the results that we are supposed to get before we commence a laboratory activity" (Open-endedness).

Notably, the SLEI was field tested and validated simultaneously with a sample of more than 5447 students in 269 classes in six different countries (the United States, Canada, England, Israel, Australia and Nigeria) to obtain comprehensive information about its cross-national validity and usefulness. Appendix 4.2 contains a copy of the SLEI.

Questionnaire on Teacher Interaction (QTI)

In research which originated in The Netherlands, a learning environment questionnaire was developed to assess the nature and quality of the interaction between teachers and students (Goh and Fraser, 1996; Wubbels and Levy, 1993). Drawing upon a theoretical model of proximity (Cooperation — Opposition) and influence (Dominance — Submission), the QTI was developed to assess student perceptions of the eight behavior aspects of Leadership, Helpful/Friendly, Understanding, Student Responsibility and Freedom, Uncertain, Dissatisfied, Admonishing, and Strict behavior. The original version of the QTI has 77 items, although a more economical 48-item version currently exists. Each item is responded to on a five-point scale ranging from Never to Always. Typical items are "S/he gives us a lot of free time" (Student Responsibility and Freedom behavior) and "S/he gets angry" (Admonishing behavior). The QTI has been found to be valid and reliable in studies among secondary school students in The Netherlands, the USA and Australia. A copy of the QTI is provided in Appendix 4.3.

Constructivist Learning Environment Survey (CLES)

Traditionally, teachers' roles have involved transmitting the logical structures of their knowledge, and directing students through rational inquiry towards discovering predetermined truths expressed in the form of laws, principles, rules, and algorithms. In contrast, the constructivist view holds that meaningful learning is a cognitive process of making sense of the experiential world in relation to the individual's already-constructed knowledge, and that sense-making involves active negotiation and consensus building. The CLES (Taylor, Fraser and Fisher, 1997) assesses the degree to which a particular classroom's environment is consistent with a constructivist epistemology, and can be used to assist teachers to reflect on their epistemological assumptions and reshape their teaching practice. The scales in the CLES are:

- Personal Relevance (the relevance of classroom experience to out-of-school experiences)
- Student Negotiation (emphasis on creating opportunities for students to explain and justify their ideas, and to test the viability of their own and others' ideas)
- Uncertainty (provision of opportunities for students to experience knowledge as arising from inquiry, involving human experience and values, evolving and insecure, and culturally and socially determined)
- Shared Control (emphasis on students negotiating and sharing control for learning activities, assessment, and social norms)
- Critical Voice (emphasis on developing a critical awareness of the prevailing curriculum and assessment policy).

The CLES contains 30 items (5 per scale) and the response alternatives are Almost Always, Often, Sometimes, Seldom and Almost Never. Examples of items are "I help the teacher to plan what I'm going to learn" (Shared Control) and "I explain my ideas to other students" (Negotiation). Appendix 4.4 contains the CLES.

School-Level Environment Questionnaire (SLEQ)

The SLEQ was designed to assess teachers' perceptions of psychosocial dimensions of the environment of the school. A careful review of potential strengths and problems associated with existing school environment instruments suggested that the SLEQ should satisfy several criteria (Rentoul and Fraser, 1983). First, relevant literature was consulted and dimensions included in the SLEQ were chosen to characterize important aspects of the school environment, such as relationships among teachers and between teachers and students and the organizational structure (e.g., decision making). Second, extensive interviewing ensured that the SLEQ's dimensions and individual items covered aspects of the school environment perceived to be salient by teachers. Third, the SLEQ was designed to provide a measure of school-level environment that had minimal overlap with these existing measures of classroom-level environment. Fourth, in developing the SLEQ, an attempt was made to achieve economy by developing an instrument with a relatively small number of reliable scales, each containing a fairly small number of items.

The above criteria could be satisfied with an instrument consisting of the eight scales shown in Table 4.1. A typical item in the Affiliation scale is "I feel that I could rely on my colleagues for assistance if I should need it". The SLEQ consists of 56 items, with each of the eight scales being assessed by seven items. Each item is scored on a five-point scale with the responses of Strongly Agree, Agree, Not Sure, Disagree, and Strongly Disagree. A copy of the SLEQ is provided in Appendix 4.5.

Preferred Forms of Scales

In addition to a form that measures perceptions of *actual* or *experienced* learning environment, the instruments in Table 4.1 have another form to measure perceptions of *preferred* or *ideal* learning environment. The preferred forms are concerned with goals and value orientations and measure perceptions of the learning environment ideally liked or preferred. Although item wording is similar for actual and preferred forms, the instructions for answering each are somewhat different. For example, whereas the actual form asks students how often a practice actually takes place in the classroom, the preferred form asks students how often they would prefer that practice to take place. An item such as "Teachers are encouraged to be innovative in this school" in the actual form would be changed to "Teachers would be encouraged to be innovative in this school" in the preferred form.

A Technique for Improving Learning Environments

Feedback information based on student or teacher perceptions can be employed as a basis for reflection upon, discussion of, and systematic attempts to improve learning environments (Fraser and Fisher, 1986). The case study described below involved an attempt at improving a classroom environment which made use of the short 25-item version of the Individualized Classroom Environment Questionnaire (ICEQ) provided in Appendix 4.1. The class involved in the study consisted of 34 eighth-grade students of mixed ability studying science at a British comprehensive school (Thorp, Burden and Fraser, 1993). The procedure incorporated the following five fundamental steps:

1 *Assessment* The ICEQ was administered to all students in the class. The preferred form was answered first, and the actual form was administered a couple of days later. The preferred form was administered first because some students in our past studies had found it difficult to remember to answer in terms of their preferred environment if they recently had answered the actual form of a questionnaire.
2 *Feedback* The teacher and researchers generated feedback information based upon student responses to the ICEQ. Class mean scores were used to construct the profiles shown in Figure 4.1, which represent differences (or discrepancies) between the means of students' preferred and actual environment scores. The distance above the "no discrepancy line" represents the amount by which the actual environment falls short of that preferred by students. The teacher used these profiles to identify which aspects of classroom environment needed to be changed to reduce major differences between the actual environment and the preferred environment. Figure 4.1 shows that relatively large differences (7–8 raw score points) occurred for all scales except Differentiation.
3 *Reflection and Discussion* The teacher thought about both the profiles and the students' additional open-ended comments, and discussed them with one of the researchers. This further clarified the interpretation and implications of the profiles and helped her to decide whether to try to change the classroom environment in terms of some of the scales. This teacher decided to attempt to increase the levels of each ICEQ dimension.
4 *Intervention* The teacher introduced an intervention over a period of approximately one month in an attempt to change the classroom environment. Because the teacher thought that it was important to base the design of this intervention on further input from her students, she talked to the class about her feelings towards them and the perceptions which she had of their interest in and commitment to her subject while at the same time, admitting that many of their comments were valid. Aspects of the intervention included the class agreeing to be more willing participants in lessons, and the teacher agreeing to mark books at least once per week, arranging a subject-based trip, encouraging cooperative work, and varying the lesson structure more.

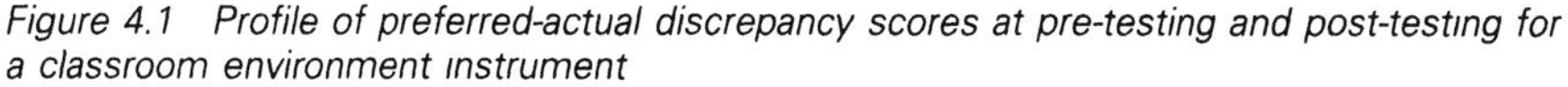

Figure 4.1 Profile of preferred-actual discrepancy scores at pre-testing and post-testing for a classroom environment instrument

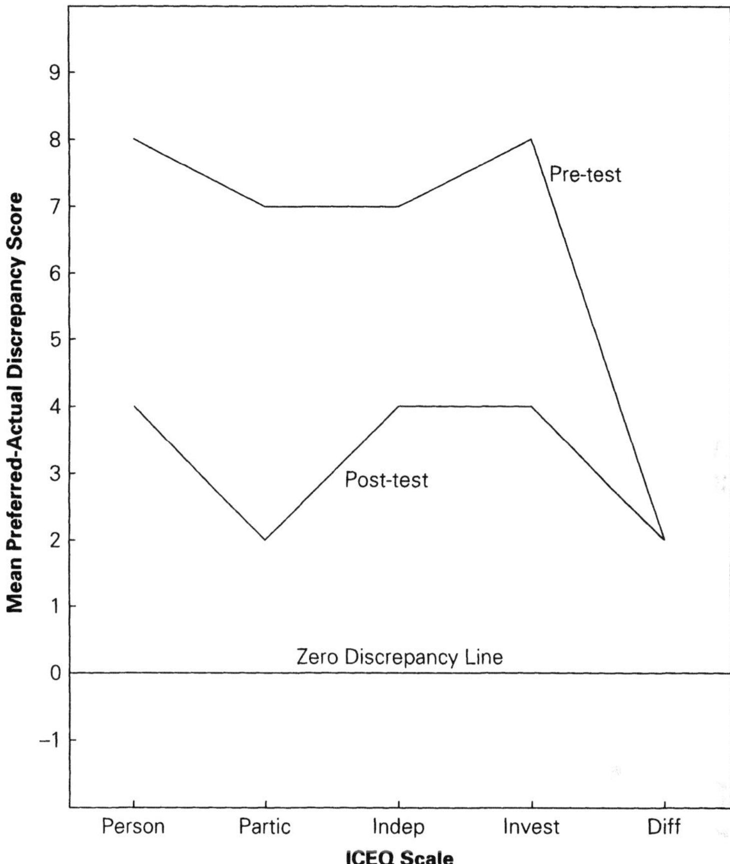

5 *Reassessment* The actual form of the questionnaire was readministered at the end of the intervention to see whether students were perceiving their classroom environments differently from before. Again, questionnaires were hand scored and mean scores were graphed to form the post-test profile of preferred/actual discrepancy scores included in Figure 4.1.

The profiles in Figure 4.1 show that a large change (ranging from one-and-a-half to three standard deviations) occurred in the preferred/actual discrepancy on every dimension except Differentiation. These differences were statistically significant ($p < 0.05$). Although the second administration of the environment scales marked the end of this teacher's formal attempt at changing her classroom environment, it might have been the beginning of another cycle. That is, the five steps could be repeated cyclically one or more times until changes in classroom environment reached the desired levels.

Generally, the results of this case study replicate the patterns found in past research in other countries (Fraser and Fisher, 1986) and illustrate the usefulness of classroom environment assessments in guiding positive changes in classroom climates. The present work is distinctive, however, because it successfully employed discussions between the teacher and the students as the basis for the environmental change attempt.

The method described above for improving classroom environments also has been used in attempts to improve school environments. For example, the School-Level Environment Questionnaire (SLEQ) (Fisher and Fraser, 1991) shown in Appendix 4.5, was used in a school improvement study involving an elementary school of 15 teachers. After pre-testing with both the actual and preferred forms of the SLEQ, mean scale scores were calculated and pre-test actual and pre-test preferred profiles were fed back to the school staff. The areas identified by the staff for initial improvement were Resource Adequacy, Work Pressure, and Innovation.

Next, the staff was divided randomly into small groups to discuss the areas in which actual-preferred discrepancies were largest. These groups were asked to consider those areas and to make suggestions for improvement. The groups then were called together and group session leaders presented a report to the whole staff. After lengthy discussion, the whole staff proposed and agreed to introduce an intervention consisting of the actions listed in Table 4.2. This intervention was implemented for approximately 10 weeks. At the end of this time, the actual form of the SLEQ was readministered to teachers to determine whether there had been

Table 4.2 Priorities for action in improving school environment

SLEQ dimension	**Priorities for action**
Resource adequacy	Conduct a survey of resources in the school. Develop a plan of attack — immediate, intermediary and long term. Check and repair already existing equipment. Develop a plan for increased sharing of resources.
Innovation	Conduct staff meetings in individual classrooms. These meetings should be rotated between elementary and infant rooms. Time should be given for the class teacher to comment on organization, display, problems, etc. Free teachers with particular skills to help in other rooms (drama, computers, science). Adopt a whole-school theme. Attempt to "spot the innovator" (particularly by senior staff).
Work pressure	Have less staff meetings. Use recess breaks for minor discussions. Draw on the community for assistance with coaching sporting teams. Provide opportunities for discussion about meeting the individual needs of children.

any changes in the work environment as perceived by teachers. The results were depicted as profiles.

An examination of the profiles revealed sizable changes in two of the priority areas. Resource adequacy increased 2.5 raw score points (about two-thirds of a standard deviation) and Innovation increased 1.7 raw score points (about half a standard deviation). The use of *t*-tests for dependent samples revealed that each of these differences was statistically significant ($p < 0.05$). However, the level of Work Pressure did not change.

Conclusions

This chapter considers the field of learning environment, including four instruments assessing students' perceptions of classroom environment (the ICEQ, SLEI, QTI and CLES) and a questionnaire for assessing teachers' perceptions of school environment (the SLEQ). With this approach, feedback to teachers is based on the perceptions of those most actively involved in the learning process — the students and teachers themselves — and, therefore, is more likely to bring about changes in environments.

This chapter has several implications about how to use the five instruments for improving and sustaining positive learning environments. Learning environment assessments derived from these questionnaires should be used in addition to student learning outcome measures to provide information about important but subtle aspects of school life. In particular, because teachers and students have systematically different perceptions of the same learning environments, student feedback should be collected using the ICEQ, SLEI, QTI or CLES. Teachers should strive to create productive learning environments as identified by research (e.g., cohesive, organized, and goal-directed classes). To improve student outcomes, classroom environments also should be changed to match students' preferred environment. Finally, teachers should use the questionnaires measuring students' perceptions of classroom environment and the instrument assessing teachers' perceptions of school environment in monitoring and guiding attempts to improve classrooms and schools.

The five questionnaires discussed in this chapter are recommended to educators wishing to assess classroom and school environment for the purpose of monitoring the development or maintenance of healthy learning environments for students and teachers. Each questionnaire is economical in terms of administration and scoring time, and each has been shown to be valid, reliable and convenient in extensive field trials. Also, each of the five instruments focuses on aspects of the learning environment which are of wide contemporary interest in education. For example, the classroom environment questionnaires assess important aspects of classroom individualization (ICEQ), science laboratory classes (SLEI), interpersonal interactions between student and teacher (QTI), and constructivist-oriented teaching and learning approaches (CLES). The school environment instrument (SLEI) taps aspects of teachers' professional interest, participatory decision making, innovation, and work pressure within their schools.

Appendix 4.1: Individualized Classroom Environment Questionnaire (ICEQ)

	Almost never	Seldom	Sometimes	Often	Very often	Teacher use only	
1 The teacher talks with each student.	1	2	3	4	5	Pe ____	
2 Students give their opinions during discussions.	1	2	3	4	5	Pa ____	
3 The teacher decides where students sit.	1	2	3	4	5	Id ____	**R**
4 Students find out the answers to questions from textbooks rather than from investigations.	1	2	3	4	5	Iv ____	**R**
5 Different students do different work.	1	2	3	4	5	D ____	
6 The teacher takes a personal interest in each student.	1	2	3	4	5	Pe ____	
7 The teacher lectures without students asking or answering questions.	1	2	3	4	5	Pa ____	**R**
8 Students choose their partners for group work.	1	2	3	4	5	Id ____	
9 Students carry out their investigations to test ideas.	1	2	3	4	5	Iv ____	
10 All students in the class do the same work at the same time.	1	2	3	4	5	D ____	
11 The teacher is unfriendly to students.	1	2	3	4	5	Pe ____	**R**
12 Students' ideas and suggestions are used during classroom discussion.	1	2	3	4	5	Pa ____	
13 Students are told how to behave in the classroom.	1	2	3	4	5	Id ____	**R**
14 Students carry out investigations to answer questions coming from class discussions.	1	2	3	4	5	Iv ____	

Appendix 4.1: (Continued)

	Almost never	Seldom	Sometimes	Often	Very often	Teacher use only	
15 Different students use different books, equipment and materials.	1	2	3	4	5	D ___	
16 The teacher helps each student who is having trouble with the work.	1	2	3	4	5	Pe ___	
17 Students ask the teacher questions.	1	2	3	4	5	Pa ___	
18 The teacher decides which students should work together.	1	2	3	4	5	Id ___	R
19 Students explain the meanings of statements, diagrams and graphs.	1	2	3	4	5	Iv ___	
20 Students who work faster than others move on to the next topic.	1	2	3	4	5	D ___	
21 The teacher considers students' feelings.	1	2	3	4	5	Pe ___	
22 There is classroom discussion.	1	2	3	4	5	Pa ___	
23 The teacher decides how much movement and talk there should be in the classroom.	1	2	3	4	5	Id ___	R
24 Students carry out investigations to answer questions which puzzle them.	1	2	3	4	5	Iv ___	
25 The same teaching aid (e.g., blackboard or overhead projector) is used for all students in the class.	1	2	3	4	5	D ___	R

		Total scale scores
Name____________________	**Class/Year**________________	Pe __ Pa__
School ____________________	**Date** ________________	Id __ Iv __ D __

Appendix 4.2: Science Laboratory Environment Inventory (SLEI)

---

*Remember that you are describing your **actual** classroom.*

---

1 I get on well with students in this laboratory class.
2 There is opportunity for me to pursue my own science interests in this laboratory class.
3 What I do in our regular science class is unrelated to my laboratory work.
4 My laboratory class has clear rules to guide my activities.
5 I find that the laboratory is crowded when I am doing experiments.

---

6 I have little chance to get to know other students in this laboratory class.
7 In this laboratory class, I am required to design my own experiments to solve a given problem.
8 The laboratory work is unrelated to the topics that I am studying in my science class.
9 My laboratory class is rather informal and few rules are imposed on me.
10 The equipment and materials that I need for laboratory activities are readily available.

---

11 Members of this laboratory class help me.
12 In my laboratory sessions, other students collect different data than I do for the same problem.
13 My regular science class work is integrated with laboratory activities.
14 I am required to follow certain rules in the laboratory.
15 I am ashamed of the appearance of this laboratory.

---

16 I get to know students in this laboratory class well.
17 I am allowed to go beyond the regular laboratory exercise and do some experimenting of my own.
18 I use the theory from my regular science class sessions during laboratory activities.
19 There is a recognized way for me to do things safely in this laboratory.
20 The laboratory equipment which I use is in poor working order.

---

21 I am able to depend on other students for help during laboratory classes.
22 In my laboratory sessions, I do different experiments than some of the other students.
23 The topics covered in regular science class work are quite different from topics with which I deal in laboratory sessions.
24 There are few fixed rules for me to follow in laboratory sessions.
25 I find that the laboratory is hot and stuffy.

---

26 It takes me a long time to get to know everybody by his/her first name in this laboratory class.
27 In my laboratory sessions, the teacher decides the best way for me to carry out the laboratory experiments.
28 What I do in laboratory sessions helps me to understand the theory covered in regular science classes.
29 The teacher outlines safety precautions to me before my laboratory sessions commence.
30 The laboratory is an attractive place for me to work in.

---

31 I work cooperatively in laboratory sessions.
32 I decide the best way to proceed during laboratory experiments.
33 My laboratory work and regular science class work are unrelated.
34 My laboratory class is run under clearer rules than my other classes.
35 My laboratory has enough room for individual or group work.

Appendix 4.3: Questionnaire on Teacher Interaction (QTI)

1 This teacher talks enthusiastically about her/his subject.
2 This teacher trusts us.
3 This teacher seems uncertain.
4 This teacher gets angry unexpectedly.

5 This teacher explains things clearly.
6 If we don't agree with this teacher, we can talk about it.
7 This teacher is hesitant.
8 This teacher gets angry quickly.

9 This teacher holds our attention.
10 This teacher is willing to explain things again.
11 This teacher acts as if she/he does not know what to do.
12 This teacher is too quick to correct us when we break a rule.

13 This teacher knows everything that goes on in the classroom.
14 If we have something to say, this teacher will listen.
15 This teacher lets us boss her/him around.
16 This teacher is impatient.

17 This teacher is a good leader.
18 This teacher realises when we don't understand.
19 This teacher is not sure what to do when we fool around.
20 It is easy to pick a fight with this teacher.

21 This teacher acts confidently.
22 This teacher is patient.
23 It's easy to make a fool out of this teacher.
24 This teacher is sarcastic.

25 This teacher helps us with our work.
26 We can decide some things in this teacher's class.
27 This teacher thinks that we cheat.
28 This teacher is strict.

29 This teacher is friendly.
30 We can influence this teacher.
31 This teacher thinks that we don't know anything.
32 We have to be silent in this teacher's class.

33 This teacher is someone we can depend on.
34 This teacher lets us fool around in class.
35 This teacher puts us down.
36 This teacher's tests are hard.

37 This teacher has a sense of humour.
38 This teacher lets us get away with a lot in class.
39 This teacher thinks that we can't do things well.
40 This teacher's standards are very high.

41 This teacher can take a joke.
42 This teacher gives us a lot of free time in class.
43 This teacher seems dissatisfied.
44 This teacher is severe when marking papers.

45 This teacher's class is pleasant.
46 This teacher is lenient.
47 This teacher is suspicious.
48 We are afraid of this teacher.

Appendix 4.4: Constructivist Learning Environment Survey (CLES)

Learning about the world

In this class . . .

1 I learn about the world outside of school.
2 My new learning starts with problems about the world outside of school.
3 I learn how science can be part of my out-of-school life.
4 I get a better understanding of the world outside of school.
5 I learn interesting things about the world outside of school.
6 What I learn has nothing to do with my out-of-school life.

Learning about science

In this class . . .

7 I learn that science cannot provide perfect answers to problems.
8 I learn that science has changed over time.
9 I learn that science is influenced by people's values and opinions.
10 I learn about the different sciences used by people in other cultures.
11 I learn that modern science is different from the science of long ago.
12 I learn that science is about inventing theories.

Learning to speak out

In this class . . .

13 It's OK for me to ask the teacher "why do I have to learn this?"
14 It's OK for me to question the way I'm being taught.
15 It's OK for me to complain about activities that are confusing.
16 It's OK for me to complain about anything that prevents me from learning.
17 It's OK for me to express my opinion.
18 It's OK for me to speak up for my rights.

Learning to learn

In this class . . .

19 I help the teacher to plan what I'm going to learn.
20 I help the teacher to decide how well I am learning.
21 I help the teacher to decide which activities are best for me.
22 I help the teacher to decide how much time I spend on activities.
23 I help the teacher to decide which activities I do.
24 I help the teacher to assess my learning.

Learning to communicate

In this class . . .

25 I get the chance to talk to other students.
26 I talk with other students about how to solve problems.
27 I explain my ideas to other students.
28 I ask other students to explain their ideas.
29 Other students ask me to explain my ideas.
30 Other students explain their ideas to me.

Appendix 4.5: School-level Environment Questionnaire (SLEQ)

Directions
There are 56 items in this questionnaire. They are statements about the school in which you work and your working environment.

Think about how well the statements describe your school environment.

Indicate your answer by circling:

SD if you STRONGLY DISAGREE with the statement;
D if you DISAGREE with the statement;
N if you NEITHER AGREE NOR DISAGREE with the statement or are not sure;
A if you AGREE with the statement;
SA if you STRONGLY AGREE with the statement.

If you change your mind about a response, cross out the old answer and circle the new choice.

1 There are many disruptive, difficult students in the school.
2 I seldom receive encouragement from colleagues.
3 Teachers frequently discuss teaching methods and strategies with each other.
4 I am often supervised to ensure that I follow directions correctly.
5 Decisions about the running of the school are usually made by the principal or a small group of teachers.
6 It is very difficult to change anything in this school.
7 The school or department library includes an adequate selection of books and periodicals.
8 There is constant pressure to keep working.

9 Most students are helpful and cooperative to teachers.
10 I feel accepted by other teachers.
11 Teachers avoid talking with each other about teaching and learning.
12 I am not expected to conform to a particular teaching style.
13 I have to refer even small matters to a senior member of staff for a final answer.
14 Teachers are encouraged to be innovative in this school.
15 The supply of equipment and resources is inadequate.
16 Teachers have to work long hours to complete all their work.

17 Most students are pleasant and friendly to teachers.
18 I am ignored by other teachers.
19 Professional matters are seldom discussed during staff meetings.
20 It is considered very important that I closely follow syllabuses and lesson plans.
21 Action can usually be taken without gaining the approval of the subject department head or a senior member of staff.
22 There is a great deal of resistance to proposals for curriculum change.
23 Video equipment, tapes, and films are readily available and accessible.
24 Teachers don't have to work very hard in this school.

25 There are many noisy, badly-behaved students.
26 I feel that I could rely on my colleagues for assistance if I needed it.
27 Many teachers attend inservice and other professional development courses.
28 There are few rules and regulations that I am expected to follow.

29 Teachers are frequently asked to participate in decisions concerning administrative policies and procedures.
30 Most teachers like the idea of change.
31 Adequate duplicating facilities and services are available to teachers.
32 There is no time for teachers to relax.

33 Students get along well with teachers.
34 My colleagues seldom take notice of my professional views and opinions.
35 Teachers show little interest in what is happening in other schools.
36 I am allowed to do almost as I please in the classroom.
37 I am encouraged to make decisions without reference to a senior member of staff.
38 New courses or curriculum materials are seldom implemented in the school.
39 Tape recorders and cassettes are seldom available when needed.
40 You can take it easy and still get the work done.

41 Most students are well-mannered and respectful to the school staff.
42 I feel that I have many friends among my colleagues at this school.
43 Teachers are keen to learn from their colleagues.
44 My classes are expected to use prescribed textbooks and prescribed resource materials.
45 I must ask my subject department head or senior member of staff before I do most things.
46 There is much experimentation with different teaching approaches.
47 Facilities are inadequate for catering for a variety of classroom activities and learning groups of different sizes.
48 Seldom are there deadlines to be met.

49 Very strict discipline is needed to control many of the students.
50 I often feel lonely and left out of things in the staffroom.
51 Teachers show considerable interest in the professional activities of their colleagues.
52 I am expected to maintain very strict control in the classroom.
53 I have very little say in the running of the school.
54 New and different ideas are always being tried out in this school.
55 Projectors for filmstrips, transparencies and films are usually available when needed.
56 It is hard to keep up with your work load.

Scoring:

Underlined items are scored 1, 2, 3, 4, and 5, respectively, for the responses SA, A, N, D, and SD. All other items are scored in the reverse manner. Invalid or omitted items are scored 3.

Scale scores are obtained by adding items scores for each of the seven items in a scale. Items are arranged in cyclic order so that the first, second, third, fourth, fifth, sixth, seventh, and eighth item, respectively, in each block measures Student Support, Affiliation, Professional Interest, Staff Freedom, Participatory Decision Making, Innovation, Resource Adequacy and Work Pressure.

References

BURDEN, R.L. and FRASER, B.J. (1993) 'Use of classroom environment assessments in school psychology: A British perspective', *Psychology in the Schools*, **30**, pp. 232–40.

Docker, J.G., Fraser, B.J. and Fisher, D.L. (1989) 'Differences in the psychosocial work environment of different types of schools', *Journal of Research in Childhood Education*, **4**, pp. 5–7.

Fisher, D.L. and Fraser, B.J. (1983) 'A comparison of actual and preferred classroom environment as perceived by science teachers and students', *Journal of Research in Science Teaching*, **20**, pp. 55–61.

Fisher, D.L. and Fraser, B.J. (1991) 'School climate and teacher professional development', *South Pacific Journal of Teacher Education*, **19**, pp. 15–30.

Fraser, B.J. (1979) 'A science-based evaluation', in Walberg, H.J. (ed.) *Educational Environments and Effects: Evaluation, Policy, and Productivity*, Berkeley, CA: McCutchan, pp. 218–34.

Fraser, B.J. (1986) *Classroom Environment*, London: Croom Helm.

Fraser, B.J. (1990) *Individualized Classroom Environment Questionnaire*, Melbourne, Australia: Australian Council for Educational Research.

Fraser, B.J. (1994) 'Research on classroom and school climate', in Gabel, D. (ed.) *Handbook of Research on Science Teaching and Learning*, New York: Macmillan, pp. 493–541.

Fraser, B.J. and Fisher, D.L. (1983) 'Use of actual and preferred classroom environment scales in person-environment fit research', *Journal of Educational Psychology*, **75**, pp. 303–13.

Fraser, B.J. and Fisher, D.L. (1986) 'Using short forms of classroom climate instruments to assess and improve classroom psychosocial environment', *Journal of Research in Science Teaching*, **23**, pp. 387–413.

Fraser, B.J., Giddings, G.G. and McRobbie, C.J. (1995) 'Evolution and validation of a personal form of an instrument for assessing science laboratory classroom environments', *Journal of Research in Science Teaching*, **32**, pp. 399–422.

Fraser, B.J. and Walberg, H.J. (eds) (1991) *Educational Environments: Evaluation, Antecedents and Consequences*, Oxford, England: Pergamon Press.

Goh, S.C., Young, D.J. and Fraser, B.J. (1995) 'Psychosocial climate and student outcomes in elementary mathematics classrooms: A multilevel analysis', *Journal of Educational Research*, **64**, pp. 29–40.

Goh, S.C. and Fraser, B.J. (1996) 'Validation of an elementary school version of the Questionnaire on Teacher Interaction', *Psychological Reports*, **79**, pp. 515–22.

Haertel, G.D., Walberg, H.J. and Haertel, E.H. (1981) 'Socio-psychological environments and learning: A quantitative synthesis', *British Educational Research Journal*, 7, pp. 27–36.

McRobbie, C.J. and Fraser, B.J. (1993) 'Associations between student outcomes and psychosocial science environment', *Journal of Educational Research*, **87**, pp. 78–85.

Moos, R.H. (1973) 'Conceptualizations of human environments', *American Psychologist*, **28**, pp. 652–65.

Rentoul, A.J. and Fraser, B.J. (1983) 'Development of a school-level environment questionnaire', *Journal of Educational Administration*, **21**, pp. 21–39.

Taylor, P.C., Fraser, B.J. and Fisher, D.L. (1997) 'Monitoring constructivist classroom learning environments', *International Journal of Educational Research*, **27**, pp. 293–302.

Thorp, H., Burden, R.L. and Fraser, B.J. (1993) Assessing and improving classroom environment', *School Science Review*, **75**, pp. 107–13.

Wubbels, T. and Levy, J. (eds) (1993) *Do You Know What You Look Like? Interpersonal Relationships in Education*, London: Falmer Press.

Chapter 5

Organizational Health Profiles for High Schools[1]

Wayne K. Hoy and John A. Feldman

This chapter contrasts the notions of organizational culture and climate, and then uses the metaphor of health to conceptualize and measure the climate of secondary schools. First, the development of an organizational health instrument is detailed and profiles of healthy and unhealthy schools are described. Next, directions for administrating and scoring the health instrument are provided, and a hands-on example and interpretation of an actual school profile are presented. Finally, the chapter concludes with a brief review of research, implications, and cautions. In sum, a useful, reliable, and valid measure of school health is ready for teachers and administrators committed to improving the climate of their schools and for researchers interested in studying and changing schools.

Although it is fashionable to use the term "organizational culture" to identify the distinctive feel or ideology of the workplace, "organizational climate" also has a rich history in the study of organizations (Pace and Stern, 1958; Halpin and Croft, 1963; Litwin and Stringer, 1968; Taguiri, 1968; Hall, 1972; Poole, 1985). Both climate and culture attempt to capture the feel of organizational life. Individual organizations may have the same mission, but traditions and organizational ideologies often differ.

Organizational culture refers to the shared orientations that bind the organization together and give it its distinctive identity. There is, however, substantial disagreement about what are shared-norms, values, philosophies, tacit assumptions, myths, or ceremonies. Another issue is the intensity of the shared orientations. Do organizations have one basic culture or many cultures? Finally, there is disagreement on the extent to which organizational culture is conscious and overt or unconscious and covert (Hoy and Miskel, 1996).

Organizational climate is a characteristic of the entire organization. Climate has a number of features:

- it is based on collective perceptions of members;
- it arises from routine organizational practices that are important to the organization and its members;
- it influences members' behavior and attitudes (Poole, 1985).

Put simply, organizational climate is the set of internal characteristics that distinguishes one organization from another and influences the behavior of its participants. More specifically, **school climate** *is a relatively enduring quality of the entire school that is experienced by members, describes their collective perceptions of routine behavior, and affects their attitudes and behavior in the school* (Hoy and Miskel, 1996).

Although the definitions of climate and culture are blurred and overlapping, one suggested difference is that culture consists of shared assumptions, values and norms, while climate is defined by shared perceptions of behavior (Ashforth, 1985). There is not a large conceptual step from shared norms (culture) to shared perceptions (climate), but the difference is real, often meaningful, and important in selecting a research strategy or in developing an organizational improvement plan. We prefer the concept of climate. Because shared perceptions of behavior are easier to map than shared values, climate is a little less abstract (more descriptive and less symbolic) than culture and measurement is less a problem.

School Climate: Conceptual Foundations of Organizational Health

A number of perspectives have been systematically developed to examine the organizational climate of schools (Halpin and Croft, 1963; Hoy and Clover, 1986; Hoy, Hoffman, Sabo and Bliss, 1996; Hoy, Tarter and Kottkamp, 1991; Pace and Stern, 1958; Stern, 1970). Perhaps the best-known conceptualization and measurement of school climate in educational administration is the pioneering work of Halpin and Croft (1963). Climate was viewed as the "personality" of the school and seen along a continuum from open to closed, much the same way that Rokeach (1960) viewed the personality and belief systems of open- and closed-minded individuals. Although the openness of organizational climate has been a useful perspective for viewing the atmosphere of the school, it has not been as successful in explaining student achievement in schools as the construct of organizational health (Hoy, Tarter and Kottkamp, 1991). Thus the focus of this paper is to view school climate in terms of its health.

Health is another metaphor for examining school climate. The idea of positive and healthy relations in an organization is not new and calls attention to conditions that foster effective organizational performance.

Miles's Perspective on Organizational Health

The health metaphor was initially used by Matthew Miles (1969) to examine the properties of schools. He defines a healthy organization as one that "not only survives in its environment, but continues to cope adequately over the long haul, and continuously develops and expands its coping abilities" (1969: p. 378). Implicit in this definition is the idea that healthy organizations manage successfully with disruptive outside forces while effectively directing their energies toward the mission and objectives of the organization. Operations on a given day may be effective or ineffective, but the long-term prognosis is favorable in a healthy organization. Miles developed a configuration of a healthy organization that consists of ten important properties. They are those which reflect the task needs (goals, communication, and power), the maintenance needs (resource use, cohesiveness, and morale), and the growth and development needs (innovativeness, autonomy, adaptation, and problem-solving capacity) of a social system. Unfortunately, attempts to operationalize Miles's formulation of organizational health with a set of reliable and valid measures have been unsuccessful (Hoy and Feldman, 1987; Kimpston and Sonnabend, 1975; Miles, 1975).

A Parsonian Perspective on Organizational Health

After the unsuccessful attempts to operationalize Miles's dimensions of organizational health, we turned our attention to the theoretical analyses of Parsons et al. (1953) and Etzioni (1975), as well as the empirical literature on school effectiveness for a scheme to conceptualize and measure school health. All social systems must solve four basic problems if they are to survive, grow, and prosper — adaptation, goal attainment, integration, and latency are essential to effectiveness. Parsons and his colleagues (1953) refer to these as the imperative functions of all social systems. In other words, schools must solve four basic problems:

(i) the problem of accommodating to their environment
(ii) the problem of setting and implementing goals
(iii) the problem of maintaining cohesiveness within the school
(iv) the problem of creating and preserving a unique culture

Healthy schools meet the instrumental needs of adaptation and goal achievement as well as the expressive needs of social and normative integration. Parsons (1967) also notes that schools, like all organizations, have three distinct levels of control over these needs — the technical, managerial, and institutional.

The *technical* level of the school is concerned with the teaching-learning process. The primary mission of the school is to produce educated students, and teachers and supervisors have primary responsibility for solving the problems associated with effective teaching and learning.

The *managerial* level controls the internal administration of the organization. Principals are the prime administrative officers of the school. They procure and allocate resources and coordinate the work effort. They must acquire the necessary resources for teaching (financial, personnel, and physical materials); find ways to develop teacher loyalty, trust, and commitment; motivate teachers; influence their own superiors; and mediate between the teachers and students.

The *institutional* or community level connects the school with its environment. Schools need legitimacy and support in the community. Both administrators and teachers need backing if they are to perform their respective functions in a harmonious fashion without undue pressure from individuals and groups from outside the school. Teachers need a buffer between themselves and hostile outside forces.

School Health: A Conceptual Framework

The preceding broad Parsonian perspective provided the theoretical underpinnings for conceptualizing and measuring school health. Specifically, **a healthy school** *is one in which the technical, managerial, and institutional levels are in harmony; and the school meets both its instrumental and expressive needs as it successfully copes with disruptive external forces and directs its energies toward it mission.* In other words, healthy schools have relatively harmonious relations among the teachers, administrators, and board members. Such schools focus their energies on the accomplishment of the instrumental goals of achievement and intellectual growth as well as expressive goals of emotional growth and development.

After a series of exploratory pilot projects (Hoy, Tarter and Kottkamp, 1991), eight dimensions of organizational health were initially identified and defined as the framework for examining school health. These aspects represented the three Parsonian levels of organization as well as the four functional imperatives of all social systems. Each dimension is defined as follows under its associated level.

Institutional level

- *Institutional integrity* (instrumental need) is the school's ability to cope with its environment in a way that maintains the educational integrity of its programs. Teachers are protected from unreasonable community and parental demands.

Managerial level

- *Principal influence* (instrumental need) is the principal's ability to influence the actions of superiors. Being able to persuade superiors, to get additional consideration, and not to be impeded by the hierarchy are important aspects of school administration.
- *Consideration* (expressive need) is principal behavior that is friendly, supportive, open and collegial. It represents a genuine concern on the part of the principal for the welfare of the teachers.
- *Initiating structure* (instrumental need) is principal behavior that is both task- and achievement-oriented. Work expectations, standards of performance, and procedures are clearly articulated by the principal.
- *Resource allocation* (instrumental need) refers to a school where adequate classroom supplies and instructional materials are allocated to teachers and extra materials are readily supplied if requested.

Technical level

- *Morale* (expressive need) is a collective sense of friendliness, openness, enthusiasm, and trust among faculty members. Teachers like each other, like their jobs, and help each other. They are proud of their school and feel a sense of accomplishment in their jobs.

- *Cohesiveness* (expressive need) is the extent to which the teachers and administrators form a coherent and integrated group. They identify with each other and the school.
- *Academic emphasis* (instrumental need) is the extent to which the school is driven by a quest for academic excellence: high but achievable academic goals are set for students; the learning environment is orderly and serious; teachers believe in their students' ability to achieve; and students work hard and respect those who do well academically.

Organizational Health Inventory for High Schools[2]

Once the conceptual framework was developed, the next step in the project was to develop a reliable and valid set of measures for the aspects of organizational health, later called the OHI (Organizational Health Inventory). The strategy to operationalize each element of school health was straightforward: write short, descriptive statements of teacher-student, teacher-teacher, and teacher-administrator interactions and then ask teachers to describe the health of their schools using an anonymous questionnaire (OHI) composed of these items.

Developing Items

Our earlier exploratory work had produced 29 items (Hoy and Feldman, 1987) that tapped some of the proposed dimensions of health. New items were needed and written by the researchers either independently or jointly, but none was included unless there was consensus on its conceptual and content validity. All descriptive statements were assessed using the following criteria:

(i) each item reflected a property of the school;
(ii) the statement was clear and concise;
(iii) the statement had content validity;
(iv) the statement had discriminatory potential.

In all, 95 items were selected for testing in another pilot study. Respondents were asked to indicate the extent to which each statement characterized their school along a four-point Likert scale as rarely occurs, sometimes occurs, often occurs, or very frequently occurs. Examples of items include the following: "Teachers are protected from unreasonable community and parental demands"; "The principal gets what he or she asks for from superiors"; "The principal looks out for the professional welfare of faculty members"; "The principal lets faculty members know what is expected of them"; "Extra materials are available if requested"; "There is a feeling of trust and confidence among the staff"; "The school sets high standards for academic performance", and "Community demands are accepted even when they are not consistent with the educational program".

Pilot Study

This preliminary version of the OHI contained 95 potential, mostly untested items. An initial task was to reduce the number of items as the factor structure of the instrument was explored. A sample of 72 secondary schools was identified, which included urban, suburban, and rural schools and represented a diverse subset of secondary schools. Data were collected from a random sample of teachers in each school. Because the unit of analysis was the school, data were aggregated at the school level for each item, and the exploratory procedures were performed to reduce the number of items and determine the factor structure of the instrument.

Three criteria were used to refine the OHI. First, the criterion of simple structure was employed in all factor analyses; only items that loaded high on one factor and weak on all others were retained. Next, in addition to their mathematical contribution to the factor (high factor loadings), items were evaluated for conceptual clarity and fit; that is, items were retained only if they were clearly related to the concept being measured. Finally, items were eliminated if they reduced substantially the internal consistency of the subtests as measured by Cronbach's coefficient alpha. School mean scores were generated for each item and the item-correlation matrices were factored.

Using the criteria specified above, a series of exploratory factor analyses of the pilot data was performed, and the number of items was reduced by one half. Ultimately, using a principal components factor analysis with a varimax rotation, a seven-factor solution was selected. Instead of the eight-factor solution that was expected, only seven factors were identified. The morale and cohesiveness items merged to produce one strong morale dimension. Forty-four items remained in the refined OHI, which defined seven dimensions of school health. The final set of items is summarized in Appendix 5.1.

A Test of the New Measure (OHI)

Having completed the data reduction and conceptualization of the OHI in the pilot study, the 44-item instrument was ready to be tested with a new data set to demonstrate the stability of the factor structure, to confirm the validity and stability of the subtests, and to explore the second-order factor structure.

Sample. Seventy-eight secondary schools in New Jersey agreed to participate in the study. A separate, new random sample of at least five teachers was drawn from each of the 72 pilot schools and from 6 additional schools that were added to the sample. Although not a random one, the school sample was diverse representing a broad range of districts and spanning the entire range of socio-economic status. Participating schools represented 17 of 21 counties in that state. If any group of schools was underrepresented it was the urban one; only 7.5 per cent of the schools came from urban districts.

Typically, data were collected by a researcher at a regular faculty meeting, but in a few schools a faculty member collected the anonymous questionnaires. The faculty, selected at random, responded to the OHI and the others responded to another battery of instruments, which was part of a larger research project (Hoy, Tarter and Kottkamp, 1991). In total, 1131 teachers and principals in 78 secondary schools participated in the study.

Factor analysis. School mean scores were calculated for each item, and the item-correlation matrix from the 78 schools was factor analyzed. Seven factors with eigenvalues form 14.28 to 1.35 explaining 74 per cent of the variance were retained. The seven-factor solution, after the varimax rotation, is summarized in detail by Hoy and his colleagues (1991).

The results strongly support the factor structure discovered in the pilot study. The items loaded on the appropriate subtest, and the reliability scores for each subtest were relatively high. The alpha coefficients were as follows: institutional integrity (0.91), principal influence (0.87), consideration (0.90), initiating structure (0.89), resource support (0.95), morale (0.92), and academic influence (0.93). A comparison of the pattern of factor loadings with those of the pilot study were remarkably similar. In fact, the factor structures for both data sets were virtually identical.

The stability of the factor structure of the OHI also supports the construct validity of the seven dimensions of school health. Factor analysis enables the researchers to study the constitutive meanings of constructs and, thus, their construct validity (Kerlinger, 1976). In the present investigation, seven hypothetical entities, dimensions of organizational health, were constructed. The relations among the items consistently held up as theoretically expected; that is, the items (variables) measuring each dimension were systematically related as predicted.

Second-order factor analysis. Next, attention turned to the underlying structure of the seven dimensions of the OHI. Is there a more general set of factors that defines the health of a school? To answer this question, subtest scores for each school were computed and a correlation matrix among the subtest was derived. Since many of the correlations among the subtests were moderate, it was appropriate to perform a second-order factor analysis on the subtest correlations.

One strong general factor emerged that accounted for 45 per cent of the variance. This factor was the only one to meet Kaiser's (1960) criterion of an eigenvalue greater than one. A scree test (Rummel, 1970) yielded the same second-order factor. All of the dimensions of organizational health had strong factor loadings on this general factor: institutional integrity (0.563), principal influence (0.747), consideration (0.633), initiating structure (0.722), resource support (0.607), morale (0.707), and academic emphasis (0.703). The factor identified schools that were relatively strong on all seven dimensions. Accordingly, the factor was called school health. An index of the health of a school can be determined simply by adding the standard scores on the seven subtests; the higher the score, the healthier the school dynamics. It is possible to sketch a description of the prototype for each of the poles of the continuum, that is, for very healthy and unhealthy schools.

Healthy School

A healthy school is protected from unreasonable community and parental pressures. The school board successfully resists all narrow efforts of vested interest groups to influence policy (high institutional integrity). The principal of a healthy school is a dynamic leader, integrating both task-oriented and relations-oriented leader behavior. Such behavior is supportive of teachers and yet provides high standards for performance (high consideration and initiating structure). Moreover, the principal has influence with her or his superiors demonstrated by the ability to get what is needed for the effective operation of the school (high influence). Teachers in a healthy school are committed to teaching and learning. They set high but achievable goals for students, maintain high standards of performance, and promote a serious and orderly learning environment. Furthermore, students work hard on their school work, are highly motivated, and respect other students who achieve academically (high academic influence). Classroom supplies, instructional materials, and supplementary materials are always available (high resource support). Finally, in healthy schools, teachers like each other, trust each other, are enthusiastic about their work, and identify positively with the school. They are proud of their school (high morale).

Unhealthy School

The unhealthy school is vulnerable to destructive outside forces. Teachers and administrators are bombarded by unreasonable parental demands, and the school is buffeted by the whims of the public (low institutional integrity). The school is without an effective principal. The principal provides little direction or structure (low initiating structure), exhibits little encouragement and support for teachers (low consideration), and has little clout with superiors (low influence). Teachers do not feel good about either their colleagues or their jobs. They act aloof, suspicious, and defensive (low morale). Instructional materials, supplies, and supplementary materials are not available when needed (low resource support). Finally, there is little press for academic excellence. Neither teachers nor students take academic life seriously. In fact, academically oriented students are ridiculed by their peers and viewed by their teachers as threats (low academic emphasis).

Administering and Scoring the OHI

The OHI is a 44-item Likert questionnaire on which educators are asked to describe the extent to which specific behavior patterns occur in the school. The responses vary along a four-point scale defined by the categories "rarely occurs", "sometimes occurs", "often occurs", and "very frequently occurs". The entire instrument is presented in Appendix 5.1.

Administering the Instrument

The OHI is best administered as part of a faculty meeting. It is important to guarantee the anonymity of the teacher respondents Teachers are not asked to sign the questionnaire, and no identifying code is placed on the form. Most teachers do not object to responding to the instrument, which takes less than ten minutes to complete. We recommend that someone other than an administrator be responsible for collecting the data. It is important to create a non-threatening atmosphere where teachers give candid responses.

Scoring the Instrument

The items are scored by assigning 1 to “rarely occurs”, 2 to “sometimes occurs”, 3 to “often occurs”, and 4 to “very frequently occurs”. When an item is reversed scored, “rarely occurs” receives a 4, “sometimes occurs” a 3, and so on. Each item is scored for each respondent, and then an average school score for **each item** is computed by averaging the item responses across the school. The school is the unit of analysis. The average school scores for the items comprising each subtest are added to yield school subtest scores. The seven subtest scores represent the health profile for the school. For example, if school A has 60 teachers responding to the OHI, each individual questionnaire is scored and then an average score for all respondents is computed for each item. Thus, the average score for the 60 teachers is calculated for item 1 and then item 2 and so on. The average school scores for the items comprising each subtest are added to yield school subtest scores. The seven subtest scores represent the health profile for the school. To score the OHI, do the following:

Step 1: Score each item for each respondent with the appropriate number (1, 2, 3, or 4). Be sure to reverse score items 8, 15, 20, 22, 29, 30, 34, 36, 39.

Step 2: Calculate an average school score for each item. In the example above, add all 60 scores on each item and then divide the sum by 60. Round the scores to the nearest hundredth. This score represents the average school item score. You should have 44 school item scores before proceeding.

Step 3: Sum the average school item scores as follows:
Institutional Integrity (II) = Items 1 + 8 + 15 + 22 + 29 + 36 + 39
Initiating Structure (IS) = Items 4 + 11 + 18 + 25 + 32
Consideration (C) = Items 3 + 10 + 17 + 24 + 31
Principal Influence (PI) = Items 2 + 9 + 16 + 23 + 30
Resource Support (RS) = Items 5 + 12 + 19 + 26 + 33
Morale (M) = Items 6 + 13 + 20 + 27 + 34 + 37 + 40 + 42 + 44
Academic Emphasis (AE) = Items 7 + 14 + 21 + 28 + 35 + 38 + 41 + 43

These seven scores represent the health profile of the school. You may wish to compare your school profile with other schools. To do so, we recommend that you use the norms developed in an earlier study of a large, diverse sample of high schools from New Jersey.[3] The average score for schools in this normative sample and their standard deviation on each health dimension (respectively) are as follows: Institutional Integrity (18.61, 2.66), Initiating Structure (14.36, 1.83), Consideration (12.83, 2.03), Principal Influence (12.93, 1.79), Resource Allocation (13.52, 1.89), Morale (25.05, 2.64), and Academic Emphasis (21.33, 2.76). To standardize your school's scores using these norms, simply take your raw score for each subtest and subtract from it the corresponding normative score (use the means above), multiply the difference by 100, divide the product by the corresponding standard deviation (use standard deviations above), and add 500 to the result.

When you have standardized your school scores against the normative data provided in the New Jersey sample, your school's score will be somewhere between 300 and 800. This standardization process makes the scores more meaningful. The scores are interpreted just like GRE or SAT scores from Educational Testing Service. An average score for each dimension is 500 and the standard deviation is 100. For example, if your school score is 700 on institutional integrity, it is two standard deviations above the average score on institutional integrity of all schools in the sample, that is, the school has more institutional integrity than 97 per cent of the schools in the normative sample. Likewise, a score of 400 indicates that the score is one standard deviation below the average. To give you a fuller understanding of these scores, examine the ranges presented below:

If the score is 200, it is lower than 99 per cent of the schools in the sample.
If the score is 300, it is lower than 97 per cent of the schools in the sample.
If the score is 400, it is lower than 84 per cent of the schools in the sample.
If the score is 500, it is average.
If the score is 600, it is higher than 84 per cent of the schools in the sample.
If the score is 700, it is higher than 97 per cent of the schools in the sample.
If the score is 800, it is higher than 99 per cent of the schools in the sample.

Computing a Health Index

Once the seven subtest scores have been standardized, an overall index of school health can be computed as follows:

$$\text{Health} = \frac{(\text{SdS for II}) + (\text{Sds for IS}) + (\text{Sds for C}) + (\text{SdS for PI}) + (\text{SdS for RS}) + (\text{SdS for M}) + (\text{SdS for AE})}{7}$$

Simply add the seven standard scores and divide by seven. This health index is interpreted the same way as the subtest scores, that is, the mean of the "average" school is 500. Thus, a score of 650 on the health index represents a very healthy school, one that is one and a half standard deviations above the average school.

School Health Profiles

After the subtest and overall index scores have been computed, it is simple to array the data as a profile of school health. To help in this regard, we have supplied prototypes for healthy and unhealthy schools. Then we provide an actual example of a health profile and its interpretation. First consider the following prototypic profiles:

	Healthy	Unhealthy
Institutional Integrity	605	443
Initiating Structure	659	404
Consideration	604	390
Principal Influence	634	360
Resource Support	598	404
Morale	603	402
Academic Emphasis	603	383
Overall Health Index	615	398

These two extreme profiles represent composite profiles of high schools with healthy and unhealthy school climates. Compare your school's profile with these prototypes to get a sense of the health of your school. To illustrate, we have changed the numbers into categories ranging from high to low by using the following conversion table:

Above 600	Very High
551–600	High
525–550	Above Average
511–524	Slightly Above Average
490–510	Average
476–489	Slightly Below Average
450–475	Below Average
400–449	Low
Below 400	Very Low

Example

A concrete example may help further. Consider the profile of the Buchanan High School, an urban school in New Jersey with nearly 1500 students:

Health Profile for Buchanan High School

Institutional Level	
Institutional Integrity	441 (Low)
Managerial Level	
Initiating Structure	463 (Below average)
Consideration	521 (Slightly above average)

Principal Influence	371 (Very low)
Resource Support	420 (Low)
Technical Level	
Morale	433 (Low)
Academic Emphasis	448 (Low)
Health Index for Buchanan High	442 (Low)

Buchanan is an unhealthy school. This is a real school, but the name has been changed. The OHI profile is a snapshot of what is wrong. Buchanan is a school in which outside groups are attempting to influence educational decisions within the school (low institutional integrity). Instructional materials and supplies are difficult to obtain (low resource support), and the principal, while seen as relatively friendly, supportive, and collegial (slightly above average consideration), has no apparent influence with superiors, who do not take him seriously (very low principal influence). The principal's attempts to maintain structure within the school are below the average of other high schools. Teachers do not get much sense of accomplishment from their jobs, nor are they confident in their fellow teachers or even friendly with them (low morale). The press for academic achievement in Buchanan is abysmal. Teachers simply have no confidence in the students to achieve.

These data about Buchanan supply some hints about its problems, but the profile simply describes the school. It does not explain the conditions. This may well be a school that is being starved for support and resources. The principal seems to be in an untenable position. He is reasonably well-liked by the teachers, but he has no influence with his superiors in the central administration. He has been unable to get what the teachers feel are the necessary instructional materials to do a good job. His faculty is demoralized. In fact, it seems as though they have given up. The problems of Buchanan may not be merely school problems; they appear to be part of a district pattern of neglect.

It would be tempting to suggest changes that ought to be made at Buchanan, but it would probably not be productive. The teachers and administrators at Buchanan are the best people to explain why this pattern of unhealthy dynamics exists, and they are critically placed to suggest and implement possibilities for change. Any program of successful change must involve the teachers at Buchanan. The OHI is a tool that can be used to describe a number of important organizational features. Once the description is made, the cooperative work of finding causes for the patterns of behavior remains. But how does one begin?

There is no one way to engage in school improvement. In cases where the health is very poor, it may be necessary to enlist the help of an outsider, one who specializes in organizational development. In other cases, the principal may take the initiative to organize change around a professional development or in-service activity for the faculty. For those who are interested in some authentic cases of principals who have initiated successful improvement activities in schools, there is help. Hoy and Tarter (in press) describe a number of such cases in detail using an organizational development approach. They predicate their change model on the following assumptions:

- Change is a property of healthy organizations. You cannot eliminate change, but you can harness it.
- Change has direction. Progressive change is movement consistent with objectives and eventual solutions.
- Organizational learning is possible. Schools can develop their own processes to solve problems.
- Schools should be learning organizations where teachers create and expand their capacity to learn.
- Healthy schools are not only ends-in-themselves, but also a means to the development of learning organizations.

Regardless of your strategy for change, it will not occur unless both teachers and administrators are committed. Ultimately, they must recognize the difficulties and take responsibility for their solution. The OHI and the health profile are tools, but they do not guarantee progress. Only the teachers and principals themselves, working together can change a school.

Some Research Findings

The OHI has proved itself a useful research instrument. Studies using the OHI have shown that dimensions of school health are consistently related to important school outcomes. We focus on three such outcomes — student achievement, teacher commitment and faculty trust.

We begin with faculty trust. Most discussions of the term occur at the global level rather than specifying its dimensions. After a careful review of the literature, Hoy and Kupersmith (1985) used the work of Rotter (1967) and Golembiewski and McConkie (1975) to conceptualize two important aspects of faculty trust. Trust is associated with a general confidence and overall optimism in occurring events. In more specific terms, trust is a generalized expectancy held by the work group that the word, action, and written or oral statement of another individual, group, or organization can be relied upon (Hoy and Kupersmith, 1985). The focus of this definition implies that trust can be viewed in relation to a variety of reference groups — student, colleague, or principal. One would trust a person, not simply in the sense of consistency of action, but in the sense of reliance to act in one's best interest. The present analysis considers two specific aspects of trust. **Faculty trust in the principal** *is the faculty's confidence that the principal will keep his/her word and will act in the best interests of the teachers.* **Faculty trust in colleagues** *is the faculty's belief that colleagues can depend and rely upon one another in a difficult situation.*

While the concepts of health and trust are not identical, they are complementary. Thus, it was assumed that the seven elements of health should predict faculty trust in the principal and in colleagues. Healthy schools should have teachers who trust each other and their principal, and they do (Tarter and Hoy, 1988).

Commitment is another important aspect of organizational life and has been associated with effective outcomes. **Organizational commitment** *is the strength of identification and involvement with the organization* (Steers, 1977). *It can be characterized by a belief in and acceptance of the organization's goals and values, a willingness to exert substantial effort on behalf of the organization, and a desire to maintain membership in the organization* (Porter et al., 1974). March and Simon (1958) argue that such commitment is commonly a function of an exchange in which the inducements offered by the organization are sufficient to prompt not merely participation in the organization, but commitment to the organization. Commitment in this sense is not simply loyalty or compliance but rather a whole-hearted support of organizational ventures and values. Again, it was assumed that the seven elements of health should predict faculty trust in the principal and in colleagues. Healthy schools should have teachers who are highly committed to the school and its mission, and they do (Tarter, Hoy and Kottkamp, 1990).

Student achievement in basic skills is one outcome that most people agree is a component of effective schools. Although there is more to school effectiveness than student achievement, few would argue that student achievement is not an important instrumental outcome of schooling. Healthy schools with their press for high academic standards, strong leadership, and cohesive interpersonal relations, should provide an organizational context for high student achievement, and they generally do (Hoy, Tarter and Bliss, 1990). Surprisingly, however, institutional integrity is not positively related to student achievement; in fact, pressure from the outside seems functional for student achievement.

Some Implications

The OHI is a parsimonious and reliable instrument ready for use by both researchers and practitioners. It is one of the few climate measures that has been designed for use in secondary schools. The health inventory provides measures of seven important attributes of student-teacher, teacher-teacher, teacher-principal, and principal-superior relationships, which fit together in a way that yields a global index of the state of organizational health.

For researchers interested in studying the school workplace, the OHI and its conceptual underpinnings provide a framework for the study of leadership, motivation, decision making, structure, communication and school effectiveness, as well as a perspective for evaluating school improvement programs. Although the OHI was developed for use in secondary schools, the framework is sound for work in elementary schools and middle schools, and versions of the health inventory are available at these levels as well (Hoy and Tarter, 1997).

For those administrators who are seriously interested in improving school effectiveness, the OHI offers a simple diagnostic tool. Improvement of instruction, curriculum development, and critical inquiry into the teaching-learning process are likely only in schools with healthy organizational climates. Healthy climates can be facilitated by enlightened and secure administrators who are willing to evaluate systematically the state of health of their schools. The OHI can be used to provide base-line data on seven critical dimensions as well as a general index of organizational health. Principals and superintendents can not only determine the health of their schools, they can compare their own perceptions of the working atmosphere with the perceptions of their teachers. Discrepancies are often at the heart of many school problems.

The position taken here is that improvement in the state of organizational health should be the prime target of change efforts in schools because only when the systems' dynamics are open and healthy will more specific change strategies be effective. Successful innovation requires self-study, security, and commitment of the professional staff. Change is a systematic process that demands not only modifying individual attitudes but also developing new relationships among members in group settings. Focusing efforts on groups and relationships, and increasing the flow of information about the organization to participants often alters existing norms that regulate interpersonal transactions in groups.

We agree with Miles (1969) that the state of organizational health will likely tell us more than anything else about the probable success of most change efforts: "Economy of effort would suggest that we should look at the state of an organization's health as such, and try to improve it — in preference to struggling with a series of more or less inspired short-run change efforts as ends in themselves" (p. 388). This is not to say that schools must be in a perfect state of health before any meaningful change can occur, but rather that the basic innovation should be one of organizational development itself.

A Conclusion and a Caution

Why use the organizational health inventory? Will it make schools better? There are no quick fixes. But healthy schools are better places to work and learn than unhealthy ones. Teachers are more productive, administrators are more reflective, and students achieve at higher levels. Academic emphasis is an integral part of a healthy school. True, the health of a school can be positive and student achievement not high, but when healthy interpersonal dynamics are linked with a press for achievement — that is, high but achievable student goals are set; the learning environment is orderly and serious; teachers believe students can achieve; and students are committed to doing well — schools are successful and students achieve at high levels.

The OHI provides administrators and teachers with an important tool to analyze sytematically the quality of their workplace. The measure is easy to use and teachers rather enjoy the experience. In fact, there is usually an initial phase of enthusiasm with the measures as administrators see both a way to capture the tone of their school and a direction for improvement. Administrators who have used the OHI testify to its usefulness. They claim they are better able to sort out how they are received by their teachers. For most of them, the news is mixed. Often the message is blunt. The principal burdens teachers with trivia and busywork and doesn't go to bat for them.

The typical principal response is "I disagree", or, "that's wrong". But the issue here is not who is right and who is wrong. The feelings of the teachers are real and based on something. The principal may indeed behave as described or may be misperceived as behaving that way. It really doesn't matter. Teachers act on their beliefs and perceptions. Principals need to come to understand the basis of the beliefs of the teachers so that they can respond directly and adroitly. The OHI does not explain, it simply describes. It is a tool for reflection and action.

We believe in the efficacy of the OHI, but we would not want to overpromise its benefits or see it used inappropriately. The health profile of a school mirrors the interaction patterns in a school. The profiles are the foundations for self-analysis and organizational improvement. We believe, and there is research evidence (see Hoy, Tarter and Kottkamp, 1991), that the OHI measures important sets of variables that are related to positive teacher and student performance. Healthy schools are good places. People like each other and they like their schools. Trust, commitment, cooperation, loyalty, and teamwork are the hallmarks of such schools. Healthy schools are transformed into educational communities where individuals come to respect each other and help each other. We caution against using the OHI for summative evaluation. To do so would be to weaken its utility as a tool for organizational development and improvement.

Rather than merely giving a vague impression of school atmosphere, the OHI provides reasonably valid and reliable descriptions of school health. The measure is relatively unobtrusive, simple to administer, and easy to score. If teachers are guaranteed anonymity, there is no difficulty in getting them to respond. In fact, teachers enjoy the opportunity to express honest opinion without fear of retaliation. The instrument requires no more than ten minutes to administer and we recommend it be given to teachers as part of a regular faculty meeting. We encourage the use of the OHI. Simply reproduce it (see Appendix 5.1) and use it.

Notes

1 This chapter draws heavily from two sources, Hoy and Feldman (1987) and Hoy, Tarter and Kottkamp (1991). For the reader interested in more of the technical details of the instrument and its development, both are good sources.

2 A similar framework and measures have been developed for elementary and middle schools (see Hoy and Tarter, 1997, elementary edition).

3 For more details on the norms and scoring directions, see Hoy, Tarter and Kottkamp (1991). The scoring is easy and simple, but for those interested, a PC computer scoring program for the OHI can be purchased from Arlington Writers, 2548 Onandaga Drive, Columbus, OH 43221. The program will automatically score the data and standardize the scores using the current norms so that comparisons can be easily made.

Appendix 5.1: Organizational Health Inventory (OHI)

Directions: the following are statements about your school. Please indicate the extent to which each statement characterizes your school by circling the appropriate response.
RO = rarely occurs SO = sometimes occurs O = often occurs VFO = very frequently occurs

1 Teachers are protected from unreasonable community and parental demands .... RO SO O VFO
2 The principal gets what he or she asks for from superiors .... RO SO O VFO
3 The principal is friendly and approachable .... RO SO O VFO
4 The principal asks that faculty members follow standard rules and regulations .... RO SO O VFO
5 Extra materials are available if requested .... RO SO O VFO
6 Teachers do favors for each other .... RO SO O VFO
7 The students in this school can achieve the goals that have been set for them .... RO SO O VFO
8 The school is vulnerable to outside pressures .... RO SO O VFO
9 The principal is able to influence the actions of his or her superiors .... RO SO O VFO
10 The principal treats all faculty members as his or her equal .... RO SO O VFO
11 The principal makes his or her attitudes clear to the school .... RO SO O VFO
12 Teachers are provided with adequate materials for their classrooms .... RO SO O VFO
13 Teachers in this school like each other .... RO SO O VFO
14 The school sets high standards for academic performance .... RO SO O VFO
15 Community demands are accepted even when they are not consistent with the Educational program .... RO SO O VFO
16 The principal is able to work well with the superintendent .... RO SO O VFO
17 The principal puts suggestions made by the faculty into operation .... RO SO O VFO
18 The principal lets faculty know what is expected of them .... RO SO O VFO
19 Teachers receive necessary classroom supplies .... RO SO O VFO
20 Teachers are indifferent to each other .... RO SO O VFO
21 Students respect others who get good grades .... RO SO O VFO
22 Teachers feel pressure from the community .... RO SO O VFO
23 The principal's recommendations are given serious consideration by his or her superiors .... RO SO O VFO
24 The principal is willing to make changes .... RO SO O VFO
25 The principal maintains definite standards of performance .... RO SO O VFO
26 Supplementary materials are available for classroom use .... RO SO O VFO
27 Teachers exhibit friendliness to each other .... RO SO O VFO
28 Students seek extra work so they can get good grades .... RO SO O VFO
29 Select citizen groups are influential with the board .... RO SO O VFO
30 The principal is impeded by the superiors .... RO SO O VFO
31 The principal looks out for the personal welfare of faculty members .... RO SO O VFO
32 The principal schedules the work to be done .... RO SO O VFO
33 Teachers have access to needed instructional materials .... RO SO O VFO
34 Teachers in this school are cool and aloof to each other .... RO SO O VFO

35 Teachers in this school believe that their students have the ability to achieve academically .... RO SO O VFO
36 The school is open to the whims of the public .... RO SO O VFO
37 The morale of the teachers is high .... RO SO O VFO
38 Academic achievement is recognized and acknowledged by the school .... RO SO O VFO
39 A few vocal parents can change school policy .... RO SO O VFO
40 There is a feeling of trust and confidence among the staff .... RO SO O VFO
41 Students try hard to improve on previous work .... RO SO O VFO
42 Teachers accomplish their jobs with enthusiasm .... RO SO O VFO
43 The learning environment is orderly and serious .... RO SO O VFO
44 Teachers identify with the school .... RO SO O VFO

References

Ashford, B.E. (1985) 'Climate formations: Issues and extensions', *Academy of Management Review*, **10**, pp. 837–47.

Etzioni, A. (1975) *A Comparative Analysis of Complex Organizations*, New York: Free Press.

Golembiewski, T.T. and McConkie, M. (1975) 'The centrality of interpersonal trust in group processes', in Cooper C.L. (ed.) *Theories of Group Process*, New York: McGraw-Hill, pp. 131–85.

Hall, J.W. (1972) 'A comparison of Halpin and Croft's organizational climates and Likert and Likert's organizational systems', *Administrative Science Quarterly*, **17**, pp. 586–90.

Halpin, A.W. and Croft, D.B. (1963) *The Organizational Climate of Schools*, Chicago: Midwest Administration Center.

Hoy, W.K. and Clover, S. (1986) 'Elementary school climate: A revision of the OCDQ', *Educational Administration Quarterly*, **22**, pp. 93–110.

Hoy, W.K. and Feldman, J.A. (1987) 'Organizational health: The concept and its measure', *Journal of Research and Development in Education*, **20**, pp. 30–8.

Hoy, W.K., Hoffman, J., Sabo, D. and Bliss, J. (1996) 'The organizational climate of middle schools: The development and test of the OCDQ-RM', *Journal of Educational Administration*, **34**, pp. 41–59.

Hoy, W.K. and Kupersmith, W.J. (1985) 'The meaning and measure of faculty trust', *Educational and Psychological Research*, **5**, pp. 1–10.

Hoy, W.K. and Miskel, C.W. (1996) *Educational Administration: Theory into Practice*, 5th edition, New York: McGraw-Hill.

Hoy, W.K. and Tarter, C.J. (1997) *The Road to Open and Healthy Schools: Handbook for Change*, elementary edition. Beverly Hills, CA: Corwin.

Hoy, W.K. and Tarter, C.J. (1997) *The Road to Open and Healthy Schools: Handbook for Change*, secondary edition in press. Beverly Hills, CA: Corwin.

Hoy, W.K., Tarter, C.J. and Bliss, J. (1990) 'Organization climate, school health, and effectiveness: A comparative analysis', *Educational Administration Quarterly*, **26**, pp. 260–79.

Hoy, W.K., Tarter, C.J. and Kottkamp, R.B. (1991) *Open School, Healthy School: Making Schools Work*, Newberry Park, CA: Corwin Press.

KAISER, H.F. (1960) 'The application of electronic computers to factor analysis', *Educational and Psychological Measurement*, **20**, pp. 141–51.

KERLINGER, F. (1986) *Foundations of Behavioral Research*, (3rd ed.), New York: Holt, Rinehart and Winston.

KIMPSTON, R.D. and SONNABEND, L.C. (1975) 'Public schools: The interrelationships between organizational health and innovativeness and between organizational health and staff characteristics', *Urban Education*, **10**, pp. 27–48.

LITWIN, G.H. and STRINGER, R.A. (1968) *Motivation and Organizational Climate*, Boston: Harvard University Press.

MARCH, J. and SIMON, H. (1958). *Organizations*, New York: Wiley.

MILES, M.B. (1969) 'Planned change and organizational health: Figure and ground', in CARVER, F.D. and SERGIOVANNI, T.J. (eds.) *Organizations and Human Behavior*, New York: McGraw Hill, pp. 375–91.

MILES, M.B. (1975) 'Comment from Miles', *Urban Education*, **10**, pp. 46–8.

PACE, C.R. and STERN, G.C. (1958) 'An approach to the measure of psychological characteristics of college environments', *Journal of Educational Psychology*, **49**, pp. 269–77.

POOLE, M.S. (1985) 'Communication and organizational climates: Review, critiques, and anew perspective', in MCPHEE, R.D. and TOMPKINS, P.K. (eds.) *Organizational Communications: Traditional Themes and New Directions*, Beverly Hills, CA: Sage, pp. 79–108.

PARSONS, T. (1967) 'Some ingredients of a general theory of formal organization', in HALPIN, A.W. (ed.) *Administrative Theory in Education*, New York: Macmillan, pp. 40–72.

PARSONS, T., BALES, R.F. and SHILS, E.A. (1953) *Working Papers in the Theory of Action*, Glencoe, IL: Free Press.

PORTER, L.W., STEERS, R.M., MOWDAY, R.T. and BOULIAN, P.V. (1974) 'Organizational commitment, job satisfaction, and turnover among psychiatric technicians', *Journal of Applied Psychology*, **59**, pp. 603–9.

RUMMEL, R.J. (1970) *Applied Factor Analysis*, Evanston, IL: Northwestern University Press.

ROKEACH, M. (1960) *The Open and Closed Mind*, New York: Basic Books.

ROTTER, J.B. (1967) 'A new scale for the measure of interpersonal trust', *Journal of Personality*, **35**, pp. 651–5.

STEERS, R.M. (1977) *Organizational Effectiveness: A Behavioral View*, Santa Monica, CA: Goodyear.

STERN, G.G. (1970) People in Context: Measuring Person-environment in Education and Industry, New York: Wiley.

TAGIURI, R. (1968) 'The concept of organizational climate', in TAGIURI R. and LITWIN G.W. (eds.) *Organizational Climate: Explorations of a Concept*, Boston: Harvard University, Division of Research, Graduate School of Business Administration, pp. 11–32.

TARTER, C.J. and HOY, W.K. (1988) 'The context of trust: Teachers and the principal', *High School Journal*, **72**, pp. 17–24.

TARTER, C.J., HOY, W.K. and KOTTKAMP, R. (1990) 'School Climate and Organizational Commitment', *Journal of Research and Development in Education*, **23**, pp. 236–42.

Chapter 6

Organizational Climate and Teacher Professionalism: Identifying Teacher Work Environment Dimensions*

Sharon Conley and Donna E. Muncey

> In this school, it's energizing and refreshing and very different to be working with a staff that is willing to do new things. I think I have a great deal more autonomy [here]. . . . There's a great deal of freedom to develop your program as long as it fits the school's curriculum and the school's policies. [When I came here] I took [my ideas] to the principal and said, "Here's what I want to do", and then he gave me free reign to do so. . . . When I come in in the morning, I don't know which skills and talents I'm going to use. (Writing teacher, 1996)

In recent years, the topic of organizational climate has been receiving increasing attention from researchers and practitioners alike. Litwin and Stringer (1968) define organizational climate as "a set of measurable properties of the work environment, based on the collective perceptions of the people who live and work in the environment and demonstrated to influence their behavior" (as Hoy and Miskel cited in 1996, p. 140).[1] Stated a slightly different way, organizational climate is concerned with aspects of the organization that shape members' behavior and attitudes concerning their work activities and the organizations in which they participate (O'Driscoll and Evans, 1988). Organizational climate research has generally addressed the identification of distinct properties of the work environment that comprise the global construct of organizational climate. With some important exceptions (Hoy, 1990), many studies of organizational climate have been conducted within business firms; analyses of organizational factors salient to climate in other organizational settings have received less attention (O'Driscoll and Evans, 1988). Such an organizational setting is schools.

The current reform movement in education has placed a strong emphasis on enhancing the performance and goal achievement of schools as work organizations. Emphasis has specifically been placed on how the work of teachers — those employees who work most closely with the system's clients, the students — should be managed (Firestone, 1996; Lieberman, 1988). There has been a shift from a belief that what is needed is to implement bureaucratic management strategies

* The authors thank Jody Brandon and Salvador Castillo for their comments on an earlier version of this chapter.

designed to control teachers to one that emphasizes the importance of creating work environments that respect teachers' professional role. In general, it has been difficult for educational managers, who are sensitive to increasing demands for public accountability, to create an ideal work environment for the professional teacher. Recently, however, numerous schools and school districts have begun to experiment with strategies designed to enhance teacher involvement in decision making (Imber and Neidt, 1990), sense of career development (Bacharach, Conley and Shedd, 1990), and quality of work life (Louis and Smith, 1991). These efforts represent attempts that begin to address the question of how to design a work environment that treats teachers as professionals.

The issues that confront professionals in work organizations are seemingly an important focus of organizational climate. Because many reform efforts are emphasizing a more professional mode of school management, climate perspectives are needed that are sensitive to the desires of teachers as professionals. Thus, this chapter examines organizational climate from the perspective of teachers as professionals. We specifically aim to identify those work environment variables that teachers believe enhance their work as professionals. We do this both to illustrate the importance of the issue as well as to document ways that this topic can become a part of organizational climate research and practice, using both quantitative and qualitative approaches.

This chapter does not do justice to the voluminous literature on professionals in organizations. Initially, we limit our discussion to a sampling of studies that outlines issues professionals confront in work organizations. We examine how some scholars have operationalized aspects of organizational climate that tap professional dimensions of the work environment in turn (e.g., Bacharach, Bauer and Conley, 1986; Conley et al., 1989; Conley and Levinson, 1993; Sutton, 1984). Finally, using organizational climate data from one elementary school in a medium-sized urban district, we provide examples of school profiles that illustrate the professional dimensions identified. Although these profiles primarily emphasize quantitative information gathered from surveys, the potential use of qualitative measures is addressed as well.

Professionals in Organizations

Research on professionals in organizations has long addressed the issue of defining a professional. Historically in education, Etzioni's (1961) characterization of "semi-professionals" has been used to depict teachers. Early sociological studies of teaching (Lortie, 1975; 1977) characterized teaching as low in status relative to other professions, marked by easy access and the lack of an arcane knowledge base. Lortie (1977) noted, for example, that a national survey ranked public school teaching "35/90 and a position below such occupations as medicine, college teaching, the clergy, dentistry, law, and engineering", (p. 348) but above journalists, welfare workers, and the skilled trades. Many people, having been pupils in schools themselves, believe that they are as knowledgeable as most teachers. As of 1977, Lortie noted that teachers have been unable to convince the public that "methods courses constitute a truly distinct and impressive body of knowledge" (p. 352). Furthermore, salaries comprise a public indication of a profession's status, and teachers' remuneration is low relative to other professional groups (Odden and Conley, 1992). Finally, members of high-status professions (e.g., law and medicine) tend to work with adults, whereas teachers work largely with children. As Lortie (1977) noted, in society in general "the care of small children is culturally defined as women's work" and thus low in status compared to other professions (p. 349).

Only during the most current reform movement have we begun to seriously rethink these assumptions. Practitioners and policy makers are now addressing the question of how to redesign schools and the work of teaching based on the assumption that teachers are full professionals (Darling-Hammond, 1996). Accordingly, it is being recognized in the general literature on organizational behavior that the question of who is a professional is more complex than earlier envisioned. Professionalism is not a unitary construct whereby an occupation is judged to be a profession or not (and where teaching is judged as something less than a full profession). Instead, professionalism encompasses several dimensions, each of which may be adhered to by a given profession to a greater or lesser extent. For example, a profession is considered to have a formalized code of ethics and a prescribed and lengthy period of training. In addition, its members should possess certain attitudinal characteristics, such as service to the public and a belief in self regulation. Finally, society in general should view the occupation as a profession (Hall, 1990). Indeed, in the educational reform movement, progress has been made on several dimensions by which teachers have typically been viewed as less than professional. Much recent emphasis has been placed, for example, on upgrading the quality and length of teachers' professional preparation (Holmes Group, 1986). There has also been an indication that the attitudinal attributes of teachers are changing; teachers, for example, are participating in peer assistance and peer review efforts that give them a greater self-regulatory role. In addition, in a recent study, Hall (1990) found that teachers ranked themselves higher on belief in public service than several other occupational groups (e.g., law and medicine) but lower than lawyers and physicians on several other attributes. Finally, the recent reform movement's concern with attracting high-quality entrants into teaching suggests that greater societal recognition is being accorded teaching. These developments suggest that teaching should not be viewed as less than a full-fledged profession.

The literature on organizations and professions has also addressed the issue of conflict between the organization and the professional and the parameters of that conflict (see, for example, Raelin, 1985; Strauss, Schatzman, Ehrlich, Bucher and Sabshin, 1963). Raelin (1985), for example, outlined some reasons why professionals' desires for autonomy sometimes clash with the preferences of organizational managers.

> Professionals wish to make their own decisions without external pressure from those outside the profession, including their managers. The right of autonomy, however, clashes with management's expectations regarding the proper role of the employee. Professional employees are expected to conform to the basic goals and procedures of the enterprise. Management is unlikely to be entirely sympathetic, therefore, with the professional's quest for autonomy. (p. 155)

This clash actually highlights opposing views about who should be responsible for reducing work uncertainty in the organization. (In schools, disagreements stem from who should reduce uncertainty concerning students.) On one hand, management would prefer to reduce ambiguity and uncertainty through rules and procedural specifications; on the other, this runs counter to the professional's desire for autonomy. The professional prefers to be responsible for handling work uncertainty in the process of carrying out the work itself.

Similarly, scholars examining school organizations (Cox and Wood, 1980; Hanson, 1996) have conceptualized a set of tensions between teachers, who view themselves as professionals, and educational managers. One manifestation of this conflict, for example, is contests for control over particular decision-making areas in the organization. Hanson (1996) noted that teachers feel that they should have primary control over determining course content, although they tend to accede decisions about other curriculum matters (e.g., textbook selection) to administrators and others. However, teachers and administrators disagree about who should have primary influence over decisions concerning special programs (e.g., bilingual and accelerated programs). Decisions in these and other areas of organizational functioning are the focus of constant negotiation and renegotiation in school organizational life.

The organizational literature has also been concerned with the outcomes of professional-bureaucratic conflict in terms of how the professional is ultimately treated in the organization, regardless of other indicators of professional status. (The professional may have excellent credentials and a strong conviction in public service. If, however, bureaucratic norms come to dominate the organizational "ethos", professionals may feel blocked in attaining their goals.) One group of scholars (e.g., Marjoribanks, 1977; Raelin, 1985) views this conflict as eventually and predominantly being resolved in favor of the professional. That is, in many organizations, professionals' preferences (e.g., autonomy and control over work) are viewed as coming to dominate the workplace. Others, however, (Cox and Wood, 1980; Organ and Greene, 1981; Lachman and Aranya, 1986) view the conflict as being resolved in favor of the organization, where administrative preferences and norms come to dominate professional ones. A third perspective maintains that the outcome of this conflict will not be resolved in favor of the professional or the organization; instead, the organizational ethos is viewed (metaphorically) as a "see-saw" that vacillates between professional and organizational domination (Bacharach, Bamberger and Conley, 1988).[2] This perpetual "see-saw" perspective is consistent with conceptions of schools as negotiated orders (Hanson, 1996). An organizational climate framework seemingly favors the first two views — (i) that ideas in the organization about how the work and the organization is designed and managed reflect professional preferences; or (ii) that over time managerial strategies pivot away from a managerially-dominant orientation (e.g., task delineation, close supervision) to a professionally-dominant orientation (e.g., work autonomy and skill variety) while recognizing that a return to the aforementioned strategies is possible.

These differing views underscore that professional-bureaucratic conflict permeates many areas of organizational functioning. The organizational climate perspective taps aspects of the organization about which members are "sensitive and which, in turn, affects their attitudes and behavior" (Taguiri and Litwin, 1968, p. 26). Because teachers view themselves as professionals, they are likely to be sensitive to ways in which bureaucratic constraints (purposed toward the reduction of uncertainty) may impede their work. Climate frameworks that take this tension into consideration appear useful in current school reform efforts. Such frameworks may reveal tensions in the workplace that are not readily apparent. Do teachers disagree that reforms have enhanced work autonomy? Does the workplace support the enhanced involvement of teachers in organizational decision making?

In addition, the violation of professional expectations of teachers has been linked to increased stress, burnout, and reduced job satisfaction in the teacher work force in general (Bacharach et al., 1986; Sutton, 1984). Contemporary observers (Hargreaves, 1992) have noted that even professional-oriented reforms are, somewhat incongruously, producing significant role stress for teachers (e.g., a sense of role overload and role conflict). Where organizational climate assessments identify significant sources of role conflict and tension in teachers' work lives, practitioners may have a basis for altering current school improvement strategies and modes of management to enhance professionals' workplace preferences and provide a greater sense of satisfaction to individual teachers. It is to these areas that we turn in the next section.

Work Environment Dimensions

As suggested above, potential conflict between the professional and the organization may manifest itself in a number of different areas. This section delineates prominent dimensions of the school work environment, taking into consideration both the nature of teachers' work as professionals and the nature of schools. These work environment dimensions are:

(i) role ambiguity and routinization;
(ii) centralization of authority and formalization;
(iii) intrinsic and extrinsic work features;
(iv) participative supervision;
(v) career development; and
(vi) involvement in decision making.

Role Ambiguity and Routinization

It is important that organizational climate assessments tap aspects of the work process. Two of these aspects are role ambiguity and routinization. In bureaucracies, an attempt is made to reduce work ambiguity and uncertainty for employees by specifying work procedures and rules. Most employees require clarity and predictability to make progress toward their work goals. Excessive ambiguity, therefore, may pose a source of frustration and anxiety for workers in meeting their goals (Kahn, Wolfe, Quinn and Snoek, 1964). Kahn et al.'s (1964) study of workers in the national labor force revealed that over one-third were "disturbed by lack of clarity about the scope and responsibilities of their jobs" (p. 74). The authors also found that role ambiguity led to "increased emotional tension and to decreased satisfaction with one's job" (p. 85). However, too much reduction of work uncertainty through, for example, the use of rules by the organization may undermine the discretion teachers require to address the unpredictable and uncertain needs of their primary clients (students). In addition, the reduction of work uncertainty may make teachers feel that their work is overly routine and mundane.

Bureaucratization of the work process, then, is manifested in the more specific work features of role ambiguity and routinization. Role ambiguity has been formally defined as "lack of the necessary information available to a given organizational position" (Rizzo, House and Lirtzman, 1970, p. 150). In a study of teachers, Bacharach et al. (1986) found that the presence of role ambiguity contributed to stress. In addition, work that was overly routine also increased stress. Thus, it seemed that a delicate balance should be maintained. Bureaucratization of the work process should be extensive enough to provide clarity about expectations and work direction, but not so much as to provide a sense that work is routine. In this context, role ambiguity and routinization appear to be important indicators of bureaucratization of the work process for professionals.

The following are some examples of role ambiguity items. They are adapted from Rizzo et al. (1970) and provide a sense of the kinds of questions used in questionnaires designed to address bureaucratization as an element of the work environment.

(i) I feel certain about how much authority I have.[3]
(ii) I know what my responsibilities are.

In addition, examples of routinization items, adapted from Bacharach and Aiken (1976), are as follows:

(i) There is something different to do in my job every day.
(ii) In my position, I need to learn to do more than one job.

Centralization of Authority and Formalization

Centralization of authority and formalization are two structural features of organizations that affect people's reactions to their jobs (Aiken and Hage, 1966). Aiken and Hage defined centralization of authority as "the locus of authority to make decisions affecting the organization" (p. 498).[4] One aspect of centralization is the hierarchy of authority or "the extent to which members are assigned tasks and then provided with the freedom to implement them without interruption from superiors" (p. 498). Workers who have little autonomy over their tasks, according to Aiken and Hage, have little sense of control over their work and thus feel dissatisfied with and alienated from their work. This may be particularly true of professionals, who expect to be involved in setting work goals (Aiken and Hage, 1966).

A second structural feature of organizations, formalization, has been defined as the extent of "work standardization and the amount of deviation that is allowed from standards" (Aiken and Hage, 1966, p. 499). When formalization is high, a preponderance of rules exist to define job procedures. The work of professionals, however, "does not lend itself to easy codification of jobs or reliance on rules without numerous exceptions" (Aiken and Hage, 1966, p. 499). Therefore, too much formalization can be expected to diminish peoples' work satisfaction. Consequently, hierarchy of authority and formalization appear to be important work environment dimensions.

Examples of hierarchy of authority items are adapted from Aiken and Hage (1966). They are:

(i) There can be little action taken here until a superior approves a decision.
(ii) Even small matters have to be referred to someone higher-up for a decision.

One item designed to measure degree of formalization was adapted from Aiken and Hage (1966). It is: People here feel that they are constantly being watched, to see if they obey all the rules.

Intrinsic and Extrinsic Work Features

Professional workers expect certain characteristics to be present in their jobs. For example, they expect to experience substantial autonomy in their work, use complex or high-level skills in carrying out their work, have the chance to utilize their own special abilities and talents, and perform whole tasks that allow them to see the results of their work (Hackman and Oldham, 1980). These can be considered *intrinsic* features of work. However, professionals, as well as other employees, are also sensitive to *extrinsic* features of work including their pay and the job security they enjoy. Both intrinsic and extrinsic features of work comprise important work environment dimensions for professionals.

Intrinsic work feature items are adapted from Martin and Shehan (1989). Sample items are:

(i) I have a lot of freedom to decide how I do my work.
(ii) I can see the results of my own work.

Extrinsic work feature items are adapted from Martin and Shehan (1989). Sample items are:

(i) I receive a good salary.
(ii) My job is secure.

Participative Supervision

In schools, principals are formally responsible for supervising and evaluating teachers. In many schools, principals can be viewed as a colleague as well as a supervisor because they provide information and support as well as evaluate work performance. Participative supervision on the part of principals — that is, requesting teachers' views and perspectives in a collegial manner — would seem to be an important work environment variable.

Participativeness of supervision items are adapted from Rosner and Tannenbaum (1987). They are:

(i) Is your principal inclined to take into account your opinions and suggestions about matters that arise in your school?
(ii) Does your principal ask your opinion when a problem comes up that involves your work?

Career Development

Professionals expect advancement opportunities in recognition of greater levels of expertise. In education, however, the "flat" career structure of teaching has provided teachers with little sense of career advancement (Lortie, 1975). Reform measures such as career ladders and career development plans have attempted to address this deficiency by creating new professional tiers to which teachers might aspire. Therefore, it seems important to include *opportunities for advancement* as a work environment dimension for professionals. In addition, a professional is likely to assess not only whether opportunities exist, but also how rational or fair the process of advancement is in the organization. Therefore, *rationality of advancement* appears to be an additional work environment concern (see Bacharach et al., 1986; Conley et al., 1989).

Two items were adapted from Bacharach et al. (1986) to measure the certainty of promotion opportunities and the rationality of the promotion process:

(i) How certain are you of the opportunities for promotion and advancement which will exist in the next few years?
(ii) To what degree do you think that promotion in this school is basically a rational process?

Involvement in Decision Making

Professionals desire a measure of influence on decisions made in the organizations in which they work, yet they may not desire equal influence in every decision-making area (Hanson, 1996). Research has identified areas in which teachers have little desire for participation and those where they would like much more influence than they currently have (Conley, 1991; Ferrara, 1992). Some education scholars (Mohrman, Cooke and Mohrman, 1978) draw a distinction between technical and managerial decisions. Applied to schools, technical decisions (such as how and what to teach) are more often those made within classrooms, while managerial decisions (such as hiring and budget) are usually made by administrators outside of classrooms. Teachers are likely to desire the most influence over technical decisions, but they are likely to want some involvement in managerial decisions as well. Research has shown teachers to be most often deprived of decision making in these areas (Ferrara, 1992). Thus, it seems important to assess the extent to which teachers are participating across a variety of areas, such as how and what to teach, discipline policies, attendance policies, and school expenditure priorities.

An item measuring teacher involvement in decision making in educational matters is:[5] How much did you actually get involved in decisions in the following areas last year? Sample areas as follows:

(a) Budget development and evaluation
(b) Teacher promotion and transfer
(c) How to teach
(d) What to teach

In summary, the above work environment dimensions are by no means the only ones that could be considered in a framework examining professionals in bureaucracies. Each of the above dimensions may be (and have been) assessed in many different ways. These and other items were included on questionnaires designed to create school profiles. We next turn to some samples of the use of these dimensions in school profiles.

Illustrations of School Profiles on Work Environment Dimensions

This section presents illustrations of school profiles on the aforementioned work environment variables. By school profiles, we mean displays of data that summarize teachers' responses to questionnaire items designed to measure the school work environment along the above dimensions. It is possible to construct a profile for a single school or any group or sub-set of schools within a district. Our illustrative case study is of a single elementary school, but to increase our analytic options, data from that school are presented along with data from four other elementary schools in the district.

We had three questions that we wanted to answer in the school profile: (i) how do teachers, on average, perceive the work environment dimensions? (ii) are work environment dimensions related to teachers' job satisfaction and organizational commitment? and (iii) how do teachers (in general or in sub-groups) respond to selected items? We have found this combination of questions to be an effective one because it allows us to look at teachers' average responses about the work environment dimensions, the relationships among those dimensions, and, finally, how teachers respond to selected items. The presentation of these questionnaire data to answer these three questions will potentially yield much rich data about the climate of the school. Now we turn to examine these questions for one school, and that school in comparison to others in the same district, to illustrate what these kind of data look like when they are profiled for an individual school in comparison with others.

Illustrative Case Study: Benjamin Davis Elementary School

We selected a single elementary school, Benjamin Davis, for this purpose. Benjamin Davis is the largest elementary school in a medium-sized urban school district in the Southwest. Benjamin Davis Elementary School is located in a transitional community, where recent arrivals to the United States live in trailers, apartments, and small homes alongside their more established blue collar neighbors. Approximately 42 per cent of the students participate in the free or reduced student lunch program, and the district and school regularly try to provide additional services (such as breakfast and clothing) for students and their families. Douglas Nichols, principal for more than five years, is respected by teachers for both his involvement in national task forces and his support of teachers' responsibilities as family members as well as their responsibilities to their students. Currently, there are 28 teachers working at Benjamin Davis, and about 560 students. We thought that a profile of this school might be of particular interest because this school and its leader were actively involved with several national and local reform and improvement initiatives. For example, the district had adopted a career ladder program and teachers at this school were involved in team planning and teaching as well.

We begin with the first question concerning how teachers perceive the work environment dimensions.

How do teachers, on average, perceive the work environment dimensions?

We wanted to ascertain for Davis Elementary School the extent to which teachers, on average, perceive the work environment dimensions to be present in their jobs. Therefore, mean scores and standard deviations were calculated for each work environment variable (see Table 6.1).

With regard to role ambiguity and routinization (1–2 in Table 6.1) teachers, on average, report that they are clear about what their responsibilities are (i.e., have low role ambiguity) and their work is not routine. (On the 7-point scale for these items, 1–3 indicates agreement that there is low role ambiguity and low routinization.) To a somewhat lesser extent, teachers report that there is a willingness for them to carry out their activities in an autonomous way, and that the work environment is not highly rule pervasive or formalized. (A score closer to the mid-point of 4 indicates a more neutral stance.) Thus, dimensions associated with a professional work environment appear to be present in teachers' jobs. This is particularly true of routinization — teachers see their work as far from routine and mundane.

*Table 6.1 Means, standard deviations and T-statistics for work environment dimensions, teacher satisfaction and organizational commitment**

		Davis Elementary School		**Other Elementary Schools**		
		Mean	*SD*	*Mean*	*SD*	*t value*
1	Role ambiguity	2.21	0.60	2.34	0.84	0.85
2	Routinization	1.72	0.71	1.85	0.86	−0.74
3	Hierarchy of authority	4.70	1.43	4.81	1.77	−0.32
4	Formalization	4.72	1.34	5.20	1.55	−1.42
5	Use of complex skills	1.76	0.88	1.79	1.23	−0.12
6	Develop special abilities	1.92	0.81	2.01	0.95	−0.44
7	Freedom to decide work	2.40	1.12	2.35	1.32	0.16
8	See the results of work	1.76	0.88	1.96	0.89	−0.97
9	Job is secure	2.48	1.58	2.67	1.52	−0.56
10	Receive a good salary	4.40	1.71	4.47	1.60	−0.20
11	Opportunities for advancement	3.36	1.71	3.27	1.83	0.22
12	Participativeness of supervision	4.21	0.75	4.15	0.91	0.29
13	Certainty of promotion opportunities	2.38	0.92	2.59	0.92	−0.92
14	Rationality of promotion	3.25	1.23	3.51	0.92	−0.95
15	Budget development	1.63	0.82	1.59	0.80	0.21
16	Promotion and transfer	1.29	0.55	1.18	0.47	0.98
17	Building maintenance	1.96	0.91	1.56	0.76	2.21*
18	School assignment	1.38	0.77	1.36	0.73	0.07
19	Classroom assignment	1.42	0.65	1.51	0.84	−0.51
20	Staff hiring	1.75	0.90	1.52	0.77	1.23
21	Performance evaluation	1.92	1.10	1.48	0.80	2.19*
22	Scheduling for teachers	1.92	0.97	2.33	1.04	−1.75
22	Scheduling for students	2.63	0.88	2.63	1.04	0.00
23	Student placement	2.75	1.07	2.43	1.03	1.33
25	Discipline policies	2.75	0.79	2.63	0.99	0.57
26	Attendance policies	1.25	0.61	1.37	0.73	−0.72
27	Promotion and retention	2.50	1.06	2.66	1.12	−0.62
28	What to teach	3.04	0.81	2.76	1.03	1.43
29	How to teach	3.29	0.81	3.21	0.92	0.41
30	Job satisfaction	1.62	0.56	1.77	0.64	−1.08
31	Organizational commitment	4.62	0.49	4.61	0.52	0.13

* $p < 0.05$
1–11 are measured on a 7 point scale; 12, 14 and 31 are measured on a 5 point scale; and the remainder are measured on a 4 point scale. A high scale value indicates a high amount of the variable, with the following exceptions: 3–11 and 30.

Concerning intrinsic and extrinsic work features (5–11), teachers, on average, agree that they use complex or high-level skills in their work, have opportunities to develop their own special abilities, and see the results of their work. To a lesser extent, they report that they have freedom to decide how to do their work, that their jobs are secure and that they have opportunities for advancement. They report the least agreement with the item, "I receive a good salary." (In Table 6.1, higher means for these are associated with lower agreement that they are present in teachers' jobs.)

Regarding involvement in decision making (15–29), teachers report that they regularly participate in deciding how and what to teach. Further, in such areas as scheduling for students, student placement, and discipline policies, their participation on average is reported between "frequent" and "occasional". Less participation is reported in the areas of teacher promotion and transfer, attendance policies, and school assignment (that is, between "occasional" and "seldom or never"). Regarding teachers' attitudinal reactions to their work, they report being "satisfied" or "very satisfied" with their jobs and committed to their school organizations (e.g., feeling that the school inspires the best from them in the way of job performance).

Finally, mean responses of Davis do not generally differ from those of teachers at all other elementary schools on the work environment variables (see Table 6.1). However, Davis teachers report greater participation in building maintenance and performance evaluation on average than do teachers in the other schools. Thus, one use of school profiles is to examine whether a school's work environment is similar to or different from those in other organizations.

In summary, teachers in these schools view many positive work environment dimensions as being present in their jobs. Teachers tend to agree, for example, that they know what their responsibilities are, have opportunities to develop their own special abilities, and know the results of their work. Organizational climate assessments then, provide a way of ascertaining whether work characteristics about which teachers are sensitive are present in particular jobs and schools. Indeed, these dimensions were found to be associated with enhanced teacher job satisfaction and/or organizational commitment.

Are work environment dimensions related to teachers' job satisfaction and organizational commitment?

It has been suggested that professionals are sensitive to several dimensions of the work environment that represent areas where the professional and the organization interface. We would expect that these work dimensions (such as bureaucratization of the work process and participativeness of supervision) affect teachers' reactions to their work. These reactions may be manifested in how satisfied teachers report they are with their jobs and how committed they are to the organization.

To examine the relationships between the work environment dimensions and job satisfaction and organizational commitment, we calculated zero-order correlation coefficients among these variables.[6] The results of this analysis (see Table 6.2) showed that in Davis school, the strongest relationships were among role ambiguity, job satisfaction, and organizational commitment. The higher the role ambiguity the teacher experiences, the less he or she is satisfied with the job and committed to the organization. That is, the more teachers lack clarity and predictability in their jobs, the more negatively they respond to their jobs and organizations. Furthermore, the more teachers feel that they have opportunities for advancement, the more committed they are to the organization. Advancement may be particularly important in this district because of its experimentation with a voluntary career ladder program. Finally, two participation-in-decision-making items are also related to teachers' reactions to their work: student scheduling and student retention and

Table 6.2 Correlations between work environment dimensions, teacher job satisfaction and organizational commitment

		Davis Elementary School		All Elementary Schools	
		Satisfact.	*Commitment*	*Satisfact.*	*Commitment*
1	Role ambiguity	0.52†	−0.48*	0.23*	−0.28*
2	Routinization	0.28	0.06	0.09	−0.23*
3	Hierarchy of authority	−0.08	0.05	−0.17	0.30†
4	Formalization	0.16	0.18	−0.02	0.32†
5	Use of complex skills	0.32	−0.13	0.28†	−0.23*
6	Develop special abilities	0.27	−0.13	0.24*	−0.37†
7	Freedom to decide work	0.20	−0.17	0.16	−0.36†
8	See the results of work	0.32	−0.03	0.35†	−0.20*
9	Job is secure	0.06	−0.02	0.21*	−0.14
10	Receive a good salary	0.30	−0.14	0.21*	−0.15
11	Opportunities for advancement	0.28	−0.41*	0.26†	−0.31†
12	Participativeness of supervision	−0.30	0.07	−0.21*	0.44†
13	Certainty of promotion opportunities	−0.32	−0.10	−0.30†	0.05
14	Rationality of promotion	−0.33	0.20	−0.24*	0.25*
15	Budget development	−0.09	0.17	0.07	0.03
16	Promotion and transfer	0.20	0.02	0.08	−0.04
17	Building maintenance	0.14	0.30	−0.05	0.13
18	School assignment	0.15	0.10	0.00	0.13
19	Classroom assignment	0.19	0.03	−0.04	0.08
20	Staff hiring	0.08	0.07	−0.05	0.12
21	Performance evaluation	0.26	0.06	−0.04	0.17
22	Scheduling for teachers	−0.16	0.07	−0.06	0.20*
23	Scheduling for students	−0.50*	0.01	−0.15	0.19*
24	Student placement	−0.15	−0.10	−0.06	0.12
25	Discipline policies	−0.05	0.08	−0.05	0.14
26	Attendance policies	0.04	−0.04	−0.07	0.07
27	Promotion and retention	−0.22	0.50*	−0.05	0.12
28	What to teach	0.20	−0.18	−0.11	0.18
29	How to teach	0.02	0.23	−0.02	0.14

* $p < 0.05$
† $p < 0.01$

promotion policies. The more input teachers feel they have into scheduling for students, the more satisfied they are with their jobs. This input may allow teachers to assemble their classes in ways that they feel they can do their jobs. Also, the greater teachers feel their input into student promotion and retention policies is, the more committed they are to the organization. It may be that this input gives teachers the feeling that their professional judgments concerning students are respected by administration, and thus teachers are more committed to the organization.

When we turned to examine correlation coefficients for teachers in the district's other four elementary schools combined, some additional work environment items achieved statistical significance.[7] Excluding the participation-in-decision-making-items (15–29), 10 of 14 work environment variables were significantly associated with job satisfaction, and 11 of 14 were associated with organizational commitment.[8] Noting the strongest relationships, the more teachers say they see the results of their work, feel certain about the promotion opportunities they have, and say they have opportunities to utilize high-level skills in their work, the more satisfied they are with their jobs. Furthermore, the greater the participativeness of supervision, chances to utilize one's own special abilities, freedom in one's work, and opportunities for advancement, the more committed teachers are to the organization. Interestingly, job security, receiving a good salary, and certainty of promotion opportunities are related to job satisfaction but not to organizational commitment. Routinized work, hierarchy of authority, and formalization (e.g., rule pervasiveness), by contrast, are associated with lower organizational commitment but not with lower job satisfaction.

In sum, these data suggest that many of the work dimensions are, in fact, related to teachers' reactions to work (in terms of job satisfaction and commitment to the organization). These findings suggest that these are climate dimensions to which teachers are sensitive. For other studies on this topic, see Bacharach et al. (1986), Conley et al. (1989), Bacharach et al. (1990), and Conley and Levinson (1993).

How do teachers respond to selected items?

It is also of interest to ascertain how teachers or sub-groups of teachers responded to particular work environment items. Three types of items were selected for examination: involvement in decision making, role ambiguity, and job satisfaction. Responses to these items are displayed in Figures 6.1–6.3.

Figure 6.1 shows arrays of teachers' responses at Davis Elementary school concerning their decision-making involvement. As discussed previously, few teachers

Figure 6.1 Percentages of teachers reporting that they are involved in decisions "Frequently" or "Almost Always" in Davis and other elementary schools

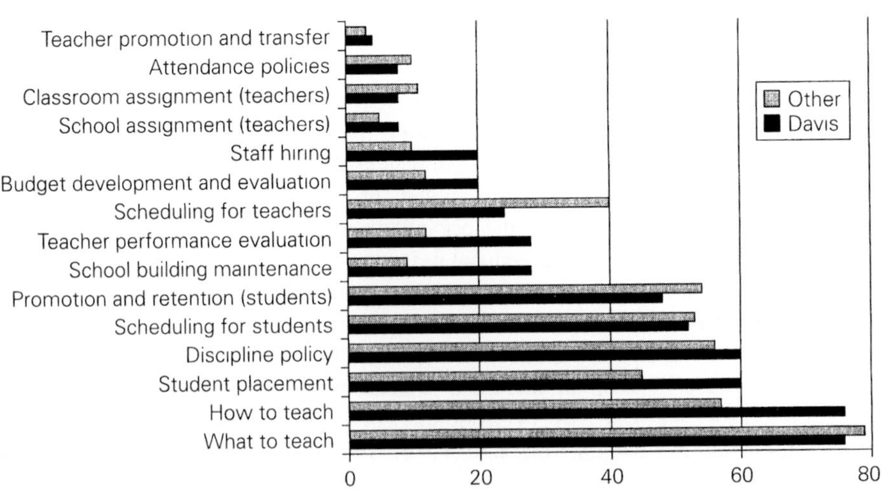

participate frequently in areas such as attendance policies and school assignment, although more do so in the areas of scheduling for teachers, teacher performance evaluation, and school building maintenance. Teacher participation is even greater in areas such as making students placements, handling discipline policies, and deciding how and what to teach.

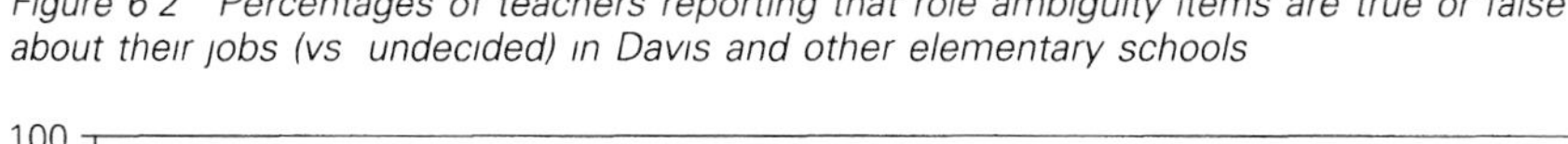

Figure 6.2 Percentages of teachers reporting that role ambiguity items are true or false about their jobs (vs. undecided) in Davis and other elementary schools

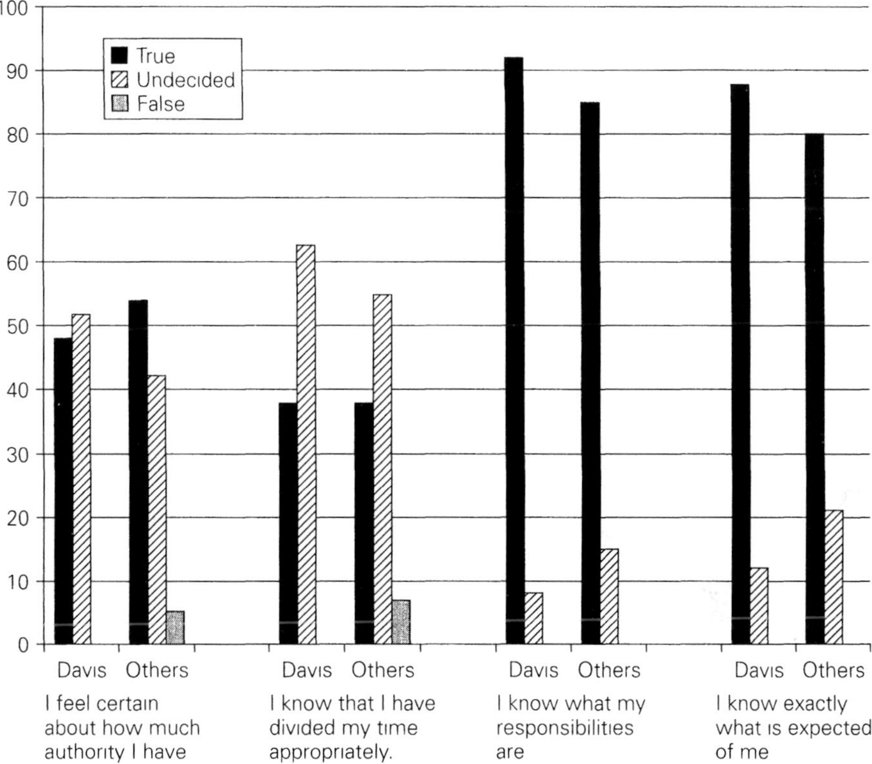

Figure 6.2 shows teachers' responses to the role ambiguity items — i.e., whether they characterized them as "true" or "false" or reported being "undecided". More teachers regard as true the statements, "I know what my responsibilities are", and "I know exactly what is expected of me", than "I feel certain about how much authority I have", and "I know that I have divided my time appropriately". Because authority over decisions is constantly negotiated in schools (Hanson, 1996), it makes sense that teachers may be uncertain about the decision-making authority they have. Furthermore, in a profession such as teaching, where time is a scarce resource, it may be difficult for teachers to feel comfortable about the way they have allocated time.

Figure 6.3 Percentages of teachers reporting that they are "Very Dissatisfied", "Dissatisfied", "Satisfied", or "Very Satisfied" with their jobs in Davis and other elementary schools

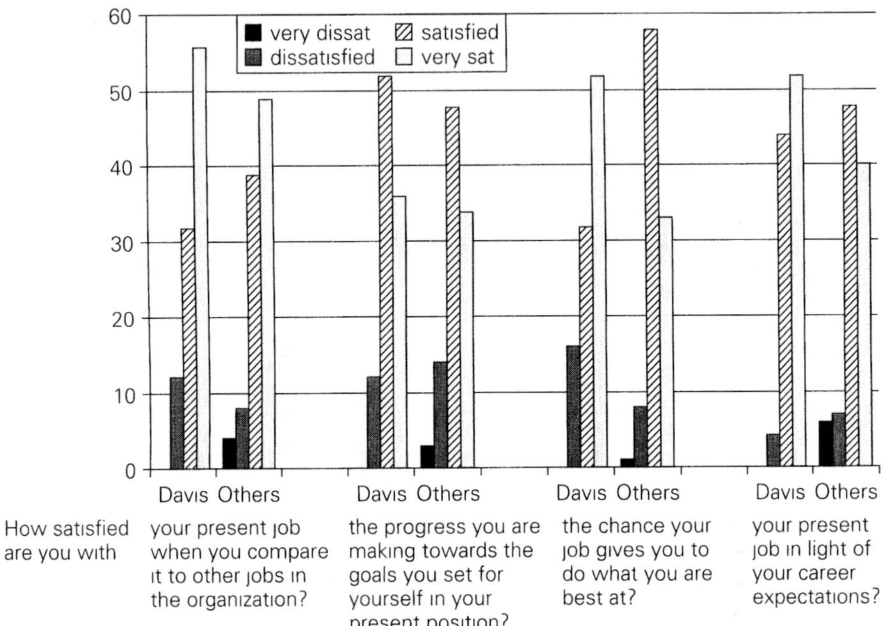

Figure 6.3 shows teachers' responses to questions about how satisfied they are with their jobs. Large proportions (e.g., about 85 to 90 per cent) of teachers in Davis and the districts' four other elementary schools report being satisfied or very satisfied with various aspects of their jobs. Just over 10 per cent of Davis teachers, however, are dissatisfied with the "goals they have set for themselves in their present positions" (second item). These teachers appear more uncertain about their progress toward work goals than about the appeal of their jobs, overall (e.g., their job in light of their career expectations).

Incorporating Qualitative Measures in the School Profile

The questionnaire results generally yield a profile that is somewhat straightforward (Calder, 1980). To flesh out the survey results, it can be useful to incorporate qualitative data techniques into the organizational climate study. Three prominent qualitative techniques that could be incorporated include: interviewing some subset of questionnaire participants; observing individual classrooms, meetings, or other relevant settings where insights about the school organizational climate are likely to be gleaned; or reviewing documents that are relevant to the topic to determine, for example, if agreed-upon decisions appear to be consistent with the profile of decision-making involvement that emerged from analysis of the questionnaire data. There are many excellent books and articles on qualitative research; certainly, describing how to do qualitative research is beyond the scope of this paper.[9] Nonetheless, we have found that targeting a topic that emerges from the quantitative data for more intensive scrutiny adds a richness to the profile.

We chose to do some follow-up interviews with experienced teachers in Benjamin Davis to try to understand how the work environment and how teacher teaming and teacher leadership looked from their perspectives. We did this because teacher teaming and teacher leadership are important components of educational reform (Lieberman, Saxl and Miles, 1988; Maeroff, 1993). What we found from our limited sampling was that teachers in the school, based on their personal experiences, preferred one mode of working (teaming or leadership) over the other. We were asking these questions to learn more about aspects of teacher professionalism (i.e., teacher leadership and teacher teaming) but our findings from the interviews also allowed us to get at teacher satisfaction and perceptions of the work environment. The teachers we interviewed, for example, cited children's learning and working with other teachers as the most important sources of satisfaction in their work. One teacher, however, emphasized autonomy as an additional source of job satisfaction; this same teacher felt more comfortable in teacher leadership than teacher teaming roles. Another teacher commented in some detail on the supervision she experienced at Benjamin Davis. Here is an excerpt of her description of her interactions with the principal:

> The principal's very supportive in sending us to workshops if we ask to go to, you know, out-of-district workshops. [He's also supportive] in following through with any kids we might send up, good or bad, coming through [our classrooms, and] keeping in contact with the kids so they know who he is and *they* know he supports what we say and what we do.

Our study examined subsets of experienced teachers and the particular issues of teacher teaming and teacher leadership but any subset of the school (e.g., the teaching population or an issue) could be looked at qualitatively. Equally, one could decide to look at the first grade team, the third grade team, or a school-wide site-based management team. Likewise, we conducted interviews to obtain additional information, but most certainly we could have done observations and/or looked at documentary material available as well.

Conclusion

The work environment dimensions presented in this chapter represent only a sampling of issues that are relevant to the work of professionals in organizations. Interested readers may refer to Sutton (1984) for the additional dimensions of interpersonal relationships and conflict between work and home and to Bacharach et al. (1986) for the topic of communication with peers and supervisors.

In the contemporary reform movement, much emphasis has been placed on treating teachers as professionals. To the degree that teachers have excessive role ambiguity in their work, limited involvement in decision making, and little sense of career advancement, they will not be regarded as full professionals regardless of the credentials they have. Teachers can excel in a school work environment that allows them to utilize their professional expertise and initiative. Organizational climate assessments provide a tool for measuring the professional satisfaction of teachers for both sustaining and improving such school work environments.

Notes

1 Similarly, Tagiuri and Litwin (1968) noted that organizational climate refers to "the quality of the organization's *internal* environment, especially as experienced by the *insider*" (p. 26).

2 See Bacharach et al. (1991) for a review of all three perspectives. The authors additionally examine factors that influence the resolution of professional conflict in favor of the organization or the professional.

3 These role ambiguity questions are asked in the negative (i.e., agreement with the items indicates low role ambiguity). These items are also measured on a scale ranging from 1 (very true) to 7 (very false), meaning that a low score is associated with low role ambiguity. How the items are worded and the scales used to measure them are important to remember when interpreting the data.

4 This definition was adapted from Pugh et al., 1963.

5 Respondents may also be asked how much they would like to get involved in decisions (see Bacharach et al., 1990, and Ferrara, 1992). For an alternative specification of decision making areas, see Ferrara (1992).

6 The correlation coefficients for Table 6.2 are available from the authors.

7 These statistics are available from the authors. Because the number of teachers in Davis is quite small (25), the correlation coefficient must be large to achieve significance. Thus, there were fewer significant correlations for Davis than for the other elementary schools combined.

8 For job satisfaction, the 10 variables were: role ambiguity, use of complex skills, special abilities, results of work, secure job, good salary, opportunities for advancement, participativeness of supervision, certainty of promotion opportunities, and rationality of promotion. Seeing the results of one's work had the strongest relationship with job satisfaction. For commitment, the 14 variables were: role ambiguity, routinization, hierarchy of authority, formalization, use of complex skills, special abilities, freedom to decide work, see the results of work, opportunities for advancement, participativeness of supervision, and rationality of promotion. Participativeness of supervision had the strongest relationship with organizational commitment.

9 It is also beyond the scope of this paper to discuss the varying views scholars hold concerning combining the use of qualitative and quantitative data collection methods in research. For a more detailed discussion of these methodological issues, see Caldwell (1980), Eisner and Peshkin (1990), Maxwell (1991), Page (1991), Seiber (1980), and Smith and Heshusius (1986).

References

AIKEN, M. and HAGE, J. (1966) 'Organizational alienation: A comparative analysis', *American Sociological Review*, **31**, 4, pp. 497–507.

BACHARACH, S.B. and AIKEN, M. (1976) 'Structural and process constraints on influence in organizations: A level specific analysis', *Administrative Science Quarterly*, **21**, pp. 623–42.

BACHARACH, S.B., BAMBERGER, P. and CONLEY, S.C. (1991) 'Negotiating the "see-saw" of managerial strategy: A resurrection of the study of professionals in organizational theory', in TOLBERT, P.S. and BARLEY, S.R. (eds) *Research in the Sociology of Organizations*, Vol. 8, San Francisco: JAI Press, pp. 217–38.

BACHARACH, S.B., BAUER, S. and CONLEY, S. (1986) 'Organizational analysis of stress: The case of elementary and secondary schools', *Work and Occupations*, **13**, 1, pp. 7–32.

BACHARACH, S.B., BAMBERGER, P., CONLEY, S.C. and BAUER, S. (1990) 'The dimensionality of decision participation in educational organizations: The value of a multi-domain evaluative approach', *Educational Administration Quarterly*, **26**, pp. 126–67.

BACHARACH, S.B., CONLEY, S.C. and SHEDD, J.B. (1990) 'Evaluating teachers for career awards and merit pay', in HAMMOND, L.D. and MILLMAN, J. (eds) *The New Handbook of Teacher Evaluation: Assessing Elementary and Secondary School Teachers*, Newbury Park: Sage.

CALDER, B.J. (1980) 'Focus group interviews and qualitative research in organizations', in LAWLER, E.E., NADLER, D.A. and CAMMANN, C. (eds) *Organizational Assessment: Perspectives on the Measurement of Organizational Behavior and the Quality of Work Life*, New York: John Wiley and Sons, pp. 399–417.

CONLEY, S. (1991) 'Review of research on teacher participation in school decision making', in GRANT, G. (ed.) *Review of Research in Education*, Vol. 17, Washington, D.C.: American Educational Research Association, pp. 225–66.

CONLEY, S.C., BACHARACH, S.B. and BAUER, S. (1989) 'The school work environment and teacher career dissatisfaction', *Educational Administration Quarterly*, **25**, 1, pp. 58–81.

CONLEY, S. and LEVINSON, R. (1993) 'Teacher work redesign and job satisfaction', *Educational Administration Quarterly*, **29**, 4, pp. 453–78.

COX, H. and WOOD, J.R. (1980) 'Organizational structure and professional alienation; The case of public school teachers', *Peabody Journal of Education*, **58**, 1, pp. 1–6.

DARLING-HAMMOND, L. (1996) 'What matters most: A competent teacher for every child, *Phi Delta Kappan*, **78**, pp. 193–200.

EISNER, E.W. and PESHKIN, A. (1990) *Qualitative Inquiry in Education: The Continuing Debate*, New York: Teachers College Press.

ETZIONI, A. (1961) *A Comparative Analysis of Complex Organizations*, New York: The Free Press.

FERRARA, D.L. (1992) Teacher perceptions of participation in shared decision making in New York State: Actual and desired participation, deviations between actual and desired participation, and domains identified from participation measures. Doctoral Dissertation, New York University. Published in UMI.

FIRESTONE, W.A. (1996) 'Images of teaching and proposals for reform: A comparison of ideas from cognitive and organizational research', *Educational Administration Quarterly*, **32**, 2, pp. 209–35.

HACKMAN, J.R. and OLDHAM, G.R. (1980) *Work Redesign*, Reading MA: Addison Wesley.

HALL, R.H. (1985) 'Professional/management relations: Imagery vs. action', *Human Resource Management*, **24**, pp. 227–36.

HANSON, E.M. (1996) *Educational Administration and Organizational Behavior*, Needham Heights, MA: Allyn and Bacon.

HARGREAVES, A. (1992) 'Time and teachers' work: An analysis of the intensification thesis', *Teachers College Record*, **94**, 1, pp. 87–108.

HOLMES GROUP (1986) *Tomorrow's Teachers: A Report of the Holmes Group*, East Lansing, MI: Author.

HOY, W.K. (1990) 'Organizational climate and culture: A conceptual analysis of the school workplace', *Journal of Educational and Psychological Consultation*, **1**, pp. 149–68.

HOY, W.K. and MISKEL, C.G. (1996) *Educational Administration: Theory, Research, and Practice*, New York: McGraw-Hill.

IMBER, M. and NEIDT, W.A. (1990) 'Teacher participation in school decision making', in REYES, P. (ed.) *Teachers and Their Workplace: Commitment, Performance and Productivity*, Newbury Park, CA: Sage, pp. 67–85.

KAHN, R.L., WOLFE, D.M., QUINN, R.P. and SNOEK, J.D. (1964) *Organizational Stress: Studies in Role Conflict and Ambiguity*, New York: John Wiley and Sons.

LACHMAN, R. and ARANYA, N. (1986) 'Job attitudes and turnover intentions among professionals in different work settings', *Organizational Studies*, **7**, pp. 279–93.

LIEBERMAN, A., SAXL, E.R. and MILES, M.B. (1988) 'Teacher leadership: Ideology and practice', in LIEBERMAN, A. (ed.) *Building a Professional Culture in Schools*, New York: Teachers College Press, pp. 148–66.

LITWIN, G.H. and STRINGER, R.A., JR. (1968) *Motivation and Organizational Climate*, Boston: Harvard University.

LORTIE, D.C. (1975) *School Teacher: A Sociological Study*. Chicago: University of Chicago Press.

LORTIE, D.C. (1977) 'The balance of control and autonomy in elementary school teaching', in ERICKSON, D.A. (ed.) *Educational Organization and Administration*, Berkeley: McCutchan, pp. 335–71.

LOUIS, K.S. and SMITH, B. (1991) *Restructuring, Teacher Engagement, and School Culture; Perspectives on School Reform and the Improvement of Teachers' Work*, Madison, WI: National Center on Effective Secondary Schools.

MAEROFF, G. (1993) *Team Building for School Change: Equipping Teachers for New Roles*, New York: Teachers College Press.

MARJORIBANKS, K. (1977) 'Bureaucratic orientations, autonomy, and the professional attitudes of teachers', *Journal of Educational Administration*, **15**, 1, pp. 104–13.

MARTIN, J.K. and SHEHAN, C.L. (1989) 'Education and job satisfaction: The influences of gender, wage-earning status, and job values', *Work and Occupations*, **16**, 2, pp. 184–99.

MAXWELL, J.A. (1991) Paradigms as ideologies: Implications for evaluation. Paper presented at a session entitled, 'Beyond the Paradigm Wars in Educational Evaluation', at the American Anthropological Association 90th Annual Meeting, Chicago, IL.

MISKEL, C. and OGAWA, R. (1988) 'Work motivation, job satisfaction, and climate', in BOYAN, N.J. (ed.) *Handbook of Research on Educational Administration*, New York: Longman, pp. 279–304.

MOWDAY, R.T., PORTER, L.W. and STEERS, R.M. (1982) *Employee-organization Linkages: The Psychology of Commitment, Absenteeism, and Turnover*, New York: Academic Press.

MOHRMAN, A.M., COOKE, R.A. and MOHRMAN, S.A. (1978) 'Participation in decision making: A multidimensional perspective', *Educational Administration Quarterly*, **14**, 1, pp. 13–29.

O'DRISCOLL, M.P. and EVANS, R. (1988) 'Organizational factors and perceptions of climate in three psychiatric units', *Human Relations*, **41**, 5, pp. 371–88.

ODDEN, A.R. and CONLEY, S. (1992) 'Restructuring teacher compensation systems', in ODDEN, A.R. (ed.) *Rethinking School Finance: An Agenda for the 1990s*, San Francisco: Jossey-Bass, pp. 41–96.

ORGAN, D.W. and GREENE, C.N. (1981) 'The effects of formalization on professional involvement: A compensatory process approach', *Administrative Science Quarterly*, **26**, pp. 237–52.

PAGE, R.N. (1991) What does combining research methods mean? Paper presented at a session entitled, 'Beyond the Paradigm Wars in Educational Evaluation', at the American Anthropological Association 90th Annual Meeting, Chicago, IL.

PUGH, D.S., HICKSON, D.J., HININGS, C.R., LUPTON, K.M., MCDONALD, K.H., TURNER, C. and LUPTON, T. (1963) 'A conceptual scheme for organizational analysis. *Adminstrative Science Quarterly*', **8**, pp. 289–315.

RAELIN, J.A. (1985) 'The basis for the professional's resistance to managerial control', *Human Resource Management*, **24**, 2, pp. 147–75.

RIZZO, J., HOUSE, R. and LERTZMAN, S. (1970) 'Role conflict and ambiguity in complex organizations', *Administrative Science Quarterly*, **15**, pp. 150–63.

ROSNER, M. and TANNENBAUM, A. (1987) 'Ownership and alienation in Kibbutz factories', *Work and Occupations*, **14**, 2, pp. 165–89.

SEIBER, S.D. (1980) 'The integration of fieldwork and survey methods', in LAWLER, E.E., NADLER, D.A. and CAMMANN, C. (eds) *Organizational Assessment: Perspectives on the Measurement of Organizational Behavior and the Quality of Work Life*, New York: John Wiley and Sons, pp. 444–70.

SMITH, J.K. and HESHUSIUS, L. (1986) 'Closing down the conversation: The end of the quantitative-qualitative debate among educational inquirers', *Educational Researcher*, **15**, 1, pp. 4–12.

SORENSON, J. and SORENSON, T. (1974) 'The conflict of professionals in bureaucratic organizations', *Administrative Science Quarterly*, **19**, pp. 98–106.

STRAUSS, A.L., SCHATZMAN, L., EHRLICH, D., BUCHER, R. and SABSHIN, M. (1963) 'The hospital and its negotiated order', in FRIEDSON, E. (ed.) *The Hospital in Modern Society* Glencoe, IL.: Free Press, pp. 147–69.

SUTTON, R.I. (1984) 'Job stress among primary and secondary school teachers: Its relationship to ill-being', *Work and Occupations*, **11**, 1, pp. 7–28.

TAGIURI, R. and LITWIN, G.H. (1968) *Organizational Climate: Explorations of a Concept*, Boston: Harvard University.

Chapter 7

Perceptions of Parents and Community Members as a Measure of School Climate

Carla J. Stevens and Kathryn S. Sanchez

Introduction

School climate is a term used to describe people's perceptions of their school. It combines beliefs, values, and attitudes of students, teachers, administrators, parents, office personnel, custodians, cafeteria workers, business partners, community members, and others who play important roles in the life of the school. Perceptions can often have as great an impact as reality. The perceptions of students, parents, and the neighboring community are key components of creating an atmosphere where teachers can teach, students can learn, parents can take an active role in the education of their children, and excellence can be achieved.

Many districts have based their measurement of school climate on the perceptions of teachers, principals, and sometimes students. As part of the progressive move in education to shift decision-making to the school level and include parental and community input, the Houston Independent School District (HISD) developed and administered a series of Student/Parent/Community Surveys during the 1991–92, 1992–93, and 1993–94 school years. The purpose of these surveys was to find out from students, parents, and other representatives of the community how *they* perceived the district. The surveys addressed such characteristics of schools as:

- expectations for student achievement;
- focus on teaching and learning;
- shared decision-making;
- parent and community involvement with, support of, and satisfaction with the educational program;
- continuous and appropriate assessment of students;
- teacher and staff interaction with students; and,
- a safe and orderly environment.

The results have been used to make policy changes on both the school and district level to improve the learning environment for students.

This chapter presents the results of the Parent and Community Surveys as one measure of school climate. It also describes efforts made by the district to improve and sustain a positive school climate based on the survey findings.

Theoretical Framework Derived From Review of Literature

For many years, research has been conducted regarding effective schools. A number of factors have been identified as contributing to effective schools. Borger et al. (1985) identified, through a review of 205 research studies, eight factors characterizing effective schools: leadership, school climate, teacher/student relations, curriculum instruction, finance, physical environment, evaluation, and parent/community. School climate and parent/community involvement are the two indicators of effective schools that will be addressed in this chapter.

Wynne (1980) and Roueche and Baker (1986) are two of many studies supporting the finding that school climate is a major indicator of effective schools. McDill and Rigsby (1973) reported that school climate accounts for significant variance in student achievement and aspirations, controlling for student background. Of the 205 studies reviewed in Borger et al. (1985), 96 per cent found school climate positively associated with academic effectiveness.

Ellis (1988) defined school climate as "an aggregate of indicators, both subjective and objective, that conveys the overall feeling or impression one gets about a school" (p. 1). According to Witcher (1993), characteristics of a positive school climate include: an emphasis on academics, an ambiance of caring, a motivating curriculum, professional collegiality, and a closeness to parents and community (p. 1). Similarly, Sweeney (1988) identified ten factors that schools with "winning" school climates have in common: supportive and stimulating environment, student-centered orientation, positive expectations, feedback, rewards, sense of family, closeness to parents and community, communication, achievement, and trust. Borger et al. (1985) stated that "a safe, orderly environment where rules are clear and consistent was the most frequently mentioned climate variable" in the effective schools studies that they reviewed (p. 15). Hoy and Tarter (1992) used a health metaphor in identifying and defining a positive school climate. They espoused the idea that schools with healthy school climates are better schools. "Relationships are more open, teachers are more productive, administrators are more reflective, and students achieve at higher levels" (p. 79).

Parent and community involvement have been found to influence academic achievement and school climate. Some of the many studies linking academic achievement to parent/community involvement include Brookover and Lezotte (1979), Edmonds and Fredericksen (1978), Klitgaard and Hall (1973a,b), Phi Delta Kappa (1980), and Wynne (1980). In their review of 205 studies, Borger et al. (1985) reported that parent and community variables played a part in effective schools according to 90 per cent of the studies analyzed. Haynes, Comer and Hamilton-Lee (1989) found that the climate of schools is considerably enhanced when parents are included in the planning and organization of school activities and contribute to important decisions about significant school events because it gives parents the opportunity to be stakeholders. Coleman's (1984) study of nine schools in British Columbia emphasizes the importance of parent perceptions, as well as teacher perceptions, both in ascertaining the climate of a school and in determining how to improve it.

Figure 7.1 Theoretical framework for student/parent/community surveys

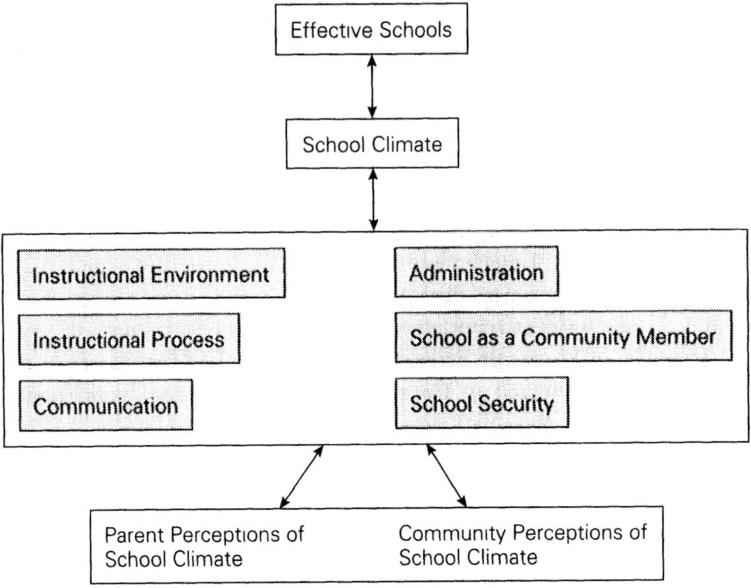

Based on what has been presented in the literature, the theoretical framework depicted above was used to guide the construction and use of the Student/Parent/Community Surveys (see Figure 7.1). Because school climate is an indicator of school effectiveness, the surveys focused on this indicator in order to assess the global construct of school effectiveness. Since student perceptions and parent and community involvement and perceptions were found to be a viable means of assessing school climate, the district chose to survey these groups. The following constructs of school climate were included in the surveys: instructional environment, instructional process, communication, administration, school as a community member, and school security. These six constructs are further defined below with the results of the surveys.

As many studies have addressed teacher and student perceptions as measures of school climate, the results from the student surveys are not presented here. The emphasis of this chapter, as stated above, is on parent and community perceptions as a useful measure of school climate.

Methods

The following discussion provides an historic perspective of the HISD Student/Parent/Community Survey development process.

Project Planning Phase

The project began with a literature review. It was determined that the surveys needed to be grounded in the most current thinking of leading experts relative to assessing the perceptions of school district patrons and students. From this review, an item bank was constructed using relevant items that had been shown in the literature to be reliable and valid. After the item bank was developed, input from site-based personnel and community members was sought on those items that best corresponded to information needed to facilitate informed decision-making at school sites. The item bank was refined and submitted for form construction. Although there are numerous instruments that have been published as valid and reliable measures of school climate, the district chose to construct its own, which would provide the specific feedback that was sought on certain facets of school climate and be more sensitive to the unique characteristics of HISD schools. According to Norton (1984), locally developed school climate assessment instruments can be quite valuable. While they lack state or national comparative norms and other standardization components, they do provide specific feedback on climate factors relative to a specific school or district. While no statistical reliability and validity checks were conducted on HISD's survey instruments, the items used reflected the concerns and issues of the district, and were firmly based on theoretical constructs garnered from the literature.

Survey Form Construction

Four surveys were developed: *HISD Student Survey: Elementary* (8 to 11-year olds), *HISD Student Survey: Secondary* (11 to 18-year olds), *HISD Parent Survey, and HISD Community Survey*. Each survey addressed a different number of items (see Table 7.1). To accommodate the needs of the two predominant language groups in the district, each survey was produced in both English and Spanish. Thus, eight surveys were assembled and distributed. Specific to each of the four survey types, the items were arranged in a random order with no two survey types having questions in the same order.

Table 7.1 Number of items by item type for each survey

Survey	**Number of Items**	
	Demographic	*Perceptual*
Student survey. Elementary	7	33
Student survey. Secondary	7	38
Parent survey	5	39
Community survey	5	19

All responses to survey statements were of a categorical format. Demographic questions such as respondent's ethnicity, grade in school (student surveys) or "grade your child is in" (parent survey), school name, and gender were asked. For the items intended to measure respondent perception(s), two response formats were adopted, one for the elementary student surveys and one for all other surveys.

Elementary level students were provided three response options: “Agree”, “Disagree”, and “Don’t Know”. To assist students in identifying an appropriate response, a happy face was used under the choice, “Agree”. A sad face was used to indicate disagreement. The “?” was used as an icon to indicate “I don’t know”. Elementary students were offered three response options in an effort to maximize the reliability of the data by providing choices similar to those used with regularity by elementary teachers.

Response options for the perception items on the remaining surveys fell into five categories: “Strongly Agree”, “Agree”, “Disagree”, “Strongly Disagree”, and “Don’t Know”. This forced-choice approach was utilized to require respondents to either indicate no knowledge, or to quantify any perception they had as either positive or negative. One reason to use the forced-choice technique is to control faking or social desirability response sets, although the benefits of this technique are under debate (Anastasi, 1988). All surveys were optically scanned.

Survey Administration and Distribution

The surveys were administered districtwide for three consecutive school years: 1991–92, 1992–93, and 1993–94. As described above, the four groups targeted to receive the surveys were elementary school students, secondary school students, parents of students who were enrolled in an HISD school, and community members. Each student in grades 3 through 12 (ages 8 to 18-year olds) were administered the survey during the spring semester. Elementary school students in grades 3–5 (typically 8–11-year olds) received the *HISD Student Survey: Elementary*, while students enrolled in grades 6–12 (typically 11–18-year olds) received the *HISD Student Survey: Secondary*. Every effort was made to survey all students and to ensure that no student was surveyed more than once. This was accomplished by the teachers distributing the surveys during homeroom, or first period in schools with no homeroom time, having the students complete the surveys during that class time, and then collecting and returning the surveys to the school office.

For 1991–92 and 1993–94, the *HISD Parent Survey* was distributed to all HISD students to be taken home to their parents. The parents returned the completed surveys to the schools via their children. The schools then mailed the student and parent surveys directly to the company contracted by the district to scan the survey forms. The procedure used in 1992–93 was somewhat different. Elementary students took the survey home with a postage-paid envelope to be used by their parents to return the survey. Parents of secondary students received the survey in the mail and returned it in the postage-paid envelope. This change in procedure was implemented to increase the response rate and to give the survey a higher profile by having the parents use the postal system instead of receiving and returning the instrument via their children. The increased cost of distributing the surveys in this manner was not justified when the response rate was substantially lower than the previous year, 21 per cent compared to 48 per cent. Consequently, the decision was made to return to the initial method of distribution.

School principals identified community members who were to complete the *HISD Community Survey*. For the 1991–92 administration of the survey, each school was provided 50 community surveys to be distributed by school staff and Parent/Teacher Organizations with a postage-paid return envelope. For the two subsequent years, principals provided the names and addresses of community members to the district's Central Office. Although the initial request to principals was for up to 20 community member names, some principals submitted more than 20 names while other principals submitted far fewer. All community members identified by the principals were mailed a survey for completion. A postage-paid envelope, addressed to the company contracted to scan the survey forms, was included and community members were directed to return the completed survey to the scanning company.

Table 7.2 Number of surveys distributed and per cent returned for each survey by year

Survey	**1991–92**		**1992–93**		**1993–94**	
	Number distrib.	*Per cent returned*	*Number distrib.*	*Per cent returned*	*Number distrib.*	*Per cent returned*
Student survey: Elementary	51,346	90	50,849	89	61,375	68
Student survey: Secondary	85,113	77	82,363	74	85,300	59
Parent survey	197,009	48	183,028	21	290,450	18
Community survey	11,322	38	4,214	29	4,033	22
Total	344,790	61	320,454	46	441,158	33

Table 7.2 documents the number of surveys distributed and the return rate for each survey by school year. The return rates for the all of the surveys declined over the three years of administration. For example, the elementary student response rate decreased from 90 per cent in 1991–92 to 68 per cent in 1993–94. Some of the lower rates of return for the 1993–94 school year may be attributed to surveys being lost in the mail between the schools and the vendor, or surveys having been received too late to be included in the results due to the national trucking strike which occurred in spring, 1994. When return rates become low, the probability of bias increases. For the parent surveys, the rates were below 25 per cent for both 1992–93 and 1993–94. The same is true for the community surveys in 1993–94. As a result, caution should be used when interpreting the data from these surveys as generalizability is reduced.

Analysis of the Surveys

Survey items were categorized into hypothesized constructs of school climate. The constructs created for the parent survey were *Instructional Environment*, *Instructional*

Process, *Communication*, and *Administration*. The *Instructional Environment* construct was composed of 12 survey questions, *Instructional Process* was composed of seven questions, *Communication* consisted of 12 questions, and eight questions comprised the *Administration* construct. For the community surveys, the constructs were *Instructional Environment*, *School as Community Member*, and *School Security*. The numbers of survey items comprising each of these constructs were eight, four, and seven, respectively. The discussions revolving around the constructs are more descriptive than inferential, as no item analysis or statistical analysis of construct validity was conducted.

Results of the Parent Survey

As indicated in Table 7.2, 197,009 parent surveys were distributed during 1991–92, 183,028 during 1992–93, and 290,450 during the 1993–94 school year. The total student enrollment for the district over these three years was 197,413, 198,209, and 200,613, respectively. The response rate decreased over that time from 48 per cent to 18 per cent. For the 1993–94 survey respondents, 4 per cent were Asian, 27 per cent African-American, 53 per cent Hispanic, and 14 per cent White. Seventy-six per cent of the parent respondents indicated they had children who were enrolled in elementary school, 16 per cent in middle school, and 9 per cent had children in high school. Demographic characteristics of the parent respondents were similar for the two previous survey administrations.

Table 7.3 presents the survey results by item for each of the three school years during which the survey was conducted. The responses for all of the survey items appeared to be consistent across time, showing no definite upward or downward trends. The highest levels of positive parental feedback concern the instructional environment and process. Although none exceeded 21 per cent, the largest consistent amount of negative feedback from parents concerns a set of statements dealing with the communication of academic expectations and strategies to parents.

Instructional Environment

The *Instructional Environment* construct was concerned with how closely parents perceived conditions at the school directly affect them or their children. Items focused on issues of safety, fairness, assistance to achieve at the highest level, and resources. For example:

- The school is a safe place to be.
- Teachers at this school believe that all their students can learn.
- Teachers expect my child to work hard.
- The school provides necessary instructional resources in the classrooms.
- Classrooms at the school are clean and well organized.

Table 7.3 Results of parent survey

Survey Item	Year	Number responding	Strongly agree	Agree	Disagree	Strongly disagree	Don't know
1 The school is clean. (IE)*	91–92	94,331	29	54	7	3	6
	92–93	37,806	31	55	8	3	4
	93–94	53,045	31	54	7	3	5
2 When I call or visit the school, I am treated with courtesy. (C)	91–92	94,178	40	52	4	2	3
	92–93	37,759	40	51	5	2	2
	93–94	52,934	39	52	5	2	2
3 This school provides a variety of activities for students. (IP)	91–92	93,803	30	53	7	2	8
	92–93	37,560	32	51	8	3	6
	93–94	52,633	31	52	7	2	7
4 The school assigns the right amount of homework. (IP)	91–92	93,983	27	54	10	3	6
	92–93	37,732	26	52	12	5	5
	93–94	52,860	28	53	10	4	5
5 The staff at the school help students with their problems. (IP)	91–92	93,890	25	49	8	3	15
	92–93	37,689	25	49	10	4	12
	93–94	52,800	25	50	8	3	14
6 The school provides necessary instructional resources in the classrooms. (IE)	91–92	93,733	24	53	6	2	16
	92–93	37,624	24	53	7	3	13
	93–94	52,676	25	53	6	2	13
7 The school is a safe place to be. (IE)	91–92	94,016	27	49	10	5	9
	92–93	37,689	26	48	11	7	8
	93–94	52,798	27	48	10	6	9
8 Teachers at this school believe that all their students can learn (IE)	91–92	94,166	37	47	4	1	10
	92–93	37,759	35	46	6	2	10
	93–94	52,901	36	48	5	2	10
9 Students at this school must work hard to get good grades. (IE)	91–92	94,238	46	46	3	1	4
	92–93	37,775	44	46	5	2	4
	93–94	52,933	46	46	4	1	3
10 Teachers at this school encourage students to do their best. (IE)	91–92	94,159	40	48	4	1	7
	92–93	37,789	39	47	6	2	6
	93–94	52,953	39	48	4	2	6

Table 7.3 (Continued)

Survey Item	Year	Number responding	Strongly agree	Agree	Disagree	Strongly disagree	Don't know
11 The school gives me suggestions of ways I can help my children learn. (C)	91–92	94,101	29	49	13	4	6
	92–93	37,775	28	47	15	6	5
	93–94	52,887	30	48	12	4	5
12 The school encourages students to stay in school and finish their education. (IE)	91–92	94,215	45	43	2	1	9
	92–93	37,830	44	42	3	2	9
	93–94	52,905	44	44	3	2	8
13 Students respect their principal/administrator and teachers. (A)	91–92	94,079	36	46	7	3	9
	92–93	37,647	33	45	9	4	8
	93–94	52,715	34	46	7	3	9
14 The school encourages my involvement. (C)	91–92	93,681	31	53	7	2	7
	92–93	37,593	31	52	9	3	5
	93–94	52,505	30	53	8	3	6
15 The principal/administrator is available for parent conferences. (A)	91–92	93,736	33	50	4	2	11
	92–93	37,519	33	48	5	3	10
	93–94	52,452	33	50	5	2	10
16 The school lets me know how my child is doing. (C)	91–92	94,017	41	50	6	2	1
	92–93	37,656	38	49	9	4	1
	93–94	52,643	41	50	6	2	1
17 Students enjoy classes at this school. (IE)	91–92	93,789	32	50	6	3	9
	92–93	37,520	29	51	8	4	8
	93–94	52,525	29	51	7	3	9
18 The school recognizes outstanding student performance. (IP)	91–92	93,740	35	49	4	1	10
	92–93	37,552	35	49	5	2	10
	93–94	52,515	35	50	4	2	9
19 My child's teacher provides comments on school work. (IP)	91–92	93,708	35	49	9	2	5
	92–93	37,546	34	46	12	4	4
	93–94	52,490	35	49	8	3	5
20 School staff respond promptly to my concerns. (C)	91–92	93,518	27	51	8	3	11
	92–93	37,498	27	50	10	5	8
	93–94	52,419	26	51	9	4	10

21	Teachers expect my child to work hard. (IE)	91–92	93,741	38	52	3	1	6
		92–93	37,569	37	52	5	1	5
		93–94	52,559	38	52	4	1	5
22	The school helps my child understand his or her school performance. (IP)	91–92	93,663	29	54	7	2	9
		92–93	37,549	27	53	9	3	8
		93–94	52,533	29	54	7	2	8
23	I have access to the principal/administrator. (A)	91–92	92,733	25	49	7	3	16
		92–93	37,245	27	49	7	4	13
		93–94	51,960	26	50	7	3	14
24	The school tells me what my children are expected to learn. (C)	91–92	93,688	27	52	13	3	5
		92–93	37,596	26	50	15	5	4
		93–94	52,488	28	51	12	4	4
25	Parents are asked to help the school make plans or decisions. (A)	91–92	93,542	25	48	11	4	12
		92–93	37,504	26	47	12	5	10
		93–94	52,397	26	49	10	4	10
26	The principal/administrator provides opportunities for parental input. (A)	91–92	93,324	24	49	8	3	16
		92–93	37,414	25	47	9	5	13
		93–94	52,305	25	50	8	3	14
27	Students are well behaved at this school. (IE)	91–92	93,464	19	45	13	7	16
		92–93	37,463	18	45	14	10	13
		93–94	52,344	19	45	13	8	15
28	The principal/administrator communicates what is happening at the school to parents. (C)	91–92	93,573	27	50	10	4	8
		92–93	37,556	27	47	12	7	7
		93–94	52,398	27	49	11	5	7
29	The teachers at this school motivate students to learn. (IP)	91–92	93,639	34	52	5	2	8
		92–93	37,537	32	50	7	3	7
		93–94	52,437	33	52	6	2	7
30	The school staff work together to improve the school. (A)	91–92	93,662	28	48	4	2	18
		92–93	37,549	28	45	6	3	18
		93–94	52,464	29	48	5	3	16
31	My child respects the school staff. (A)	91–92	93,762	42	50	3	1	4
		92–93	37,569	41	50	4	2	4
		93–94	52,498	42	50	3	1	4
32	Teachers expect my child to learn. (IE)	91–92	93,673	42	52	2	1	3
		92–93	37,551	40	53	2	1	4
		93–94	52,493	41	53	2	1	3

Table 7.3 (Continued)

Survey Item	Year	Number responding	Strongly agree	Agree	Disagree	Strongly disagree	Don't know
33 The school gives parents written information about rules, meetings, and other issues. (C)	91–92	93,871	46	47	3	1	2
	92–93	37,654	43	47	5	3	2
	93–94	52,574	44	48	4	2	2
34 The people who work at the school work together as a team. (A)	91–92	93,619	28	43	4	2	23
	92–93	37,569	27	43	5	3	22
	93–94	52,402	28	45	5	2	20
35 I can discuss my child's progress with his/her teachers. (C)	91–92	93,728	44	50	3	1	3
	92–93	37,586	43	50	4	2	2
	93–94	52,476	43	50	3	2	3
36 The school asks parents to help students prepare for tests. (C)	91–92	93,731	35	45	9	3	7
	92–93	37,559	33	42	12	5	7
	93–94	52,517	35	46	10	4	6
37 The school keeps me informed about my child's school progress. (C)	91–92	93,832	40	50	6	2	2
	92–93	37,587	37	49	9	4	1
	93–94	52,513	39	50	6	3	2
38 Classrooms at the school are clean and well organized. (IE)	91–92	93,862	32	49	6	3	10
	92–93	37,644	31	50	7	4	8
	93–94	52,561	32	49	6	3	9
39 The school makes sure students know when a project or assignment is due. (C)	91–92	93,610	34	53	3	1	9
	92–93	37,618	33	53	4	2	8
	93–94	52,486	35	52	3	2	8

* The parenthetical code identifies the related construct for each survey item.
IE = *Instructional Environment*
C = *Communication*
IP = *Instructional Process*
A = *Administration*

An underlying theme was parent perceptions of the student as an integral part of the school.

The responses to the survey indicated that most of the parents held a positive view of the Instructional Environment provided by HISD schools with few parents disagreeing to survey questions. For example, over the three survey years, 86–88 per cent of the parents responded that teachers encouraged students to do their best. The same percentages of parents indicated that their child's school encouraged students to stay in school and finish their education. A majority of parents (77–78 per cent) believed that the schools provided the necessary instructional resources. Eighty-one per cent of parents for all three years responded that classrooms at the school were clean and well organized, 83–86 per cent agreed that the school was clean, and 74–76 per cent thought the school was a safe place to be. However, only 63–64 per cent believed that students were well behaved. These last two items regarding safety and behavior received the largest percentage of disagreement from the parents. While 15–18 per cent of the parents disagreed that the school was a safe place to be, 20–24 per cent of the parents were of the opinion that the students at the school were not well behaved. Thus, while many parents believed that students could behave better, a somewhat larger majority indicated that despite mediocre behavior on the part of students, the schools are basically safe.

Over the three survey years, 93–94 per cent of parents agreed that teachers expected their children to learn, while 89–90 per cent responded that teachers expected students to work hard. Interestingly, 80–82 per cent of parents responded that their children enjoyed classes at their school. This is in sharp contrast to 26–29 per cent of secondary students who responded favorably to this same question and 71–76 per cent of elementary students who indicated that they liked going to their school. It should be noted that the parent responses were not disaggregated by their child's grade level in school. If this analysis was to be done, it is possible that the responses of parents with secondary students would be more similar to their children's responses to this question.

Instructional Process

The *Instructional Process* construct concerned activities and planning by teachers that directly impact student learning in the classroom. For example, items revolved around teachers: planning instruction for maximum effect, communicating what is expected of students, reinforcing the belief that students are capable of learning, and presenting stimulating lessons. Overall, the construct showed parent perceptions of the ability of teachers to motivate students through the use of effective practices. The items used on the survey included:

- The school recognizes outstanding student performance.
- My child's teacher provides comments on school work.
- The teachers at this school motivate students to learn.
- The school assigns the right amount of homework.

Most parents agreed that the instructional process was a positive factor in HISD. Accordingly, 84–85 per cent of parents believed that the schools recognized outstanding student performance. Eighty-three per cent of parents agreed that the schools provided a variety of activities for students.

A substantial number of parents agreed that teachers provided the attention needed to help students achieve academically. For example, 80–84 per cent of the parents agreed that teachers provided comments on school work, and 80–83 per cent also agreed that the school helped their child to understand his or her school performance. Additionally, 82–86 per cent of parents responding believed that the teachers motivated students to learn. Seventy-four to seventy-five per cent of the parents indicated that the school staff helped students with their problems.

Although several of these items solicited strong positive responses, they also evoked some negative perceptions, as well. Parents disagreed at the rate of 13–17 per cent that the school assigns the right amount of homework. Eleven to sixteen per cent of the parents disagreed that the teachers provided comments on school work, and 11–14 per cent disagreed that the school staff helped students with their problems.

Communication

The *Communication* construct focused on how the school and its agents directly interact with students and parents. Items addressed issues of access to school administrators, communication of student progress and performance, and distribution of information concerning school activities. Communication items included:

- When I call or visit the school, I am treated with courtesy.
- The school gives me suggestions of ways I can help my children learn.
- The school gives parents written information about rules, meetings, and other issues.
- I can discuss my child's progress with his/her teachers.

The information provided by the survey indicated that the majority of parents believed they were informed about what goes on at school and indicated that their opinions were solicited for the school's decision-making process. Specifically, 83–84 per cent of the parents responding agreed that the school encouraged their involvement. While 74–76 per cent believed that school administrators communicated school happenings to them, 14–19 per cent of the parents disagreed. In addition, 90–93 per cent of the parents agreed that the school provided written information about rules, meetings, and other issues. When parents called or visited the school, 91–92 per cent responded that they were treated with courtesy; yet, 77–78 per cent believed that the staff responded promptly to their requests, with 11–15 per cent disagreeing.

The majority of the parents also indicated that the schools were keeping them informed regarding their children's academic performance. This is evidenced by the fact that 87–91 per cent of the parents responded that the school informed them on how their children were performing. Ninety-three to ninety-four per cent responded that they could discuss their children's progress with the teachers. According to 75–78 per cent of the parents, the schools provided them with suggestions of ways they could help their children learn. And in 75–81 per cent of the cases, parents indicated that the school asked for their help in preparing students for tests. Nevertheless, three of these items received relatively strong negative remarks. The percentage of parents disagreeing that the school gives parents suggestions of ways to help their children learn was 16–21 per cent, and 16–20 per cent indicated that the school did not tell them what their children are expected to learn. Twelve to seventeen per cent of the parents reported that they were not asked to help their children prepare for tests.

Regarding communication, a majority of HISD elementary school students responded that teachers and administrators kept them and their parents informed. For example, 86–87 per cent of the elementary students indicated that teachers let them know how well they were doing and 88–89 per cent responded that teachers kept their parents informed about their progress. However, only 48–51 per cent of the secondary students responded that the school kept their parents informed on student progress.

The percentage of elementary students who indicated that their parents were asked to help with the school was 66–68 per cent. Furthermore, 67–71 per cent of the elementary students agreed that their parents discussed their progress with their teachers. Similar to the parent responses, 73–75 per cent of elementary students indicated that their teachers asked their parents to help them get ready for tests.

Sixty-six to seventy per cent of the secondary students responded that their parents or guardians could contact teachers at will, and 70–74 per cent agreed that their teachers were available to discuss their progress with their parents. These results indicated that a majority of both the elementary and secondary students were of the opinion that their school afforded parents access to teachers. Nevertheless, more than 25 per cent of the elementary school students and 34 per cent of the secondary students felt that the schools were not keeping their parents informed of their progress.

Administration

The *Administration* construct identified parent perceptions of the school's ability to involve them in the decision-making process. Specifically, items identified participant viewpoints about school management, efforts by the principal to cast positive images of the school's administrators and staff, and aspects of good school management. For example:

- The principal/administrator is available for parent conferences.
- Parents are asked to help the school make plans or decisions.
- The people who work at the school work together as a team.

Parent responses in the area of administration were, for the most part, positive. In particular, 81–83 per cent of the parents agreed that the principal was available for parent conferences, and 74–76 per cent responded that they had access to the school principal. An interesting finding regarding the district's emphasis on shared decision-making was that 73–75 per cent of the parents reported that they were asked to help the school make plans or decisions, while 14–17 per cent reported that they were not asked. Also, 72–75 per cent agreed that the principal provided opportunities for parental input, yet 11–14 per cent disagreed. Concerning the apparent working climate of the schools, 73–77 per cent of the parents believed that the school staff worked together to improve the school, and 70–73 per cent reported that the school staff worked together as a team.

Analysis of the Community Survey

Community surveys were distributed to community members who lived or worked near HISD schools. The number of surveys distributed decreased from 11,322 in 1991–92 to 4,214 in 1992–93 and 4,033 in 1993–94. The response rate also declined from 38 per cent for 1991–92 to 22 per cent in 1993–94. One per cent of the community respondents in 1993–94 were Asian, 29 per cent African-American, 14 per cent Hispanic, and 59 per cent White. Sixty-three per cent of the community respondents were female and 37 per cent were male. Of those community members who responded, 44 per cent lived near the school, 28 per cent worked near the school, and the remaining 28 per cent lived and worked near the school. The demographic characteristics for the 1993–94 respondents resembled those of the 1991–92 and 1992–93 respondents.

Responses from the community survey by item for each of the three years are presented in Table 7.4. As with the parent responses, most were consistent across time. Only a few items showed any visible trends. Areas of concern arising from the community survey seem to center around safety, traffic problems, and student behavior. Statements dealing with the Principal's involvement in neighborhood activities and concerns showed lower levels of agreement, with large numbers of respondents indicating that they did not have enough information to specify agreement or disagreement. This response pattern indirectly suggests that community members found the level of communication with their neighborhood schools to be deficient.

Instructional Environment

The *Instructional Environment* construct was concerned with how closely community members perceive conditions at the school directly affect them. Items focused on issues of academic expectations, fairness, assistance to achieve at the highest level, and resources. Several of the items included were:

Table 7.4 Results of community survey

	Survey Item	Year	Number responding	Strongly agree	Agree	Disagree	Strongly disagree	Don't know
1	The school is an asset to this community. (CM)*	91–92	4,325	58	35	3	1	3
		92–93	1,214	60	33	3	1	3
		93–94	887	57	36	3	1	3
2	I would pay to increase security in the neighborhood around the school. (S)	91–92	4,311	32	38	12	5	12
		92–93	1,203	28	36	18	6	12
		93–94	874	25	34	17	8	15
3	The school encourages students to stay in school and finish their education. (IE)	91–92	4,335	49	34	3	2	12
		92–93	1,221	53	32	2	1	12
		93–94	894	49	36	3	2	11
4	The school honors students who do well with their studies. (IE)	91–92	4,341	42	37	3	1	17
		92–93	1,220	46	35	2	1	16
		93–94	890	44	37	3	1	15
5	People from the community (other than parents) are asked to help the school. (CM)	91–92	4,342	35	39	7	2	17
		92–93	1,224	40	40	4	2	14
		93–94	892	38	37	6	3	16
6	The principal supports neighborhood activities. (CM)	91–92	4,319	34	31	5	3	26
		92–93	1,207	40	29	5	2	24
		93–94	886	36	30	6	3	24
7	The school provides adequate supervision for students before and after school. (S)	91–92	4,332	27	39	9	5	20
		92–93	1,216	25	38	8	4	24
		93–94	887	26	38	8	4	24
8	Students are well behaved at this school. (S)	91–92	4,318	21	47	11	5	17
		92–93	1,209	21	48	12	5	14
		93–94	889	19	46	13	5	16
9	The school grounds are kept clean. (IE)	91–92	4,324	36	53	6	2	3
		92–93	1,220	40	51	5	1	3
		93–94	894	36	54	4	2	3
10	Students show respect for the people who live and work near the school. (S)	91–92	4,312	20	48	12	6	14
		92–93	1,214	20	46	13	5	16
		93–94	879	16	48	13	4	19

Table 7.4 (Continued)

Survey Item	Year	Number responding	Strongly agree	Agree	Disagree	Strongly disagree	Don't know
11 The traffic around the school is a problem. (S)	91–92	4,320	25	28	29	9	10
	92–93	1,219	18	27	37	7	11
	93–94	891	17	27	37	6	13
12 I often see students loitering in the neighborhood while school is in session. (S)	91–92	4,319	9	15	39	24	13
	92–93	1,220	6	13	43	24	14
	93–94	885	7	14	43	22	14
13 The school is a safe place. (S)	91–92	4,325	23	50	9	4	13
	92–93	1,221	22	53	8	4	13
	93–94	891	21	53	9	3	14
14 The students appear excited about school. (IE)	91–92	4,323	23	45	10	4	18
	92–93	1,215	21	46	10	3	20
	93–94	887	16	45	14	4	21
15 The school places emphasis on learning. (IE)	91–92	4,331	39	41	3	1	15
	92–93	1,221	42	41	4	1	12
	93–94	891	37	45	3	2	13
16 The school recognizes outstanding student performance. (IE)	91–92	4,322	37	39	3	1	20
	92–93	1,216	41	38	2	1	18
	93–94	888	38	40	2	2	18
17 The people who work at the school work well as a team. (IE)	91–92	4,334	27	36	5	3	30
	92–93	1,220	28	36	6	3	26
	93–94	892	26	35	8	4	28
18 Teachers at this school encourage students to do their best. (IE)	91–92	4,330	37	39	3	2	19
	92–93	1,221	38	39	4	2	17
	93–94	892	35	41	5	2	17
19 The school responds to neighborhood concerns. (CM)	91–92	4,321	27	38	8	4	24
	92–93	1,218	28	36	7	3	25
	93–94	891	23	41	8	4	23

* The parenthetical code identifies the related construct for each survey item.
CM = *School as Community Member*
S = *School Security*
IE = *Instructional Environment*

- The school places emphasis on learning.
- The students appear excited about the school.
- The school recognizes outstanding student performance.
- The school grounds are kept clean.

Results of the 1993–94 community survey indicated a general approval of the instructional environment in HISD. This finding was supported by 80–83 per cent of the respondents who agreed that the school placed an emphasis on learning. In addition, 76–77 per cent of respondents agreed that HISD's teachers encouraged students to do their best. Seventy-six to seventy-nine per cent agreed that their school recognized outstanding student performance, while 79–81 per cent reported that the school honors students who do well with their studies. Of interest, 83–85 per cent indicated that students were encouraged to stay in school and finish their education. In contrast, only 61 per cent of the 1993–94 community respondents agreed that the students in their community appeared excited about school, showing a downward trend from 68 per cent in 1991–92. Likewise, 13–18 per cent of the community respondents disagreed that the students appeared excited about school.

As far as the schools' physical appearance is concerned, 89–91 per cent of the community respondents believed that the school grounds were kept clean.

School as Community Member

The *School as Community Member* construct was centered on issues of the school's interaction with neighborhood patrons. For instance, questions focused on whether community members were brought into the school as volunteers and conversely whether the school participated in community events and activities. The four items comprising this construct were as follows:

- People from the community (other than parents) are asked to help the school.
- The principal supports neighborhood activities.
- The school responds to neighborhood concerns.
- The school is an asset to this community.

The percentage of respondents in agreement that people from the community, other than parents, were asked to help at the school varied from 74 per cent to 80 per cent over the three survey years. Only 65–69 per cent agreed that principals in their community supported neighborhood activities. However, for this question, 24–26 per cent responded "Don't Know". As a result, it should be noted that only 7–9 per cent indicated that the principal did not support community activities. In a similar light, 64–65 per cent of community members believed that their school responded to neighborhood concerns, with 23–25 per cent answering "Don't Know". Nevertheless, an overwhelming 93 per cent of the community respondents for each of the three years agreed that their neighborhood school was an asset to their community.

School Security

The *School Security* construct focused on a critical element of education. The question addressed was whether or not community members perceived the school as a safe place that added to, or detracted from, their community's image. Items inquired about perceptions of student loitering, behavior, and respect for community residents. A second component was concerned with the patrons' willingness to pay additional taxes for increased security at the school. Several of the survey items were:

- Students are well behaved at this school.
- The traffic around the school is a problem.
- I often see students loitering in the neighborhood while school is in session.
- I would pay to increase security in the neighborhood around the school.

School security was a concern for community members, although not as great a concern as might be expected. Regarding the question, "The school is a safe place to be", 73–75 per cent agreed and 13–14 per cent responded "Don't Know". Only 12–13 per cent of the community respondents indicated that the school was not a safe place. While the responses regarding safety remained consistent, there was a sharp downward trend in the percentage of community members who were willing to pay for increased security around the school. In 1991–92, 70 per cent were willing to pay additional taxes for security, with 17 per cent unwilling to pay, where as in 1993–94, the percentage of respondents willing to pay had dropped to 59 per cent, with 25 per cent unwilling to pay.

Although the community's image of HISD's schools appears to be fairly positive, it is not surprising, though somewhat disappointing, that a higher percentage of community respondents answered "Don't Know" to more questions on their survey than did any of the other response groups. Not surprisingly, 65–69 per cent agreed that students were well behaved at the school, 16–18 per cent disagreed, with 14–17 per cent responding "Don't Know". With regard to students showing respect for the people who live and work near the school, 64–68 per cent indicated agreement, 17–18 per cent indicated disagreement, and 14–19 per cent answered "Don't Know". The percentages of community members who believed that adequate supervision was provided by the schools for students before and after school was 63–64 per cent, yet 20–24 per cent did not have enough knowledge concerning the issue to answer the question. It was of some concern, however, that 19–24 per cent of the community respondents indicated that they often see students loitering in the neighborhood while school is in session.

A positive trend was witnessed over the three years regarding traffic around the schools. In 1991–92, 53 per cent of the community respondents indicated that traffic was a problem. By 1993–94, the percentage had declined to 44 per cent, showing that some improvement or a change in perceptions had taken place, although this issue still appears to be problematic.

Discussion

The Student/Parent/Community Surveys were part of HISD's effort to evaluate and improve the effectiveness of Houston public schools. The district continues to strengthen its schools and serve the youth of the district with input from teachers, parents, students, business partners, community leaders, and other interested Houstonians. The surveys pointed out strengths and areas of dissatisfaction and provided the district and the schools with a unique perspective of how the district's "customers" viewed the services received.

This survey process was instituted at a time when the district was actively seeking input and support from parents and the community. In accordance with state and national trends towards local control of education, the school board and superintendent at that time made great strides in decentralizing the district, shifting the decision-making to the school level, and providing parents and community members with an opportunity to get involved in this process. To more effectively design educational programs geared to meet the specific needs of their students and their local community, accessing parent and community perceptions was essential.

The Student/Parent/Community Surveys provided feedback to the schools on which to base planning and operational decisions. This feedback was incorporated into the schools' School Improvement Plans required by the district as part of the accountability process. Many of the School Improvement Plans reflected not only student outcome variables such as academic achievement, discipline, attendance, etc., but also perceptions of school climate as measured by the Student/Parent/Community Surveys. Individual schools utilized the data collected from the surveys to increase communication with parents, plan parent and community involvement activities, and improve safety and traffic issues related to their school. It was evident from the survey results that these were areas of concern to parents and community members.

From a district perspective, the information obtained from the surveys provided additional feedback on issues relative to school climate. One aspect of such was the focus on safety and security. As a result, the district adopted a "zero-tolerance" attitude toward student behavior in October, 1993. Under the zero-tolerance policy, any student possessing a weapon, or any object used in a threatening manner, on school property or at a district-related activity, would be immediately suspended and recommended for expulsion. Furthermore, in cases where middle or high school students commit a Level IV offense (e.g., arson, assault, criminal mischief, sale/delivery/possession of illegal substances, persistent serious misbehavior), the district will pursue charges, arrests, and removal to a juvenile detention facility or county jail. This focus was continued through a comprehensive safety and security program implemented during the 1994–95 school year. This program added more officers to the district's police department, enhanced officer training, improved incident reporting procedures, and facilitated more cooperation between the district's and the city's police departments.

The survey results also provided the district with a gauge of the parent and community support for its decentralization policies and efforts. Parents' and community members' support and involvement supplied the impetus for continuing an assertive process of decentralization through the Shared Decision-Making process. As a result this necessitated an increase in the role that parents and community members play in the education of students, giving them a personal stake in HISD.

After having witnessed three years of fairly consistent attitudes among survey respondents, the Student/Parent/Community Surveys were discontinued after the 1993–94 school year. The district's emphasis shifted from measuring parent and community perceptions to improving and sustaining them. As the next step in this direction, HISD implemented the Peer Examination, Evaluation, and Redesign (PEER) program. Groups of professionals representing the fields of finance, law, communications, human resources, and ten other fields, along with parents, community members, and district personnel, volunteered their expertise to evaluate HISD's support services and programs and make recommendations for improvement in each review area.

According to the Superintendent, "The single most important function and reason for HISD's existence is education. The face-to-face contact between teacher and student is the central event and the rest of HISD exists only to support that function. In light of the decentralization initiative, a review of programs and processes in place indicated that some were not operating at optimal levels and were not as responsive as they should be" (HISD, 1994, p. 5). The purpose of the PEER committees was to utilize business and community feedback for a thorough, systemic examination, evaluation, and redesign of support services and programs. The fourteen committees that produced reports from April, 1995, through January, 1996, were Child Study/Psychological Services, Communications Services, Counseling Services, Criminal History Background Checks, Discipline Management, Exceptional Education, Financial Systems, Legal Services, Parental Involvement, Personnel, Plant Operator Professionalization, Staff Development, and Transportation Services. Committees are being formed on Employee Hearing Procedures, Food Services, and Reading. The general activities of the PEER committees were gathering data through surveys, interviews, and focus groups, benchmarking performance against other organizations, and formulating recommendations. By acting upon recommendations made by these community-based committees, HISD focused its efforts on improving and sustaining a positive school climate and successful learning environment for students.

One such recommendation from the Discipline Management PEER Committee was to increase the number of alternative schools serving students with special needs such as academic deficiencies and behavior problems. In response, the Belfort Alternative Middle School and Ninth Grade Skills Enhancement Center were opened at the beginning of the 1996–97 school year. Belfort Alternative Middle School was designed to meet the special needs of middle school aged children who were experiencing serious disciplinary problems. The school offers a comprehensive academic, social, behavioral, and developmental program based on mutual respect and trust for self, adults, and the law. The goal of the Ninth Grade Skills Enhancement

Center was to serve students who were placed into the ninth grade due to multiple academic failures and improve their attendance and academic level so that they would be able to successfully complete high school. By providing a supportive and nurturing environment for both the students and their parents, these schools have attempted to improve the learning environment of students who were not successful in the traditional classroom.

A number of schools have also taken the initiative to improve school climate by improving student behavior. One such program supported by the University of Houston at several HISD schools is the Consistency Management Project. By empowering students with specific "job" responsibilities in the classroom, teachers have witnessed remarkable improvement in student behavior, as well as increased attention to learning.

In compliance with state law and in response to the Parent Involvement PEER Committee, HISD has begun a comprehensive plan for promoting and increasing parent involvement in district schools. The main component of HISD's parent involvement efforts, Project Reconnect, is in the process of being implemented. This project calls for the creation of community centers at thirty HISD schools. The purpose of these centers is to offer parent/adult education programs, increase parent and community involvement in the schools, and refer parents and community members to appropriate social services agencies. In addition, the centers will maintain a roster of motivational and educational speakers who are available to make presentations at any HISD school. Each center will be staffed by a full-time parent educator, along with parent and teacher volunteers.

Another component of the district's parent involvement efforts is to establish a Parent Community Participation Team (PCPT) on each HISD campus with the intent of increasing parent involvement at each school and establishing an effective parent communication network. The PCPT at each school will encourage parents to participate in parent involvement activities, parent/teacher membership groups (PTA/PTO), school-related community activities, and HISD's Volunteers in Public Schools (VIPS) program.

Although HISD has focused efforts on improving and sustaining a positive and learning climate in its schools, more can still be done to improve parent and community perceptions of HISD schools and the district as a whole. With this in mind, the Superintendent identified four goals for the 1996–97 School Budget. These goals were to: (i) Address the facilities crisis; (ii) Increase student achievement; (iii) Increase management efficiencies; and (iv) Increase public support. With the failure of a bond election in the spring of 1996, it became quite salient to district administrators that parental and community involvement and support, not only in the schools but in the district as a whole, is necessary to maintain healthy learning environments for children. These conclusions are predicated on the effect that being involved and investing time and effort in the education process have on perceptions. By allowing parents and community members the opportunity to express their views and expand their involvement, school districts provide these stakeholders with a definitive role, predisposing them toward a more positive attitude about their children's education.

As M. Scott Norton (1984) notes, "While such attention [to improving school climate] will not likely achieve desired results immediately, such emphasis will bring about a gradual improvement in personal interactions and result in a healthy atmosphere for student learning and personal growth" (p. 45). It is this attention to the perceptions of not only teachers, school administrators, and students, but also to parents and community members that will lead to improvements in school climate. And, it is within a positive school climate that teachers will more effectively teach, students will more effectively learn, and academic excellence will be achieved.

References

ANASTASI, A. (1988) *Psychological testing*, (6th edn.), New York: Macmillan Publishing Company.

BORGER, J.B., LO, C., OH, S. and WALBERG, H.J. (1985) 'Effective schools: A quantitative synthesis of constructs', *Journal of Classroom Interaction*, **20**, 2, pp. 12–17.

BROOKOVER, W.B. and LEZOTTE, L.W. (1979) *Changes in School Characteristics Coincident with Changes in Student Achievement*, Occasional Paper No. 17, Michigan State University, Institute for Research on Teaching.

COLEMAN, P. (1984) *Elementary School Self-improvement Through School Climate Enhancement*, Vancouver, BC: Simon Fraser University. (ERIC Document Reproduction Service No. ED 251 961)

EDMONDS, R.R. and FREDERICKSEN, J.R. (1978) *Search for Effective Schools: The Identification and Analysis of City Schools that are Instructionally Effective for Poor Children*, Cambridge, MA: Harvard University, Center for Urban Studies.

ELLIS, T.I. (1988) 'School climate', *Research Roundup*, **4**, 2.

HAYNES, N.M., COMER, J.P. and HAMILTON-LEE, M. (1989) 'School climate enhancement through parental involvement', *Journal of School Psychology*, **27**, 1, pp. 87–90.

HOUSTON INDEPENDENT SCHOOL DISTRICT [HISD] (1994) *State of the Schools*, Houston, TX: Author.

HOY, W.K. and TARTER, C.J. (1992) 'Measuring the health of the school climate: A conceptual framework', *NASSP Bulletin*, **76**, 547, pp. 74–9.

KLITGAARD, R.E. and HALL, G. (1973a) *Are there Unusually Effective Schools?* Santa Monica, CA: The Rand Corporation.

KLITGAARD, R.E. and HALL, G. (1973b) *A Statistical Search for Unusually Effective Schools*, Santa Monica, CA: The Rand Corporation.

MCDILL, E.L. and RIGSBY, L.C. (1973) *Structure and Process in Secondary Schools: The Academic Impact of Educational Climates*, Baltimore, MD: Johns Hopkins University Press.

NORTON, M.S. (1984) 'What's so important about school climate?' *Contemporary Education*, **56**, 1, pp. 43–5.

PHI DELTA KAPPA (1980) *Why Do Some Urban Schools Succeed?* Bloomington, Indiana: The Phi Delta Kappa Study of Exceptional Urban Elementary schools. (ERIC Document Reproduction Service No. ED 107 736)

ROUECHE, J.E. and BAKER, G.A., III. (1986) *Profiling Excellence in America's Schools*. Arlington, VA: American Association of School Administrators. (ERIC Document Reproduction Service No. ED 274 062)

SWEENEY, J. (1988) *Tips for Improving School Climate*, Arlington, VA: American Association of School Administrators. (ERIC Document Reproduction Service No. ED 303 869)

WITCHER, A.E. (1993) 'Assessing school climate: An important step for enhancing school quality', *NASSP Bulletin*, **77**, 554, pp. 1–5.

WYNNE, E.A. (1980) *Looking at Schools: Good, Bad, and Indifferent*, Lexington, MA: D.C. Health.

Chapter 8

The Teachers' Lounge and its Role in Improving Learning Environments in Schools*

Miriam Ben-Peretz, Shifra Schonmann and Haggai Kupermintz

Teachers' lounges constitute an almost uncharted territory in the educational environment of schools. What happens in the lounge behind its closed doors? What kinds of interactions occur there? What functions does the lounge serve beyond being a place to rest between classes and maybe drink a cup of coffee? Is it a meaningless "non-place", lacking any real importance in the culture of schools? Or is it an integral part of school life, with far-reaching consequences for the well-being and success of teachers, administrators and students? What is the nature of the climate of teachers' lounges and what, if any, is their impact on the school climate and on students' achievement?

These are some of the questions addressed in this chapter. We shall start with a brief introduction of our conceptual framework, focusing on the role of teachers' lounges in generating a professional community of teachers. The relationship between the environment of teachers in their lounges and the learning environment of students in their classrooms will be discussed, based on empirical evidence. The instruments, developed by us, for studying teachers' perceptions of the climate of their lounges will be presented, and their possible uses for understanding school environments and structures will be discussed.

The Conceptual Framework: The Relationships Between School Climate and Life in Teachers' Lounges

Schools are different from other bureaucratic organizations (Bidwell 1965). One of the main differences concerns the importance of interpersonal relationships which characterize teaching and express themselves in the dealings between

* Based on: *Behind Closed Doors: Teachers and the Role of the Teachers' Lounge* by Miriam Ben-Peretz and Shifra Schonmann, by permission of the State University of New York Press, October 18, 1996.

teachers and students as well as among adults. We shall see that teachers' workplace, the school, is a world in which peer relationships play a major role. Zak and Horowitz (1985) claim that one of the difficulties of describing and analyzing the organizational climate of schools has to do with the fact that most functions of teaching are carried out behind the closed doors of classrooms. In schools where teachers tend to meet in their lounge, we are afforded a glimpse into some of the overt and covert features of the school climate, as it affects teachers' interpersonal relationships, their pedagogical views, and their overall perceptions of their professional environment.

"School climate" is a multidimensional concept composed of interpersonal relations, norms of behavior, levels of autonomy, styles of leadership, sense of belonging, job satisfaction and status. Friedmann (1989) suggests that an "open" school climate is characterized by a high level of intimacy among teachers who feel part of a community, autonomous and unpressured by too many directives. Zak and Horowitz (1985) have shown that relationships among teachers influence their choices of instructional strategies, thus having potential impact on student achievement. Teacher autonomy is considered to be of utmost importance in the overall expression of school climate. In schools in which teachers felt stressed by the burden of their work, the relationships among teachers were found to be unsatisfactory and their sense of autonomy weak. Teachers' positive feelings toward job satisfaction were more pronounced in schools with more teacher autonomy and better interpersonal relations (Zak and Horowitz 1985).

Two basic assumptions guide our analysis of teachers' lounges as sites for improving the learning environment of schools:

(i) The lounge is a defined and separate space in school which is usually considered to be teachers' territory. The teachers interacting in the lounge create their own social organization.
(ii) The lounge is the natural site for the development of professional communities in school.

The notion of schools consisting of loosely coupled systems was developed by Weick (1976). According to his theory, the different units in educational systems interact with each other while keeping their identity and the manner in which the members of each unit view the organizational climate. Goldring (1987) has studied the organizational climate of eleven different units in a large junior high school and found that the climate of each unit was perceived distinctively by its members. Six were teacher units, such as math or history teachers, and five were administrative units, such as department heads or counselors. We contend that the teachers' lounge is one of the separate units in the school's organizational system with its own social organization and distinctive climate. Yet, the lounge has the potential to fulfill an important role in strengthening the links among the different units, promoting a more cohesive school ethos which is conducive to school improvement and effectiveness.

Professional Communities in Schools

One way of achieving the enhancement of the overall school network is through the formation of active professional communities in schools. Strong teacher communities evolving in lounges bear the promise of shared norms of practice and stronger teachers' professional commitments. The data of Talbert and McLaughlin (1994) reveal

> that teachers who participate in strong professional communities within their subject area departments or other teacher networks, have higher levels of professionalism, as measured in this study, than do teachers, in less collegial settings. (pp. 142–43)

The prospects for enhancing professionalism are perceived by Talbert and McLaughlin (1994) to be determined locally as colleagues come to share standards for educational practice, including strong commitments to students and to their profession. In this view, local communities of teachers are the vehicles for enhanced professionalism in teaching (Talbert and McLaughlin, 1994, p. 145). According to Lieberman (1991) "teachers must have opportunities to discuss, think about, try out, and hone out new practices" (p. 593). She suggests several ways of enabling teachers to do this in a school-based environment, for instance, by creating new structures such as problem-solving groups or decision-making teams, and by creating a culture of inquiry as an ongoing part of teaching. The movement is toward "long-term, continuous learning in the context of school and classroom and with the support of colleagues" (p. 596).

It is highly probable that lounges, as sites for teachers' interactions, provide the necessary conditions for the development of strong teacher networks and the generation of communal knowledge about teaching. This knowledge might lead to more effective teaching modes.

Teachers' Perceptions of the Climate of their Lounges

It is important to emphasize that teachers' lounges are part of the social reality of teachers in Israel. Their perceptions and understanding of this reality shape the nature of their experiences in the lounges. The study of teachers' perceptions of their lounges is based on two factors:

(i) the teachers' lounge is a regular meeting place of people who share common interests;
(ii) teachers' participation in the various activities of the lounge is determined by their need to cooperate with their colleagues, and is not compulsory.

The study was conducted in 19 Israeli elementary schools. Teachers in Israel at all levels of schooling usually spend the breaks between classes in a common lounge as there are no private spaces for them, and it is not customary for them to stay in their classrooms. The school day in Israel, at all levels, generally starts around 7 or 8 a.m. and finishes around 1 or 2 p.m for six days during the week. During this time there are 3 short breaks of 10 minutes each, and one long break of 20–30 minutes. Usually no lunch is served at school.

Teachers' Lounges Questionnaire

A self-report questionnaire (see Appendix 8.1) was designed to uncover teachers' perceptions of their lounges. The questionnaire was composed of two parts, compiled on the basis of preliminary interviews with teachers:

(i) A list of twenty characteristics of lounges was compiled (e.g., noisy, pleasant atmosphere, competitive environment, lessons are prepared, a place to talk with students). Participating teachers were asked to indicate on a Likert-type scale the appropriateness of each of the characteristics to their own teachers' lounge (range 1–5; 1 indicating "not true or very seldom true for the teachers' lounge in my school" and 5 indicating "very often true for the teachers' lounge in my school").

(ii) Teachers were asked to assess the perceived impact of teachers' lounges on ten school-related domains (e.g., improving school climate, developing interpersonal relationships between teachers, developing educational activities). Responses were indicated on a Likert-type scale (range 1–5; 1 indicating "no impact" and 5 indicating "great impact").

The two questionnaires are included in the Appendix of this chapter.

Demographic and School Background Data

A total of 409 elementary school teachers (95 per cent female) responded to the teachers' lounge questionnaire. Most of the teachers from urban schools (84 per cent), had a mean of 12 years (SD = 7.7) teaching experience and a mean of 7 years (SD = 5.6) in their current school. On the average they reported five workdays a week (SD = 1) and visited their lounges more than twice a day (SD = 1). The time teachers actually spend in the lounge exceeds one hour (three recesses) and may in fact be more whenever teachers have an unscheduled free period. The data collected for this study was part of a larger survey conducted in 19 elementary schools in Israel.

The Characteristics of Teachers' Lounges — Their Perceived Climate

The structure of teacher responses to the teachers' lounge questionnaire was first examined by employing a factor analysis (based on principal components and a varimax rotation of extracted factors). The factor analysis provides a useful and parsimonious summary of responses to individual items, clustered in meaningful

Table 8.1 Teachers' lounge characteristics factors

Social function (Alpha = 0.74)
Pleasant atmosphere
Expansive space
A great deal of information communicated
Humor
Colorful
The principal drops in
Tolerance
A place to talk with colleagues
A place to rest
Political function (Alpha = 0.64)
Noisy
Overflowing with students
Competitive environment
Regular seating arrangement
Leadership is established
Sharing of secrets
Professional competitiveness
Work function (Alpha = 0.73)
Lessons are prepared
Tests are graded
A place to talk with parents
A place to talk with students

groups (factors) based on the pattern of item intercorrelations. Three factors emerged from the analysis of teachers' responses to the first questionnaire section presenting 20 lounge characteristics. Table 8.1 presents the extracted structure and internal consistency reliability estimates (alpha coefficients) for each factor.

This three-factor solution of the teacher lounge characteristics is best described in terms of the distinct function teachers attribute to their lounge. The first factor was labeled **social function**. Most of the items on this factor describe the teachers' lounge as a place to relax and socialize, such as "pleasant atmosphere", "tolerance", and "a place to rest". The perceived atmosphere is pleasant, colorful, a place to rest and to talk with one's colleagues. Visits of the principal and communication of information are understood to refer mainly to social interactions. The social function of the lounge is exemplified by comments concerning the lounge made by a teacher in one of the interviews which preceded the questionnaire:

> "I am totally convinced that for teachers, school becomes a second home. Teachers' work at school deals mainly with emotions and the teachers' lounge offers them support and serves as a place where one can laugh or cry without anyone interfering".

The second factor was labeled **political function**. In a clear distinction from the first factor, items belonging to this factor describe the stressful, challenging, reality of the profession. Items in this factor are, for example, "competitive environment", "leadership is established", and "sharing of secrets". The lounge is perceived as a place where professional power struggles are played out, characterized by competitiveness, secrecy, and the establishment of leadership. Regular seating arrangements are likely to be associated with the social-hierarchy structure among teachers. Sometimes the power struggles in the lounge cause great pain, as is the case of Sarah.

> Sarah was celebrating the wedding of her daughter, who was a graduate of the school. Sarah was so relaxed she could admit that she was "fed up with working. I'm ready to retire, and help bring up my own grandchildren". Ron, a school executive, responded: "The students will happily agree with you". The peaceful atmosphere immediately changed. Sarah controlled her anger and hurt but became tense. Her friend tried to save the situation by loudly joking: "Of course the students would be happy if all of us retired". Teachers began to laugh. They continued eating and talking as usual, but it was clear that for Sarah the intimacy of the teachers' lounge was lost, as was the sense of belonging to the community.

The third factor was labeled **work function**. Items belonging to this factor describe the teachers' lounge as a place to carry out professional duties. Some items in this factor were: "lessons are prepared", "tests are graded" and "a place to talk with students". Since teachers in the Israeli school system usually do not have their own office in school, they use the lounge to communicate with students and parents, to prepare for lessons or correct exams. The lounge appears to be the place for teacher cooperation, for sharing professional tasks, for creating a working community even in sites where teachers do have individual offices. It may be that the informal environment opens opportunities for teachers to form *ad hoc* associations which are oriented toward specific tasks, such as the preparation of a school commemoration day. The work function is exemplified by Jane in one of our interviews:

> "There is a great paradox in this matter of lounges. On one hand, it is a place to hide from work, we enter the lounge to 'clean our heads'. But if we listen to what we are talking about there, we can clearly see that only a few of us are not talking about work. It is rare that the subject is about anything but work. In fact we continue working even during our free periods, and despite this we love being there. I don't know how to explain it, however, I feel that I rest, even though I am working".

Thus, our analysis suggests that multiple functions are associated with the teachers' lounge. These functions coexist simultaneously and present a multifaceted perception of the lounge — it is a place to socialize and relax, to engage in internal politics and to carry out professional duties. The complex and often conflicting realities of the teaching profession are reflected in these findings.

However, these seemingly conflicting functions do not have equal weights. Based on the factor analysis results, three scores were computed for each teacher, indicating the magnitude of responses on each factor or lounge function on a 1–5 scale. The social function, according to teachers' reports in our study, describes the reality of teachers' lounge much better than do the other two functions. The average score for the social function was 3.7 (SD = 0.64) compared to average scores of 2.2 (SD = 0.60) and 2.3 (SD = 0.80) for the political and work functions respectively. In the wording of the response options on the teacher questionnaire, the social function items describe, on the average, the teachers' lounge "often", while the political and work functions only apply "seldom or sometimes". Teachers, therefore, perceive their lounge first and foremost as a place for social interaction with their peers, a place where they can relax in a pleasant atmosphere and have supportive exchanges with colleagues. This finding might reflect a tendency of women as teachers, to attribute much importance to interpersonal relations. The lesser emphasis the political and work functions receive in teachers' perceptions of their lounge is meaningful. It should not, however, be interpreted as indicating the insignificance of these functions. The reality of the teachers' lounge is complicated and the political and work functions are potent and powerful elements in determining the climate of the teachers' lounges and the nature and atmosphere of interactions in the lounge.

Teachers' responses portray their sense of the reality of lounges, the kind of environment they are, as well as what they are not, and what they could be. The responses to the social function part of our questionnaire describe the social aspects of the climate. The organizational aspect of climate is expressed in the political and work functions. The physical characteristics of the environment of lounges, which are mentioned in the questionnaire, provide the background in which the unique climate of the lounge originates.

The distinction among the functions is often blurred in the concrete, existential, ongoing, and shifting situations in teachers' lounges. However, beyond the kaleidoscopic events in teachers' lounges, the various aspects of the functions might become dominant at different times during the school day, or school year. The introduction of an innovative curriculum might result in more emphasis on the work function of the lounge. Before the end of the school day, the lounge might turn into an arena of social interactions. At other times, for instance, when a new principal is appointed, the political function of the lounge might become most pronounced.

We are interested in the climate of teachers' lounges as a part of the overall climate of the school and not as an isolated sphere. We turn now to the teachers' own perceptions of the influence of lounges on life in schools.

Spheres of Perceived Influence of Teachers' Lounges on Life in Schools

We again employed factor analysis on the second section of the teachers' lounge questionnaire. When asked about the influence of the teachers' lounge on their school, teachers presented a unidimensional factor structure, which was rather surprising given the range of topics covered by the items. Some of the items address peer relationships, while others deal with relationships with students or with Principals. The task of identifying perceived links between the lounge and other domains of school life appeared to be one of low resolution: while the intensity of perceived influence could be measured it was harder for teachers to isolate the targets of that influence. The overall average score (on a 1–5 scale based on the single factor extracted earlier) for the influence items was 3.5 (SD = 0.73), which indicates that teachers perceive their lounge to have "certain" or "considerable" influence on school life. This finding supports the notion that schools constitute loosely coupled

Table 8.2 Correlations between teachers' lounge functions and domains of influence, by school achievement level

Function / **Achievement level**	Social		Political		Work	
	Low	High	Low	High	Low	High
Developing educational activities	0.34*	0.28*	0.09	−0.03	−0.07	0.01
Individual treatment of students	0.22*	0.04	−0.06	−0.03	0.17	0.36
Developing interpersonal relationships among teachers	0.54*	0.39*	−0.09	0.05	−0.03	0.11
Management of professional problems	0.39*	0.31*	−0.21*	0.04	0.01	0.29
Management of administrative problems	0.22*	0.31*	−0.01	0.03	−0.02	0.14
Improving school climate	0.45*	0.40*	−0.05	0.03	−0.01	0.04
Promoting motivation for work	0.36*	0.17	−0.09	0.01	−0.03	0.02
Improving relationships between teachers and principal	0.28*	0.09	0.11	−0.06	−0.00	0.04
Improving communication	0.53*	0.40*	−0.13	0.06	−0.02	−0.01
Collaboration between colleagues	0.52*	0.40*	−0.19*	−0.00	−0.01	0.02

Note: * $p < 0.01$

systems in which separate units, while characterized by their distinctive climate, are interlinked with other units and might impact a variety of school domains.

When correlating the influence scale with the three factors of lounge characteristics, a strong positive correlation ($r = 0.52$; $p < 0.001$) was found with the social function scale. No significant correlations were found with the other two scales ($r = -0.01$ and $r = 0.06$ with the political and work function respectively). This finding suggests that the amount of influence teachers attribute to their lounge is strongly linked to its perceived social function. Teachers who view the lounge as a place to relax and to engage in positive social interactions with colleagues also view it as a considerable source of influence on school life in general. This finding stresses the importance of the affective dimension of teachers' worklife, their need for interpersonal relations with their peers. The social context appears to constitute a pre-requisite for the establishment of a professional community of teachers and the development of a sense of efficacy and potency with regard to various aspects of school life. Looking at the items which make up the social function factor (see Table 8.1) we might gain some insights into the reasons for its strong positive correlation with the lounge impact scale. The perceived characteristics of the lounge that contribute to its social function point to an unthreatening, unstressful atmosphere which promotes networking and the creation of teacher teams without undue pressure. Teachers might talk with their colleagues and with the principal and a great deal of information communicated, but all this happens in a restful, tolerant and pleasant environment. It is interesting to note that humor appears to play a role in creating links between the lounge and school events. One teacher said:

> "Sometimes as I teach I find myself looking forward to the saving bell that will save me from the seriousness and the tension of the lesson. I like the atmosphere in the lounge and I want to be there".

The lightness and sometimes lack of seriousness in the lounge seems to give this teacher the strength to continue with her classroom teaching.

Professional issues are woven into the fabric of the social interactions in the lounge. Such exchanges, when accompanied by an atmosphere of collegial trust and support, might help teachers reshape and examine their professional identities and, in turn, have a direct influence on classroom practice.

Just as important is the finding of the overall lack of correlation between the political and work functions and the perceived influence of the lounge. While the social function is directly associated with the significance teachers ascribe to the lounge in their workplace, the "harsher" aspects of the lounge characteristics are not perceived as inhibiting factors regarding its influence. One might have expected that the overall atmosphere which marks the political function — a noisy, competitive, secretive, and hierarchical environment — might be perceived as counterproductive to any concerted attempt to influence school life. Conflicts and dilemmas, which are apt to rise in such environments, might be perceived by teachers as prohibiting any positive influence of the lounge for improving interpersonal relationships or creating professional cooperation. The empirical evidence, however, does not confirm such expectations.

The pattern of correlations suggests that when teachers reflect upon the influence their lounges have on school life, the primary reference point is the extent to which the lounge promotes social interactions. Acknowledging the existence of tougher and sometimes unpleasant aspects of life in the lounge (e.g., Sarah's experience) does not seem to be a chief concern in terms of the lounges' importance to the broader school life. It is possible that the community-building nature of the social function is weighted heavily as a crucial component for exerting influence throughout the school, while the more destructive or counterproductive elements of lounge life are perceived as an inevitable evil and, for the most part, a natural aspect of any human interaction. It is also important to note that the meaning and relative importance different descriptions of the teachers' lounge hold should be considered within the larger context of the school climate. As we shall see later, teachers in different schools attach different meanings and importance to the contrasting descriptions of their lounges.

Teachers' Lounges and Students' Achievement

Our purpose in this section is to investigate the relationships between teachers' perceptions of their lounge's climate and functions and the lounge's influence on school life and their students' achievement.

Data on students' academic achievement in two standard tests, one in math and one in reading comprehension, was collected for each school in the study (aggregated to the school level). These tests were administered by the Ministry of Education in grades 3 and 5 in all elementary schools in Israel. Based on test results, the 19 schools in our study were divided into two groups: low-achieving and high-achieving, according to their place below or above the average test score. Because the correlation between math and reading test scores was about 0.9, the results were averaged across the two subjects. In low-achieving schools (8 schools, 181 teachers) the average failure rate was 42 per cent, while in high-achieving schools (11 schools, 228 teachers) the average failure rate was 14 per cent. The two groups of schools were comparable with respect to size, teachers-students ratio, and physical characteristics, such as relative classroom space with respect to total school space and space per student. We then investigated the patterns of teachers' perception of their lounges in low versus high-achievement schools.

Two empirical questions guided our data analysis in this section:

(i) Are there differences between teachers in low and high-achievement schools in their perceptions of the teachers' lounge functions and influence?
(ii) How do teachers in low and high-achievement schools associate the teachers' lounge functions with specific domains of influence on school life?

The schools included in our study were part of the total population of Israeli schools which participated in the state-wide achievement testing. There were schools with mainly low SES students which did well on the tests, while other schools, with mainly high SES students, were low achieving.

To answer the first question, we compared the mean scores of the three lounge functions and the influence scale between the two groups of teachers. Figure 8.1 depicts these average scores by school achievement level.

Statistically significant differences were found between the two groups of teachers in their emphasis of the social function of the teachers' lounge ($t(344) = 5.0$; $p < 0.001$) and the overall impact of teachers' lounge ($t(327) = 4.2$; $p < 0.001$). Teachers in high-achievement schools perceive the characteristics of the social function as a more appropriate description of their lounge than do their low-achievement school counterparts. They also perceive the lounge to be a more influential source on school life. The political and work functions were perceived as much less characteristic of the teachers' lounges by teachers from both achievement levels.

The perceived prominence of the social function and influence of lounges by high-achievement school teachers might support a hypothesis of a positive impact of a strong teacher community on student achievement. As a plausible explanation consistent with our findings, the prominence of the social function in the eyes of teachers could be interpreted as indicating a strong community ethos with positive consequences reflected in student achievements. Several statements of teachers highlight the importance of the social function of lounges. "It's a nice place, my lounge, and you don't feel how time passes because I feel very comfortable with my friends". Another teacher says: "I spend a lot of time in the lounge beyond working hours, just to talk, share ideas, to work, to plan or just to chat".

Figure 8.1 Teachers' lounge functions and influence by school achievement level

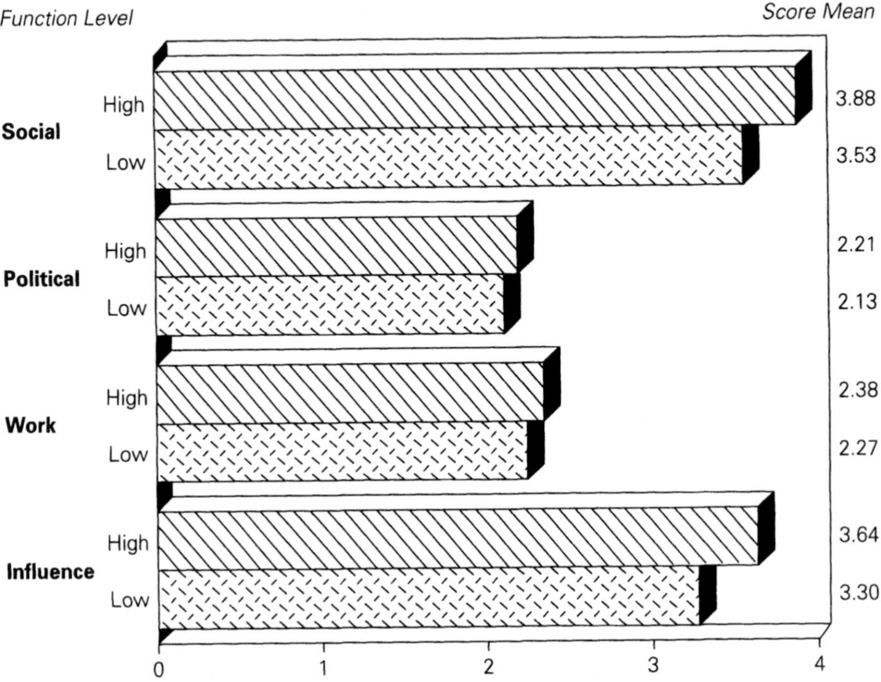

Note: *High* — stands for high-achievement schools — 11 schools, 228 teachers.
Low — stands for low-achievement schools — 8 schools, 181 teachers.

While we cannot offer a conclusive causal interpretation of these findings, it is reasonable to entertain a conjecture which links the quality of teacher relations, and the strength of the local teacher community, as reflected in their teachers' lounge climate, to the facilitation of student learning. At the very least, we can infer substantial differences in school climate between low and high-achieving schools emerging as a result of the reciprocal influences between teachers and students. The strongest correlations with the social function, in both school achievement levels, were found with influence on professional cooperation, communication channels, interpersonal relations, and overall school climate. These correlations support the interpretation of the social function specified earlier, namely the emphasis on interpersonal relations and communication among teachers. It is clear that a supportive atmosphere in the teachers' lounge is associated, for most teachers, with enhanced quality of professional and personal relations in school.

The differences in the magnitude of correlations between low and high-achievement schools were especially pronounced for influence related to treatment of individual students, relationships between teachers and the principal, and increased motivation for work. Teachers in the high-achievement schools did not associate influence on these domains with the social function of the teachers' lounge.

These differences and the overall pattern of stronger correlations between the social function and the teachers' lounge influence in low-achievement schools are puzzling given the overall stronger emphasis of high-achievement school teachers on the social function. The importance of the social function of teachers' lounges to specific aspects of influence on school life in low-achievement schools might be best understood against the background of a possible lack of established, effective ways to deal with individual students and their needs. In such schools, the relationships between teachers and principals might be strained, and there might be a generalized feeling of teacher burn-out. Under such circumstances, the social function of the teachers' lounge might be extremely important for overcoming existing limitations. Thus, for teachers who experience an unpleasant and, many times, unfriendly and hostile workplace, a positive and supportive teachers' lounge holds special value. Contrasting the lounge to other domains of professional life in low-achievement schools might contribute to its perceived importance as an enabling force in promoting a better school climate. What teachers in high-achievement schools accept as the norm cannot be taken for granted by teachers in low-achievement schools. In the absence of other supportive school structures, teachers in low-achievement schools seem to be more aware of the domains of influence of lounges. It may well be the case that, for many of these teachers, the lounge is one of the few places in their work environment with the potential to offer a sense of cooperation, sharing, and encouragement. A teacher who rushes into the lounge crying: "I have never come across such stupid students before", might find encouragement when her colleagues share their experiences with her and create a sense of collegiality.

Differences in correlations were also found between the two groups of teachers with respect to the political function. No correlations were found between this function and the high-achievement school teachers' perceptions of lounge influence. For teachers in low-achievement schools, there were negative correlations between the political, competitive function and the perceived influence on professional issues and professional cooperation. We suggested above that professional competition may be considered a natural part of the professional climate in school and, as such, its manifestations in the teachers' lounge does not inhibit the overall influence of the lounge on school life. We now qualify this general pattern. In low-achievement schools, manifestations of professional competitiveness in the teachers' lounge might be interpreted as insurmountable obstacles in the daily work of the school. Again, we see that for these teachers, things that take place in the lounge echo in broader school domains. Professional cooperation among teachers and effective problem solving mechanisms are likely to be sensitive, often painful, issues in low-achievement schools, so that overt threats to them in the teachers' lounge are more readily viewed as symptomatic of the entire school climate.

The work function of the teachers' lounge was found to influence the treatment of individual students and professional issues for teachers in high-achievement schools, but not for teachers in low-achievement schools. A possible explanation for this finding is that low-achievement schools lack the kind of professional work climate which characterizes the life of teachers in high-achievement schools. As their work environment is not learning-enriched (Rosenholtz 1989), they may not perceive specific links between lounges and professional growth, or professional activities, such as treatment of individual students. We saw earlier that for these teachers the professional domain is influenced more by the intensity of the political function of the teachers' lounge. Teachers in high-achievement schools, however, are able to identify the benefits of productive professional activities in the lounge, especially for promoting communication with and treating individual students. We find a hint of this relationship in a statement by a teacher who says: "the teachers' lounge is a community characterized by a break without a break, break from the students with the students". The community of teachers in the lounge thus continues to be involved in student matters, even during breaks. This involvement might express itself in actual communication of teachers with students who come into the lounge. It might also be served by what another teacher called "consultancies concerning students, carried on in the lounge".

Overall, it seems that teachers in high-achievement schools are better able to differentiate among the teachers' lounge functions in terms of their influence on various aspects of school life. They associate the social function with the interpersonal-relations dimension, and the work function with aspects of their professional activities. On the other hand, teachers from low-achievement schools tend to give a broader interpretation to the effects of the social functions of the teachers' lounge including influence on the professional and interpersonal domains. They also perceive displays of professional competitiveness as constraining factors of the lounges' influence. Teachers are aware of the interpersonal struggles going on in the lounge: "There are quarrels among different members as in any place". One teacher expressed her perception of such situations as follows: "I sensed tense relations among teachers, especially a hostile attitude towards the principal who would at times go in to hand out materials".

Through uncovering the importance teachers assign to the social function of lounges, we gain an understanding of the conditions involved in creating communities of teachers. Especially revealing in this context is the significant difference in the way teachers in high- and low-achievement schools view the social functions of their lounges. This supports the arguments of Talbert and McLaughlin (1993) for the important role that institutional factors play in establishing teacher professionalism. It is important to note that the perceived power of the social elements of teachers' lounges seems to extend over the work function. Teachers are members of a community of practice. Their professional development takes place in a social environment and depends on social interactions. The natural site for these interactions is the teachers' lounge.

Concluding Comments — Potential Uses of the Analysis of the Climate of Teachers' Lounges

Some of the specific conditions of school organization which might foster developing strong professional communities of teachers through social interactions in the teachers' lounge are noted by teachers in our study. Their responses in interviews and our questionnaire indicate that the social function of their lounges is determined by physical aspects of space and color, as well as affective aspects, such as tolerance and humor, and by providing opportunities to rest, to talk with colleagues, and to share information. The lounge also presents occasions for strengthening the relationships between teachers and the principal.

Teachers' perceptions of their lounges and the role lounges play is closely linked to, and possibly dependent on, the school context. High-achievement schools constitute a positive workplace with more social interactions in the lounge, and there is a positive awareness of the lounge's overall influence on school life. It might well be that the relationship between teachers' perceptions of lounges and student achievement is reciprocal, that is the more intensely social function of lounges, by enabling and facilitating teachers' professionalism, leads to high achievement, and higher achievement, in turn, strengthens the social function of the lounge. These potential patterns are presented schematically in Figure 8.2 which highlights some important components of this process. Furthermore, teachers in high-achievement schools experience their lounge as a potent source of influence on school life.

Figure 8.2 A model for describing the relationship between teachers' perception of their lounge and student achievement

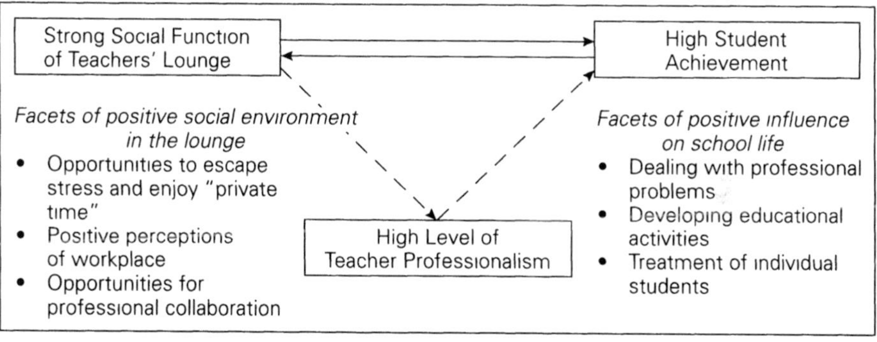

Note:
The solid-line arrows reflect the empirical finding of correlation between perception of the social function and student achievement. The broken-line arrows refer to the hypothesized process behind the empirical correlation.

In low-achievement schools conditions seem to exist that hinder the development of powerful communities of teachers. As noted above, negative correlations were found for teachers in low-achievement schools between the political, competitive, function of their lounges and the perceived influence of the lounge on dealing with professional issues. Here, too, we suggest a reciprocal relationship between the political function of the lounge and student achievement. The more competitive and less accepting the lounge is, the smaller the chances for establishing a productive professional community of teachers, resulting in lower student achievement. Also, low student achievement might lead to high levels of political competitiveness in the lounge coupled with a perception of limited influence of teachers' experiences in their lounge on professional aspects of school life.

Breaking the mold of competitiveness in the lounge and promoting positive social interaction might help establish professional communities of teachers in schools. Our study highlights the importance of the teachers' lounge in facilitating this process of professional development with its contribution to student achievement.

The instruments used in this study can be used by school administrators or by the teachers themselves to determine the climate of teachers' lounges as perceived by their occupants. They can be focused on a specific function of the lounge, such as the social or work function, or on the overall characteristics of the lounge. The correlations between the different functions and the various domains of influence can be investigated separately or comprehensively. Also, the instruments used in our study might serve as triggers for asking school-based questions concerning the nature and climate of the lounge. Educators, administrators and decision-makers, concerned with the quality of teaching and learning can thus examine one of the school sites which might be essential to their efforts to improve schooling, namely, the teachers' lounge.

Appendix 8.1: Self-report Questionnaire

Dear Teacher,

We would be grateful if you could take some time to respond to the enclosed questionnaire. We are conducting a research project on the functions of teachers' lounges, and your assistance is greatly appreciated.

Sincerely yours,
Professor Miriam Ben-Peretz
Dr Shifra Schonmann
School of Education
University of Haifa

Part A: Characteristics of Teachers' Lounges

The following is a list of characteristics of teachers' lounges.

Please note for each, on a scale from 1 to 5, how closely it describes the teachers' lounge in your school.

1 is **not true** or **very seldom true** for the teachers' lounge in my school
2 is **seldom true** for the teachers' lounge in my school
3 is **sometimes true** for the teachers' lounge in my school
4 is **often true** for the teachers' lounge in my school
5 is **very often true** for the teachers' lounge in my school

Characteristics	**Rate of Fit**
1 Pleasant atmosphere	
2 Expansive space	
3 A great deal of information communicated	
4 Noisy	
5 Humor	
6 Overflowing with students	
7 Competitive environment	
8 Regular seating arrangements	
9 Colorful	
10 Leadership is established	
11 Sharing of secrets	
12 The principal drops in	
13 Tolerance	
14 Professional competitiveness	
15 Lessons are prepared	
16 Tests are graded	
17 A place to talk with parents	
18 A place to talk with students	
19 A place to talk with colleagues	
20 A place to rest	

Part B: Domains of Impact of Teachers' Lounges

What is the extent of impact of the teachers' lounge on different domains of school life. Please note your estimate in the table.

Domains	**no impact**	**little impact**	**certain impact**	**considerable impact**	**very great impact**
1 Developing educational activities					
2 Individual treatment of students					
3 Developing interpersonal relationships among teachers					
4 Management of professional problems					
5 Management of administrative problems					
6 Improving school climate					

Domains	no impact	little impact	certain impact	considerable impact	very great impact
7 Promoting motivation for work					
8 Improving relationships between teachers and principal					
9 Improving communication					
10 Collaboration between colleagues					
Please give a concrete example in any domain you choose.					

Part C: Demographic Details

Part D: Open-ended Opportunities to Write About the Lounge, and to Provide a Metaphor Describing It

References

Bidwell, C.E. (1965) 'The school as a formal organization', in March, J.G. (ed.) *Handbook of Organizations*, Chicago, Rand McNally.

Friedmann, I. (1989) 'The role of organizational climate and school culture in the evaluation of schools', *Studies in Educational Administration*, **16**, pp. 187–92.

Goldring, E. (1987) 'Organizational climate as a component in the loosely coupled system of schools', *Studies in Educational Administration*, **14**, pp. 27–40.

Lieberman, A. and Miller, L. (1991) 'Revisiting the social realities of teaching', in Lieberman, A. and Miller, L. (eds) *Staff Development for Education in the '90s*, New York, Teachers College Press.

Rosenholtz, S.J. (1989) *Teachers' Workplace: The Social Organization of Schools*, New York and London, Teachers College Press.

Talbert, J.E. and McLaughlin, M.W. (1994) 'Teacher professionalism in local school contexts', *American Journal of Education*, **102**, pp. 123–53.

Weick, K. (1976) 'Educational organizations as loosely coupled systems', *Administrative Science Quarterly*, **21**, pp. 1–19.

Zack, I. and Horowitz, I. (1985) *Schools as the World of Teachers*, Tel-Aviv, Ramot Publishers, Tel-Aviv University. (Hebrew)

Chapter 9

The Impact of Principal Change Facilitator Style on School and Classroom Culture

Gene E. Hall and Archie A. George

In our studies of change in schools, one of the inescapable conclusions has been that the formal leader makes a significant difference. No matter what the leader does (and does not do), the effects are detectable throughout the organization. In visiting schools we all have experienced a difference in "feel", which, in large part, has been shaped by the principal.

Just as the teacher establishes the climate for the classroom, the school principal plays the significant role in establishing the climate for the school. How teachers perceive and interpret the actions of the principal leads to the construction of the culture of the school and, in part, each teacher's classroom culture.

A discussion of healthy environments should deal not only with what is healthy for students, but also with what is healthy for adults. In the case of schools, the health of the environment for students and for adults, in large part, is determined by the principal. In our studies we have identified critical differences in how principals lead that result in some schools perceived as being more healthy than others. We have developed a measure that teachers fill out regarding how they see their principal leading the school. The findings from this measure provide direct information to the principal and teachers about the role and effects of the principal as shaper of the climate.

This chapter presents a conceptual framework for thinking about and describing differences in how principals lead, and introduces a measure for assessing these differences, *The Change Facilitator Style Questionnaire (CFSQ)* (see Appendix 9.2). The chapter begins with a brief summary of research on change in schools upon which the conceptual framework is based. The concept of change facilitator style is introduced and three basic change facilitator styles are described. Six underlying dimensions that, in aggregate, form the Change Facilitator Styles represented in the CFSQ scales are presented next. Following this, the design and development activities, the psychometrics of the CFSQ, and interpretation of CFSQ data are described. The chapter concludes with a set of recommendations, discussion points and implications related to the Change Facilitator Style concepts and use of the CFSQ.

Early Observations of the Connection Between Leaders and Climate

The overall goal of our studies is to learn more about the change process and what happens to the people who are engaged in it. The conceptual framework for the work is the Concerns Based Adoption Model (CBAM), which consists of a number of concepts including three diagnostic dimensions and related measures that can be used to better understand how the change process works (Hall, Wallace and Dossett, 1973; Hall and Hord, 1987; Hall and Hord, In press). The concepts and related measures can be used to plan for change, to facilitate the change process, and to assess the degree and rate of success.

In our studies, we have been especially interested in learning about what happens to teachers in classrooms as they implement the innovations that are introduced. Thus, studies of school leaders and their effects grew out of previous research on the educational change process. This research focused on the front line users of innovations, i.e., teachers and professors. We were inextricably drawn into studying leadership and climate, however, as it became increasingly clear that the activities of the front line participants (e.g., teachers) is determined largely by what the leaders (e.g., principals) do.

The Role of the Principal is Discovered

About 1983, our research team could not explain a set of findings from one large study. We had compiled concerns profiles for teachers in nine different schools within the same district. The concerns profiles seemed to cluster into three distinct patterns. However, the schools were similar in terms of SES. The same innovation was used in all schools. All teachers had attended the same inservice training workshops and they all had the same materials, district office support and time to implement. The concerns data documented that teachers in these different schools had had varied degrees of success in implementing the innovation. Why were the teachers in different schools so different in their degrees of implementation success?

Since this was a collaborative effort with the school district, we consulted with our practitioner colleagues. We posed the problem of the three different groups of teacher concerns data and asked if they could explain the differences in implementation success our district colleagues observed. “It’s the principals. In Group 1 schools principals provide a great deal of leadership. In the Group 2 schools the principals talk a good game but don’t do a lot. In the Group 3 schools the principals are really well organized, but they do not push beyond the minimum”. This discussion implied a direct link between what the principal did and the extent of teacher success in implementing educational innovations. This led our research team into a decade of studies about school leaders and their effects on teacher success with change.

The Concept of Change Facilitator Style

The first step in examining the role of the principal in influencing teacher success with change was to examine the existing literature. Leaders and leadership have been studied and written about for a long time. For example, Machiavelli's classic, *The Prince* (1532) could be described as an ethnographic study of leadership. In the twentieth century, there have been many studies of leaders and their behaviors. Earlier in the century there were extensive studies of the traits and characteristics of leaders. No consistent patterns were found.

A shift in focus from studying traits and behaviors began to occur in the 1930s. For example, in 1938 Lewin and Lippitt proposed their concept of Democratic, Autocratic and Laissez-faire leaders. In the 1950s, two dimensions to leadership were proposed by a number of theorists. For example Consideration and Initiation were identified in the classic work at Ohio State University (Hemphill, 1950). Nomothetic and Idiographic dimensions were proposed by Getzel and Guba (1957), and Task Orientation and Relations Orientation by Blake and Mouton (1964).

As more has been learned, the models have become more complex and subtle. For example, Fiedler (1977) proposed that leadership needed to be contingency based. Depending on the situation, the effective leader needs to do different things. A useful summary of these and other studies of leaders and leadership is *Stogdill's Handbook of Leadership* (Bass, 1981).

In our research, we distinguish between the concept of style, the gestalt or holistic pattern to a leader's actions, and leader behaviors, the moment-to-moment and day-to-day actions of the leader. The style of the leader is the cumulative total of all of his or her individual actions (Rutherford, 1985.)

School district practitioners suggested that there was a correlation between teacher implementation success and the style of the principals in the different schools. In other words, the principal's overall approach to leadership seemed to be directly related to successful implementation of the education innovation by the teachers. Testing this hypothesis became a major piece of the CBAM researchers' agenda in the 1980s. There were two major findings out of these studies.

1 Three Change Facilitator Styles could be distinguished in terms of the behaviors that were used.
2 Teacher success in change were directly correlated with their principal's Change Facilitator Style.

As these findings were confirmed in the subsequent studies of colleagues in the US, Australia and Belgium, we began work on a measure to assess the Change Facilitator Style of principals. The first step was to develop careful and clear definitions of each identified CF Style.

Three Change Facilitator Styles

The first major study of Principal Change Facilitator Style was the Principal Teacher Interaction (PTI) Study (Hall, Hord and Griffin, 1980; Hall, Rutherford, Hord and Huling, 1984; Hall, 1988). In this year-long study, an attempt was made to document every innovation related intervention made by nine elementary school principals. The principals were located in three school districts, each in a different part of the

United States. The study confirmed the existence of the three Change Facilitator Styles, and also documented the extent of Teacher Implementation Success. Implementation Success was found to correlate 0.74 with the Principal's Change Facilitator Style.

The three identified Change Facilitator Styles are the Initiator, Manager and Responder. Definitions of each Change Facilitator Style (CFS) are presented in Appendix 9.1 which summarizes the different ways that principals lead change processes on a moment-to-moment and day-to-day basis. The effects of these differences in intervention behaviors is that teachers receive not only a different quantity of innovation related interventions, but a different quality as well.

The Initiator has a clear and strongly held vision about where the school is headed and what is best for students. The Initiator sees how the innovation being implemented fits into the vision. Their priority is on doing what is best for students, even when teachers may be overly busy or not fully ready for the change. Initiators guide everyone and everything in the school in the same direction. They expect all of the school staff to work to make the school better and to support the school. Initiators will often interpret policies and rules in flexible ways or ignore them altogether. They often work with the philosophy that it is easier to seek forgiveness than prior approval.

The Manager's first priority is keeping the school well organized and running smoothly. Managers are skilled at devising efficient operating systems, procedures and routines. Their teachers know how to access materials and are well informed about school procedures. When a change is first proposed, the Manager Principal usually delays implementation. He or she prefers to learn more about the change, what is expected and what it would mean for the school. One consequence of a delay is that when the school does implement a change, everyone is ready and prepared. Teachers are also protected from having too many changes simultaneously. Manager principals tend to arrive early in the morning and stay until late in the afternoon. They strive to attend all workshops and school activities, and most likely, they come back to their school offices on the weekend.

Responder principals attend to the current concerns and perceptions of teachers, the community and others. They engage in many "one legged interviews" with teachers checking perceptions and feelings. They talk with parents and community members about their concerns. They check with other principals to get a reading on their understanding of what the superintendent meant in the last principals' meeting. Typically, Responders will state that an innovation is similar to what their teachers are currently doing. "What's the big deal here? Yes, there is a different name. But we are already doing most of it". Responders make significantly fewer interventions. They also are willing to have others take the lead.

Researching the Change Facilitator Style of Principals

Studies by other researchers have also documented the quantity and quality of interventions made by principals and other change facilitators and related these to differences in teacher success. For example, Schiller (1991) conducted a study of nine elementary school principals and teacher success in implementing computer education. Hougen (1984) completed a study of the Change Facilitator Style of high school principals. In each of these studies the three Change Facilitator Styles were observed in terms of the quantity and quality of their interventions and associated with similar differences in teacher implementation success. In a cross cultural study, Shieh (1996) documented the intervention behaviors of a set of elementary school principals in Taiwan and observed similar CFS characteristics, intervention behavior, and related differences in teacher implementation success.

Studies of principal CF Style have been conducted by Roland Vandenberghe and his colleagues at the Katholeik University in Leuven, Belgium. Vandenberghe documented differences in what he calls "local innovation policy". The underlying assumption was that schools that are confronted with a comprehensive or large-scale innovation project will develop an "organizational reaction". (Vandenberghe, 1988, p. 3) He observed that in schools with principals with long-term vision (i.e., Initiators) a *Planning Local Innovation Policy* was established.

The Need to Know More About Change Facilitator Style

Following the original and confirming studies, our interest shifted to exploring ways to measure Change Facilitator Style. One early strategy had been to use the definitions (see Appendix 9.1) and a number line that ranged from zero to one hundred (see Figure 9.1). The researchers would meet with two or three observers who were knowledgeable of the principals, such as district office administrators, and ask them to rate the CF Style of each principal and place them at points along the number line. The stereotypic Responder would be a "30" on the number line, a Manager would be a "60", and an Initiator would be a "90". An individual that was seen to be a combination could be placed at an in-between point.

Figure 9.1 Initial measure of principal change facilitator style

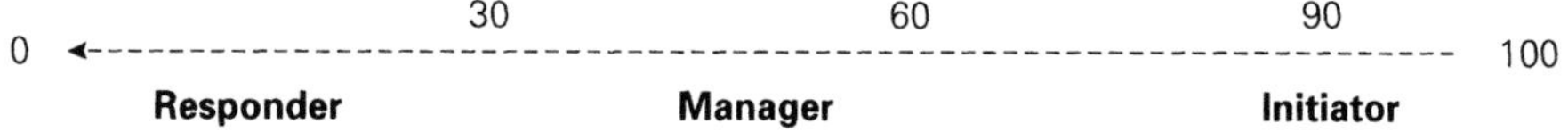

For example, a principal who behaved much like a Manager but who exhibited some of the characteristics of an Initiator could be placed at some point between the two, such as "73". This process worked reasonably well, but clearly is dependent on the extent of first hand knowledge of the raters. A more reliable and less subjective measure was needed. We decided to let teachers provide information about what principals did. Teachers are the most direct observers. In addition, they can provide a consensus or diversity of opinion, which is also valuable.

Another concern was that summarizing all that a principal does to facilitate change into one of three style categories is too restrictive. The vast quantity of studies on leaders and leadership makes the case that the phenomena is very complex and multivariate. In response, Hall and George (1988) and Vandenberghe

(1988) began refining the conceptual framework and developing a reliable measurement tool.

Six Underlying Dimensions of Change Facilitator Style

Based on the literature review and continued study of their databases, Hall and Vandenberghe hypothesized six concepts that appeared to underlie Change Facilitator Style. At first these were hypothesized as ends, or poles, on each of three continua. However, once a prototype of the measure was tested, it became clear that instead of having three continua with six poles, the clearest descriptions could be derived from defining and measuring six independent dimensions. The original three continua became the organizing clusters for pairs of dimensions. Thus, the conceptual framework for change Facilitator Style consists of three clusters, with each cluster having two dimension (see Figure 9.2). Each of these is defined and described below.

Figure 9.2 Change facilitator style profile

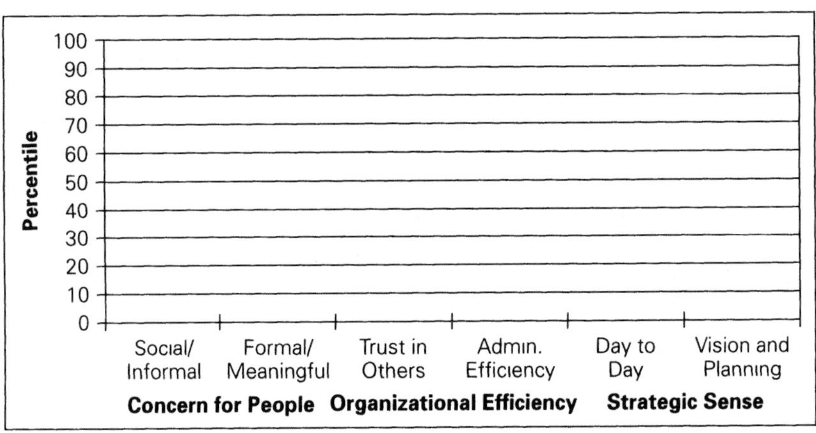

Cluster 1: Concern for People

People have feelings and attitudes about their work and how a change process is going. They have personal needs, too. From day-to-day, facilitators can monitor, attend to and affect these concerns and needs in different ways and with different emphases. For example, it is possible to spend little time in directly addressing the feelings of others or to become preoccupied with listening to and responding to each concern that is expressed. The emphasis can be on attending to individual concerns as they are expressed day-to-day, or focus on more long-term needs of all staff, with attention to individual concerns on an as-needed basis. The first cluster of CFS behaviors deals with how the principal, as change facilitator, addresses the personal side of change.

The Concern for People cluster is composed of two dimensions that weigh the degree to which the moment-to-moment and daily behaviors of a facilitator emphasizes *Social/Informal* and *Formal/Meaningful* interactions with teachers. The Social/Informal dimension addresses the extent to which the facilitator engages in informal chat and casual social discussions with teachers. Many of these discussions may not be related, even remotely, to the work of the school or a specific innovation. The Formal/Meaningful dimension addresses brief task-oriented interactions that deal with specific aspects of the work and the details of the innovation implementation.

Social/Informal This dimension addresses the frequency and character of informal and personal talk between the facilitator and teachers and staff. Facilitators who emphasize this cluster of interactions engage in frequent social chatting. They attend to feelings and perceptions. Their emphasis is more on listening, trying to understand, and acknowledging immediate concerns than in providing answers or anticipating long-range consequences. There is a personable, friendly, almost chatty tone to these interactions. When concerns are addressed, it is done in ways that are responsive rather than anticipatory and the emphasis is on being personal, friendly and accepting.

Formal/Meaningful Facilitators are centered on school tasks, priorities and directions. Discussions and interactions are focused on teaching and learning and substantive issues. Interactions are primarily intended to support teachers in their school related tasks and the facilitator is almost always looking for solutions that are lasting. The interactions and emphases are not overly influenced by superficial and short-lived feelings and needs of people. Instead, teaching and learning activities and issues directly related to use of the innovation are emphasized. However, personal concerns and feelings are addressed in ways that are personally meaningful.

Cluster 2: Organizational Efficiency

The work of the organization can be facilitated with varying degrees of emphasis on obtaining resources, increasing efficiency and consolidating or sharing responsibilities and authority. Principals can try to do almost everything themselves or they can delegate responsibility to others. System procedures, role clarity, and work priorities can be made more or less clear and resources organized in ways that increase or decrease availability and effectiveness. In this cluster the principal's administrative focus is examined along two dimensions, *Trust in Others* and *Administrative Efficiency*.

Trust in Others This dimension examines the extent to which locating resources, establishing procedures and managing schedules and time is left to others. When there is delay in making decisions, administrative systems and procedures are allowed to evolve in response to needs expressed by staff and in response to external pressures. The principal assumes that teachers know how to accomplish their jobs and that there should be a minimum of structuring and monitoring by the principal. As needs for additions or changes in structures, rules, and procedures emerge, they are gradually acknowledged and introduced as suggestions and guidelines rather than by directly establishing new procedures and policies. Formalizing procedural and policy changes is left to others and to time.

Administrative Efficiency This dimension addresses the extent to which establishing clear procedures and resource systems to help teachers and others do their jobs efficiently is a priority. The emphasis is on having clear procedures, available resources and a smoothly running organization. Administration, scheduling and production tasks are clearly described and understood and used by all members of the organization. Emphasis is placed on having a high level of organizational efficiency so teachers can do their jobs better. As needs for new structures and procedures emerge, they are formally established.

Cluster 3: Strategic Sense

To varying degrees, principals keep in mind the long-term view and its relationship to their own monthly, weekly, daily, and moment-to-moment activities and those of their school. Some principals are more "now" oriented, while others think and act with a vivid mental image of how today's actions contribute to accomplishing long-term goals. Some reflect about what they are doing and how all of their activities can add up, while others focus on the moment, treating each event in isolation from its part in the grand scheme. Planning and visiting encompasses the entry into the schools and role of external facilitators as well. The principal encourages or discourages external facilitators entry and prescribes their role in the schools.

Day-to-day At the high end of this dimension there is little anticipation of future developments and needs or possible successes or failures. Interventions are made in response to issues and needs as they arise. Knowledge of the details of the innovation is limited and the amount of intervention with teachers is restricted to responding to questions and gradually completing routine steps. Images of how things could be better and how more rapid gains could be made are incomplete, limited in scope, and lack imagination. There is little anticipation of longer term patterns, trends or consequences. External facilitators come and go as they wish and spend extraordinary effort in advising the principal.

Vision and Planning The facilitator with a high emphasis on this dimension has a long term vision that is integrated with an understanding of the day-to-day activities as the means to achieve the desired end. The facilitating activity is intense, with a high degree of interaction related to the work at hand. There is depth of knowledge about teaching and learning. Teachers and others are pushed to accomplish all that they can. Assertive leadership, continual monitoring, supportive actions, and creative interpretations of policy and use of resources to accomplish long-term goals are clear indicators of this dimension. Also present is the ability to anticipate the possible systemic effects of interventions and the longer term consequences of day-to-day actions. Effects are accurately predicted and interventions are made in anticipation of likely trends. Moment-to-moment interactions with staff and external facilitators are centered on the work at hand within a context of the long-term aspirations. The focus is on tasks, accomplishing school objectives and making progress. External facilitators are encouraged to be involved in the school according to the principal's perception of their expertise and worth.

Development of the Change Facilitator Style Questionnaire

Development of the CFSQ took place over a period of several years in the late 1980s and early 1990s. This was a collaborative effort involving Gene Hall and Archie George in the United States and Roland Vandenberghe in Belgium.

Developing the Items on the CFSQ

In 1987, Gene Hall and Roland Vandenberghe developed a set of 77 short statements describing change process related intervention behaviors of school principals. Each of these items was intended to represent one of the six dimensions of the Change Facilitator Style. For example, "Chats socially with teachers" should be characteristic of a principal high on the Social/Informal Scale, while "Discusses school problems in a productive way" should be characteristic of a principal high on the Formal/Meaningful Scale. Both English and Dutch language versions of the items were constructed. Items were re-worded or rejected if it was judged that the connotation would be different in translation or if the behavior would be viewed differently in the other's school culture.

These items were included in a questionnaire which was completed by 657 teachers in the US and 900 teachers in Belgium and The Netherlands. Each teacher was asked to reflect on his or her principal's behaviors regarding the implementation of a particular innovation. The teachers then read each item and indicated, on a six point Likert scale, whether the statement was (1) Never or not true, (2) Rarely, (3) Seldom, (4) Sometimes, (5) Often, or (6) Always or very true. The resulting data were then analyzed independently by Vandenberghe in Belgium and George in the United States. Results of the item analyses were shared along with discussions of the techniques (Alpha factor analysis, with or without orthogonal rotation, item-scale correlations, and scale inter-correlations). Out of these data analyses and interpretation processes a common set of five items per scale, thirty items in total, was selected for the final measure.

Characteristics of the CFS Questionnaire

The resulting instrument was used in a variety of studies from 1988 through 1991. Several different scoring techniques were explored for analyzing and interpreting data. In all of these, the responses to the five items on each scale were added together to obtain six scale scores. The individual teacher scores were frequently averaged within each school, and the averages converted to percentile scores based on previously collected data.

CFSQ Profile Interpretation

As each teacher completes the CFS Questionnaire, each response indicates an opinion about the change facilitator's behaviors and perceived intents. The scales on the CFSQ are simply groups of items with a common thread of meaning. Thus, when the responses to the items on a scale are combined, the concept which ties those items together is given a numerical value. To interpret the CFSQ, these values are examined. The sum of the response values is not often as useful as the relative value of that sum, in comparison with other respondents. Thus, the raw scale scores are converted to percentiles based on an established norm group. The six percentile scores form the basis for a bar chart, or CFSQ Profile.

To interpret the meaning of each scale score, it is necessary to understand the concept which ties the items on that scale together. Here the data from each scale will be described and the scale concept discussed individually. However, the scales do not function independently, but rather as a whole. The overall pattern of responses is often as important as the individual scale scores, which is an additional reason for displaying the scale data as a profile.

Scale 1 was designed to measure the **Social/Informal** nature of the change facilitator's *Concern for People* dimension. The items on this scale are as follows:

- Is friendly when we talk to him or her.
- Is primarily concerned about how teachers feel.
- Being accepted by teachers is very important to him/her.
- Attending to feelings and perceptions is his or her first priority.
- Chats socially with teachers.

Each of these items has been written for the respondents to rate the degree to which the change facilitator is sociable and informal in communications with the respondents. High values on this scale indicate friendly, social interactions. Note that for all scales a high score is clearly neither good nor bad, but simply indicates the tone, or Change Facilitator Style.

Scale 2 was designed to measure the **Formal/Meaningful** nature of the change facilitator's *Concern for People* dimension. The items on this scale are as follows:

- Discusses school problems in a productive way.
- Shares many ideas for improving teaching and learning.
- Asks questions about what teachers are doing in their classrooms.
- Supports his or her teachers when it really counts.
- Takes the lead when problems must be solved.

Each of these items has been written to allow the respondent to rate the degree to which the change facilitator is formal, task oriented, production oriented and supportive of activity with the innovation in communications with the respondents. High scores reflect task and production oriented interactions. Originally, this concept was thought to be incompatible with the **Social/Informal** scale. However, the results of our studies indicate that these two scales have a positive correlation.

Scale 3 was designed to measure the **Trust in Others** aspect of the change facilitator's *Organizational Efficiency* dimension. The items on this scale are as follows:

- Seems to be disorganized at times.
- Plans and procedures are introduced at the last moment.
- Allocation of resources is disorganized.
- Explores issues in a loosely structured way.
- Delays making decisions to the last possible moment.

High scores on this scale indicate a reactive style. The change facilitator leaves a lot to others, including the determination of resource allocations, organizational structures, and decision making. Ratings on this scale were hypothesized to be uncorrelated with ratings on the *Concern for People* dimension. Our research data indicates that high ratings on both the **Social/Informal** and **Trust in Others** scales are associated with low scores on this dimension.

Scale 4 was designed to measure the **Administrative Efficiency** aspect of the change facilitator's *Organizational Efficiency* dimension. The items on this scale are as follows:

- Procedures and rules are clearly spelled out.
- Keeps everyone informed about procedures.
- Provides guidelines for efficient operation of the school.
- Efficient and smooth running of the school is his or her priority.
- Is skilled at organizing resources and schedules.

High ratings on these items reflect a proactive style to structure and tasks. Procedures and rules are in place and well understood. Problems are anticipated and dealt with easily. It was thought this aspect of the change facilitator style would be incompatible with the Social/Informal style, but research to date indicates that there is a positive correlation between the Social/Informal ratings and ratings on this scale. However, there is a much stronger positive correlation between the Formal/Meaningful ratings and the Administrative Efficiency ratings, which is what was predicted. Thus, we have found that efficient, procedures-oriented change facilitators, while not unfriendly, are supportive, task-oriented and more knowledgeable about the innovation than those with another style.

Scale 5 was designed to measure the **Day-to-day** approach of the change facilitator's *Strategic Sense* dimension. The items on this scale are as follows:

- Proposes loosely defined solutions.
- Has few concrete ideas for improvement.
- Knows very little about programs and innovations.
- Has an incomplete view about the future of his or her school.
- Focuses on issues of limited importance.

Change facilitators with high marks on this scale are perceived to lack vision. The day-to-day label refers to a short-term focus underlying decision making. Change facilitators who have received high scores on this scale have generally received low marks on the Social/Informal scale. They tend to have high ratings on scale 3, Trust in Others, and low marks on both the Formal/Meaningful and the Administrative Efficiency dimensions.

Scale 6 was designed to measure the *Vision and Planning* aspect of the change facilitator's *Strategic Sense* dimension. The items on this scale are as follows:

- Knows a lot about teaching and curriculum.
- He or she is heavily involved in what is happening with teachers and students.
- Uses many sources to learn more about the new program or innovation.
- He or she sees the connection between the day-to-day activities and moving toward a long-term goal.
- Has a clear picture of where the school is going.

Change facilitators who receive high marks on this dimension are perceived to be knowledgeable, involved, and informed. They have the long-term in mind, but connect this with moment-to-moment actions and events. High marks on this scale are correlated highly with the Formal/Meaningful and the Administrative Efficiency scales, as was predicted in the original concept papers. High marks on this scale are indicative also of low marks on the Trust in Others and Day-to-day scales, as predicted. Only the first scale did not correlate as expected, indicating again that Social/Informal actions are compatible with proactive, vision-oriented leadership.

When examining CFSQ profiles, the researcher should keep in mind that the pattern across all scales is as important as the absolute values of each dimension. Look at the patterns in the three profiles (Figure 9.3) based on the norm groups' Initiator, Manager, and Responder data. Initiators have lower scores on scales 3 and 5 (Trust in Others, and Day-to-day) and higher scores on scales 1, 2, 4, and 6 (Social Informal, Formal/Meaningful, Administrative Efficiency, and Vision and Planning). The pattern is high-high, low-high, low-high. Managers are relatively flat across all six scales. Responders have a pattern that in large part is the reverse of the Initiators, with high scores on scales 1, 3 and 5 (Social/Informal, Trust in Others, and Day-to-day), and lower scores on scales 2, 4 and 6 (Formal/Meaningful, Administrative Efficiency, and Vision and Planning). The pattern is high-low, high-low, high-low. Notice also that scales 1 and 2 are both much higher on the Initiator profile than on the Responder profile. Initiators are more social than Responders, but their conversations are much more meaningful!

Figure 9.3 Three change facilitator style profiles

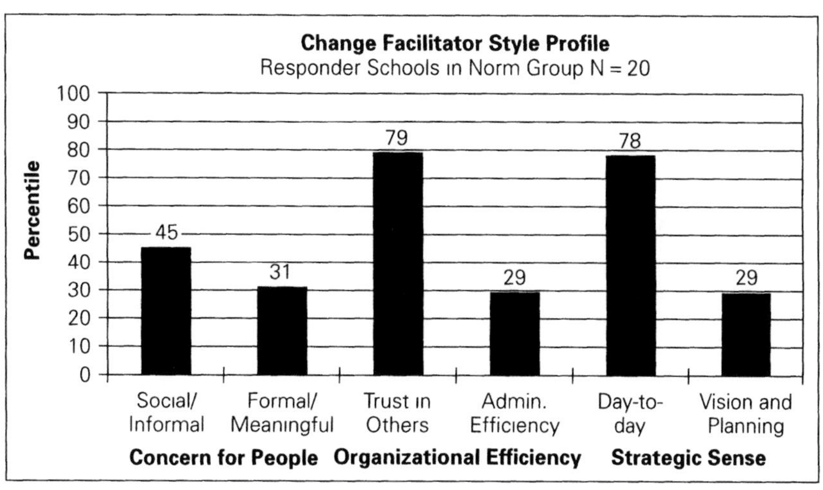

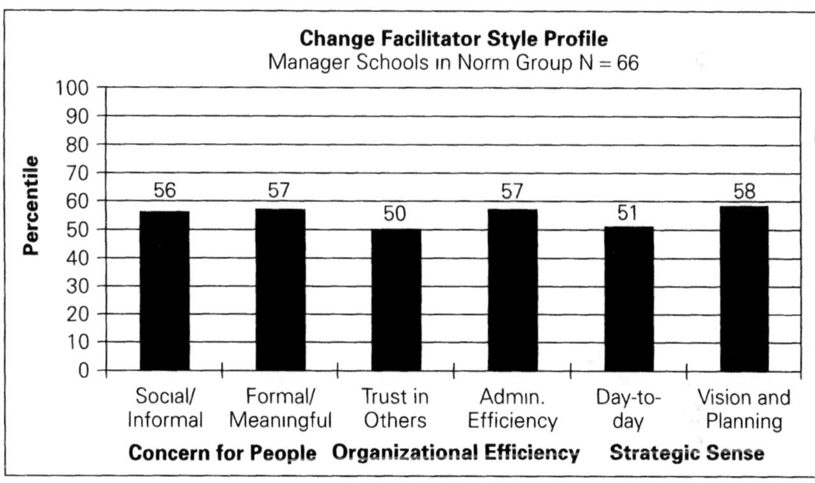

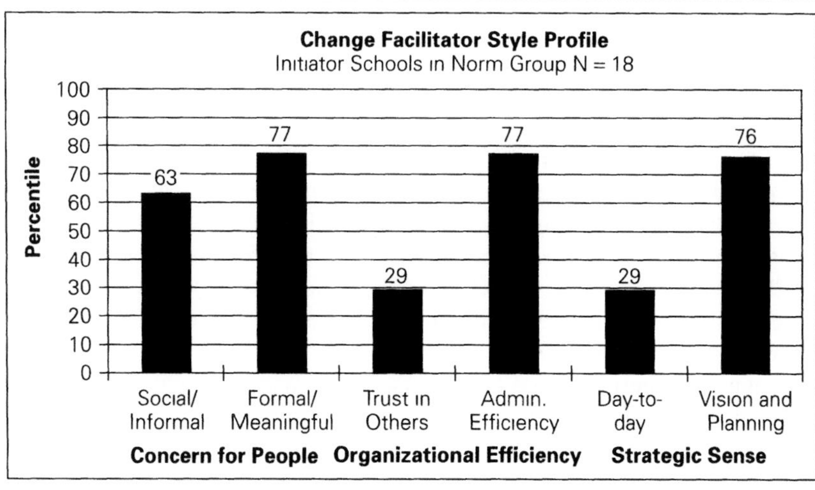

Psychometric Qualities of the CFSQ

The scale characteristics based on the norm group of 1,189 CFSQ ratings collected in a variety of studies from 1989 through 1994 (representing 104 schools) are as follows:

Means, Standard Deviations and Alpha Coefficients

	Means	*Standard Deviations*	*Alpha Coefficients*
Scale 1	22.70	4.44	0.83
Scale 2	24.31	4.17	0.83
Scale 3	13.28	5.27	0.84
Scale 4	24.95	3.95	0.87
Scale 5	12.09	4.74	0.76
Scale 6	25.54	3.98	0.88

Scale Score Intercorrelations

Scale	*2*	*3*	*4*	*5*	*6*
1	0.64	−0.28	0.44	−0.39	0.56
2		−0.58	0.76	−0.68	0.86
3			−0.72	0.75	−0.60
4				−0.68	0.79
5					−0.72

The alpha coefficients are all very high, which indicates very good internal reliability on the scales. (All items on each scale contributed positively to the alpha coefficients, which is remarkable.) The scale intercorrelations are all statistically significant, which might be undesirable in some instruments. However, in this case, we are more interested in the pattern, which fits the high-low theory quite well. Scales 1 and 2, however, have a positive correlation (0.64), while the theory predicts they should have a negative correlation. Notice that scale 1's correlation with scales 3 through 6 are lower (closer to zero) than scale 2's correlation with the same. The only correlations below 0.50 in the entire table occur in this area. This indicates that scale 1 is more independent of other scales on the instrument than any other scale.

Estimating Overall CF Style

Researchers who had been drawn to the concept of three separate and distinct CF Styles requested a classification procedure which put each principal in one category. In other words, was a particular principal most like a Responder, Manager or Initiator?

The procedure we have found most satisfactory for classification purposes is as follows. The responses to each item on a scale are totaled to obtain six raw scale scores. These values are entered into a mathematical formula, a classification function, which produces a single value for each respondent. As is the case in the original number line procedure (Appendix 9.1), low scores represent Responder Styles, middle values represent Manager Styles, and high numbers represent Initiator Styles. Thus, the CFSQ responses for each teacher provide an individual rating of the principal's overall CF Style. If most of the teachers under a given principal place the person in one category, then that is the assigned style. For example, in one school 25 teachers completed CFSQ ratings on their principal. Fifteen of these ratings were classified as Initiator, eight were Manager, and two were Responder. Since more than half (15/25 = 60 per cent) rated the principal as Initiator, that is the rating for the unit.

The classification formula was based on a discriminant analysis in which each of 1,189 CFSQ forms in the norm group was assigned a tentative classification based on a least-squares fit to a theoretical pattern of scores on the six scales. The expectation was the Initiator ratings would have low scores on scales 1, 3, and 5, and high scores on scales 2, 4, and 6. Responder ratings would be high on 2, 4, and 6, and low on 1, 3, and 5. Manager ratings would be average on all six scales. For the initial classification, high was defined as one standard deviation above the mean in the norm group, average was the mean of the norm group, and low one standard deviation below the mean. One significant discriminant function was found which can be used to classify each CFSQ rating into one of these groups. The raw canonical coefficients of this discriminant function were multiplied by 100 and rounded to integers, resulting in the following classification procedure. In this formula, CLF is the classification function value and S1 through S6 are the CFSQ raw scale scores:

$$\text{CLF} = (-10 \times \text{S1} + 8 \times \text{S2} - 13 \times \text{S3} + 8 \times \text{S4} - 20 \times \text{S5} + 9 \times \text{S6})/100$$

Values of CLF above 1.50 indicate Initiator ratings, CLF values below –1.50 indicate Responder ratings, and all others (–1.49 through +1.49) are Manager ratings. This classification procedure resulted in the same assignment to "style" in more than 95 per cent of the individual 1,189 teacher ratings as the least-squares procedure described previously.

If there is no majority in a school, calculate the average CLF value for the group, and use the same rule as for the individuals: 1.50 and above implies Initiator, –1.50 and below implies Responder, and –1.49 through +1.49 implies Manager. For example, in one school there were eight teachers and four rated the principal as Initiator and four as Manager. The average CLF was 1.70, so the principal would be classified as Initiator. In another school, twenty-one teachers' ratings were split with two Initiator, nine Manager, and ten Responder ratings. Since none of these is over 50 per cent (10/21 = 48 per cent), the average CLF value of –1.68 was used to classify the principal as Responder.

Obviously, the degree to which individual ratings agree is very important information about differences in perceptions within the group. In most cases, a majority is found in one category. This was true for 77 of the 104 schools (74 per cent) in the normative sample. In a few cases, however, a wide divergence of opinion existed. In one school, six out of eighteen teachers' ratings were Initiator, four were Manager, and six were Responder. Even though the CLF was –1.03, putting the school into the Manager category, it would be wise to recognize that teachers at this site do not agree on the principal's style.

This classification procedure resulted in 18 of the 124 schools classified as Initiator, 66 as Manager, and 20 as Responder styles. This overall distribution is fairly consistent with our clinical impressions of the distribution in the principal population. The CFSQ profiles for these three groups have been plotted using MS EXCEL[tm] and are shown in Figure 9.3.

Improving School Climate

There were three overall purposes in writing this chapter, which we restate here as summary points:

1 The climate of classrooms is nested inside the climate of the school.
2 The Change Facilitator Style of the principal is highly correlated with teacher success in implementing classroom innovations.
3 Principal Change Facilitator Style is composed of three dimensions and six concepts which can be reliably measured.

One conceptual and one pragmatic point need to be kept in mind when considering the CFSQ. First, the CF Style concepts are based on a long tradition of concepts, models and theories about leaders and leadership. There have been extensive studies of leaders and leadership in many contexts, especially industry. As was noted in the brief references to the literature, much of that work, especially in the last forty to fifty years, has centered on two dimensions of leadership, a people-oriented dimension and job or task dimension. These dimensions can be seen readily in the *Concern for People* and *Organizational Efficiency* dimensions of Change Facilitator Style. We feel we have contributed definitions of two independent scales within each of these dimensions and developed a reliable measure for assessing them in relation to leaders of change processes in school settings.

The *Strategic Sense* dimension originated out of our intensive studies of school leaders at work. The many Initiators who shared their actions and visions with us taught us that there is a critical third dimension of leadership. Empirical confirmation has come through the establishment of the two scales within Strategic Sense that emphasize the significant differences in leader scope and coherence that we have observed. Initiators have taught us that there is more to leadership than being concerned for people and having organizational efficiency.

Our concluding pragmatic discussion point is a word of caution. When teachers complete the CFSQ they are *evaluating* their principal. This can be very uncomfortable for both teachers and principal. The use of the CFSQ and the interpretations of the data analyses must be done responsibly, with respect, and with preservation of confidentiality. The CFSQ has been designed expressly for use in research and for professional development of change facilitators. The CFSQ should *not* be used for evaluation or any other form of personnel action. Perhaps the most practical use of the CFSQ would be as a tool to select leaders and sites for initial introduction of innovations into school districts. Research has indicated that initiator principals have more success with innovation adoption. It might be possible to enhance innovation adoption by introducing innovations into the most likely schools first, the schools with principals rated as initiators by their teachers.

Appendix 9.1: Descriptions of three change facilitator styles

Initiators have clear, decisive long-range policies and goals that transcend but include implementation of the current innovation. They tend to have very strong beliefs about what good schools and teaching should be like and work intensely to attain this vision. Decisions are made in relation to their goals for the school and in terms of what they believe to be best for students, which is based on current knowledge of classroom practice. Initiators have strong expectations for students, teachers and themselves. They convey and monitor these expectations through frequent contacts with teachers and clear explication of how the school is to operate and how teachers are to teach. When they feel it is in the best interest of their school, particularly the students, Initiators will seek changes in district programs or policies or they will reinterpret them to suit the needs of the school. Initiators will be adamant but not unkind, they solicit input from staff and then decisions are made in terms of the goals of the school, even if some are ruffled by their directness and high expectations.

Managers represent a broader range of behaviors. They demonstrate both responsive behaviors in answer to situations or people and they also initiate actions in support of the change effort. The variations in their behavior seem to be linked to their rapport with teachers and the central office staff as well as how well they understand and buy into a particular change effort. Managers work without fanfare to provide basic support to facilitate teachers' use of an innovation. They keep teachers informed about decisions and are sensitive to teacher needs. They will defend their teachers from what they perceive as excessive demands. When they learn that the central office wants something to happen in their school, they then become very involved with their teachers in making it happen. Yet, they do not typically initiate attempts to move beyond the basics of what is imposed.

Responders place heavy emphasis on allowing teachers and others the opportunity to take the lead. They believe their primary role is to maintain a smooth running school by focusing on traditional administrative tasks, keeping teachers content and treating students well. They view teachers as strong professionals who are able to carry out their instructional role with little guidance. Responders emphasize the personal side of their relationships with teachers and others. Before they make decisions, they often give everyone an opportunity to have input so as to weigh their feelings or to allow others to make the decision. A related characteristic is the tendency toward making decisions in terms of immediate circumstances rather than in terms of longer range instructional or school goals. This seems to be due, in part, to their desire to please others and, in part, to their more limited vision.

Appendix 9.2: Change facilitator style questionnaire

The purpose of this questionnaire is to let you give your perspective on how the principal or other leader in your school manages school improvement efforts. These items were selected from a collection of comments made by teachers and others involved in schools where new programs were being implemented. Research has indicated that responses to these particular statements can be used to build a good picture of how your leader, in this case ________________________________ manages the change process. Please think about a particular program while responding, ________________________________.

Please indicate how accurately each statement describes your leaders:

	1 Never or Not True	2 Rarely True	3 Seldom True	4 Sometimes True	5 Often True	6 Always or Very True
1 Is friendly when we talk to him or her	1	2	3	4	5	6
2 Knows a lot about teaching and curriculum	1	2	3	4	5	6
3 Procedures and rules are clearly spelled out	1	2	3	4	5	6
4 Discusses school problems in a productive way	1	2	3	4	5	6
5 Seems to be disorganized at times	1	2	3	4	5	6
6 Shares many ideas for improving teaching and learning	1	2	3	4	5	6
7 Plans and procedures are introduced at the last moment	1	2	3	4	5	6
8 Keeps everyone informed about procedures	1	2	3	4	5	6
9 He or she is heavily involved in what is happening with teachers and students	1	2	3	4	5	6
10 Proposes loosely defined solutions	1	2	3	4	5	6
11 Is primarily concerned about how teachers feel	1	2	3	4	5	6
12 Asks questions about what teachers are doing in their classrooms	1	2	3	4	5	6
13 Has few concrete ideas for improvement	1	2	3	4	5	6
14 Provides guidelines for efficient operation of the school	1	2	3	4	5	6
15 Supports his or her teachers when it really counts	1	2	3	4	5	6
16 Allocation of resources is disorganized	1	2	3	4	5	6
17 Efficient and smooth running of the school is his or her priority	1	2	3	4	5	6
18 Uses many sources to learn more about the new program or innovation	1	2	3	4	5	6
19 Being accepted by teachers is very important to him/her	1	2	3	4	5	6
20 He or she sees the connection between the day-to-day activities and moving toward a long-term goal	1	2	3	4	5	6
21 Knows very little about programs and innovations	1	2	3	4	5	6
22 Is skilled at organizing resources and schedules	1	2	3	4	5	6
23 Has an incomplete view about the future of his or her school	1	2	3	4	5	6
24 Attending to feelings and perceptions is his or her first priority	1	2	3	4	5	6
25 Explores issues in a loosely structured way	1	2	3	4	5	6
26 Chats socially with teachers	1	2	3	4	5	6
27 Delays making decisions to the last possible moment	1	2	3	4	5	6
28 Focuses on issues of limited importance	1	2	3	4	5	6
29 Takes the lead when problems must be solved	1	2	3	4	5	6
30 Has a clear picture of where the school is going	1	2	3	4	5	6

Your School ______________________________ Years at This School ____

Years Working with This Innovation __________ Total Years Teaching ____

Scoring the Change Facilitator Style Questionnaire

The procedure for scoring the Change Facilitator Style Questionnaire consists of the following steps:

1) Transfer the item responses into the table below.
2) Sum the five items on each scale to obtain six "raw scale scores." If any items were left blank, compute the average of the non-blank items on that scale, round to an integer (i.e. 4.6 → 5), and use for the missing values.
3) Multiply each raw score by the number shown below each sum, enter each value on the "product" row.
4) Sum the six products to obtain a "total score." Be sure to add or subtract according to the sign of the products.
5) Divide this sum by 100, which should result in a value near zero (the formula was developed to produce results with a mean of 0.00 and standard deviation of 1.00, so most values are between –3.00 and +3.00).
6) If the result is below –1.50, the classification is "responder". If the value is higher than +1.50, the classification is "initiator". Values between –1.50 and + 1.50 are classified as "manager".
7) Base the overall rating of the change facilitator on the majority of the teacher's ratings. If less than 50 per cent of the teachers' ratings agree, average the classification values and assign the overall rating based on this average, using the rule outlined in (6).
8) To construct a CFSQ profile, find the raw scale score in the first column of the "CFSQ Percentile Table". The percentile for each scale is the value in the table in that scale's column.
9) Draw a vertical bar on the chart provided, or construct a similar chart using commercial software such as Harvard Graphics[tm] or Microsoft Excel[tm].

	Scale 1		Scale 2		Scale 3		Scale 4		Scale 5		Scale 6	
	1	___	4	___	5	___	3	___	10	___	2	___
	11	___	6	___	7	___	8	___	13	___	9	___
	19	___	12	___	16	___	14	___	21	___	18	___
	24	___	15	___	25	___	17	___	23	___	20	___
	26	___	29	___	27	___	22	___	28	___	30	___
Total:		___		___		___		___		___		___
times:		–10		8		–13		8		–20		9
product:		___		___		___		___		___		___

Sum of products: ___ divided by 100: ___

Responder	Manager	Initiator
(less than –1.50)	(–1.50 through +1.50)	(greater than 1.50)

Percentiles ___ ___ ___ ___ ___ ___
(see table below)

Percentile Scores and Profile Template for The Change Facilitator Style Questionnaire

Raw Scale Score	Percentile equivalent					
	S1	S2	S3	S4	S5	S6
5	1	1	6	1	7	1
6	1	1	10	1	13	1
7	1	1	15	1	19	1
8	1	1	21	1	26	1
9	1	1	28	1	33	1
10	2	1	35	1	42	1
11	2	1	42	1	50	1
12	3	2	49	1	57	1
13	4	2	55	1	64	2
14	5	3	60	2	69	2
15	7	4	66	2	76	3
16	9	5	71	3	80	3
17	12	6	77	5	85	4
18	16	8	81	7	88	6
19	20	12	86	9	91	7
20	27	16	90	12	95	10
21	34	21	92	18	97	14
22	43	28	95	24	99	19
23	52	36	97	31	99	26
24	62	45	98	40	99	33
25	71	56	99	50	99	42
26	81	66	99	60	99	53
27	87	75	99	71	99	63
28	92	85	99	79	99	72
29	97	93	99	87	99	84
30	99	99	99	99	99	99

References

BASS, B.M. (1981) *Stogdill's handbook of leadership, a survey of theory and research*, (rev. and expanded edn.) New York: The Free Press.

BLAKE, R.R. and MOUTON, J.S. (1964) *The Managerial Grid*, Houston: Gulf Publishing.

FIEDLER, F.E. (1978) 'The contingency model and the dynamics of the leadership process', in BERKOWITZ, L. (ed.), *Advances in Experimental and Social Psychology*, New York: Academic Press, pp. 59–112.

GETZELS, J.W. and GUBA, E.G. (1957) 'Social behavior and the administrative process', *School Review*, **65**, pp. 423–44.

HALL, G.E. (1988) 'The principal as leader of the change facilitating team', *Journal of Research and Development in Education*, **22**, 1, pp. 49–59.

HALL, G.E. and GEORGE, A.A. (1988) Development of a framework and measure for assessing principal change facilitator style. Paper presented at the American Educational

Research Association annual meeting. (ERIC Docum... No. ED 336 401).

Hall, G.E. and Hord, S.M. (1987) *Change in Schools Facilitating the Process*, Albany: State University of New York Press.

Hall, G.E. and Hord, S.M. (in press) *Implementing Change: Patterns and Principles*, Boston: Allyn and Bacon.

Hall, G.E., Hord, S.M. and Griffin, T.H. (1980) *Implementation at the School Building Level: The Development and Analysis of Nine Mini-case Studies*, (Report No. 3098). Austin: The University of Texas at Austin, Research and Development Center for Teacher Education. (ERIC Document Reproduction Service No. ED 207 170).

Hall, G.E., Rutherford, W.L., Hord, S.M. and Huling, L.L. (1984) 'Effects of three principal styles on school improvement', *Educational Leadership*, **41**, 5, pp. 22–9.

Hall, G.E., Wallace, R.C. and Dossette, W.A. (1973) *A Developmental Conceptualization of the Adoption Process within Educational Institutions*, (Report No. 3006). Austin: The University of Texas at Austin, Research and Development Center for Teacher Education. (ERIC Document Reproduction Service No. ED 095 125).

Hemphill, J.K. (1950) *Leader Behavior Description*. Columbus: Ohio State University, Personnel Research Board, (mimeo).

Hougen, M.C. (1984) High School Principals: An analysis of their approach to facilitating implementation of microcomputers. Doctoral dissertation, The University of Texas at Austin.

Lewin, K. and Lippitt, R. (1938) 'An experimental approach to the study of autocracy and democracy: A preliminary note', *Sociometry*, **1**, 292–300.

Machiavelli, N. (1532) *The Prince* (P. Bandanella and M. Musa, Trans.) Oxford University Press, 1984.

Rutherford, W.L. (1985) School principals as effective leaders, *Phi Delta Kappan*, **69**, 1, pp. 31–4.

Schiller, J. (1991) 'Implementing computer education: The role of the primary principal', *Australian Journal of Educational Technology*, **7**, 1 Winter, pp. 48–69.

Shieh, W. (1996) Environmental Factors, Principals' Change Facilitator Style and Implementation of Cooperative Learning Project in Selected Schools in Taiwan. Greeley: University of Northern Colorado, doctoral dissertation.

Vandenberghe, R. (1988) Development of a questionnaire for assessing principal change facilitator style. Paper presented at the American Educational Research Association annual meeting. (ERIC Document Reproduction Service No. ED 297 463).

Chapter 10

The Phoenix Rises From its Ashes . . . Doesn't It?

Sam Stringfield[1]

In ancient Egyptian mythology, the phoenix was a beautiful, lone bird that lived in the desert for many years, then consumed itself in fire. The phoenix would rise renewed from its ashes, and begin another, beautiful life.

Introduction

This chapter presents qualitative implementation/institutionalization data, quantitative outcome data, and the author's interpretations of events from pre-implementation through year seven of an effort to improve student outcomes at an inner-city school. Over the first four implementation years the project was characterized by diverse groups' well-orchestrated, focused effort to implement a thoroughly-specified school model. During those years, the school rose from mediocre standing within the lowest achieving district in its state, to the highest academic achievements in the district, and to international acclaim. Over the following three years, the school maintained its considerable state and international status. However, the unity and shared focus that had characterized the first four years disappeared, and evidence of less-than-stellar performance has mounted. Although the future of reform at the school is uncertain, data gathering is continuing. This is, therefore, a chapter of a work in progress.

Phoenix School

Phoenix School[2] was not the most plausible candidate for successful school reform. Phoenix is a neighborhood public school serving nearly 500 (K–8) students in a large east coast city. Key student population demographics in this school included 82 per cent participation in the free or reduced-price lunch program (a standard measure of poverty) and 94 per cent minority status (almost exclusively African-American). The 82 per cent free lunch figure is more than triple the 26 per cent rate for the entire state. Phoenix is three blocks from one of the city's larger drug hot spots. Over the three years before reform was attempted, Phoenix's fourth graders had produced mean reading achievement scores on the Comprehensive Test of Basic Skills (CTBS–4, CTB/Macmillan/McGraw Hill, 1989) that ranged from the 20th to the 25th percentile. Average daily attendance rates had hovered around 90 per cent. As with the test scores, this rate was low even compared to the city's other inner-city schools. However, these data had not caused the district's central administration to take steps to improve the long-standing academic problems within the school.

Observations made at Phoenix prior to the school improvement effort indicated that the school was clean, that by-and-large the students were well behaved and often remarkably quiet. Class sizes were large, often with a student-teacher ratio greater than 35–1. Classes that were visited featured teachers standing at the front of the room lecturing and occasionally asking a question. The students listened and worked ditto sheets. They generally seemed compliant, passive, and disinterested.

The school received some Chapter 1 funding,[3] and that money was used for pull-out services for large numbers of students. The criterion for being labeled "gifted and talented" (GATE) in the city was a CTBS score above the 50th percentile nationally, and even at that, Phoenix was in danger of losing it's one part-time GATE teacher for lack of qualifying students.

In the early 1980s, the school climate had deteriorated to the point that members of the surrounding community had gone to the system's administration and pleaded for a new principal. The system responded by bringing in a principal with prior experience in social work and community involvement. The principal, Ms. Sparks,[4] proved exceptionally skilled at re-uniting the community behind the school. However, after nearly 10 years as principal at the school, she oversaw a largely orderly, but academically very troubled school.

The principal's training and skills lay in working with groups of people, not with curriculum. Ms. Sparks recognized that the city's curriculum clearly was not helping her students excel academically, and sought other options.

On two occasions in the 1980s Ms. Sparks petitioned the district's administration for permission to use the curriculum of an élite private school, and twice she was turned down. In 1990, a private foundation directed by the former president of the school board offered to fund the entire effort, so the new superintendent was petitioned. He again refused. The principal and the foundation took their case to the mayor. The state's largest newspaper and several other groups immediately endorsed the experiment and refused to let the issue die. After a lively public debate lasting several months, the mayor intervened, and Phoenix School was allowed to initiate its experiment with the Calvert School program.

Calvert School is a private elementary school founded in 1897. For 100 years, the school has offered a remarkably consistent and rigorous educational experience to children from many of Baltimore, Maryland's leading families. One reason for the constancy of content was Calvert's Home Instruction Program. The Home Instruction Program was born in 1907 out of the need to send lessons home to the day school students during a whooping cough epidemic. (At the turn of the century, whooping cough required students to remain at home for six weeks.) Teachers had been required to write fully detailed lessons for all courses so that parents could keep their children from falling behind at school. Over time, this detailed instructional program, complete with materials for every content area, grew into a service for children of Americans in government or business who needed a portable, temporary curriculum during their overseas assignments.[5]

The program includes a manual that is written by teachers for parents. In developing the manual, teachers taught the material to their in-school students first, then wrote instructions to parents in such detail that they could be successful no matter what. This means that the teachers have been required to conduct very detailed analyses of and reflection upon the year's material. Both the desired end and one very detailed route map exist for and by each teacher. The manuals have been revised over the years. However, their existence, combined with the reticence of the Calvert School's board to radically alter a curriculum they have always viewed as successful, has resulted in unusually consistent teaching at Calvert and an unusually articulated written instructional program.

Calvert's first Head Master was firmly convinced that an education was only as good as the skills training that formed its base. He stressed accuracy and speed, among other things, and much that he stressed continues to be observed in the daily work of Calvert's teachers and students. In 1899, he declared that a student's work was the best assessment of the student's progress. Students began collecting their work into monthly folders, and to this day the Calvert administrators conduct monthly folder checks of each student's work. This Calvert practice preceded "authentic" and "portfolio assessment" by nearly 90 years.

Fads, which at Calvert means practices that haven't been proven successful for at least 10 years, simply aren't tolerated. Neatness, accuracy, orderliness, punctuality, politeness, consideration, respect for others, and similar traits are integral parts of the Calvert ethos. Having fun learning things is, too.

The Calvert Curriculum is notable for its insistence on several specific processes:

(i) Students read a great deal, and reading is taught with an emphasis on deriving meaning from the written word. In addition to continuously exposing students to interesting text, teachers formally instruct young children in phonics.

(ii) All students *produce* a great deal of work. In the Calvert curriculum, students write every day. In the early grades, the school uses a modeled writing approach. This assumes that there is a correct way to write and that there is little reason to write something incorrectly five times before getting it right. In the first year of formal instruction (Calvert's equivalent of first grade), students often imitate teachers' writing of the letters. Then teachers immediately use those letters to write short sentences, which the children also imitate. Over time, students make increasingly original contributions to their daily writing assignments. They write about their reading, about paintings, field trips, and what is happening in their lives.

(iii) Teachers check students' work, and students correct all their own work. Each primary grade class has an assisting teacher who walks around the room while the lead teacher is instructing. If the assisting teacher sees something wrong on a paper, she or he guides the student to make the correction immediately. For longer student work where it is impractical for them to correct mistakes as they occur, the teacher reads over each student's work after school, and students make corrections early the next day. At Calvert, an assignment is not finished until it is correct. The goal at Calvert is not acceptable work, but perfect work.

(iv) Calvert believes in the importance of teaching history and geography, and, like the Core Knowledge Curriculum (See Hirsch, 1996), begins teaching them early. Students study art history and diverse traditions of music. The upper grades curriculum is rich in history, art, music, and hands-on sciences. Because public speaking skills are valued at Calvert, the school holds monthly assemblies. Over the course of the year, all Calvert students make presentations.

(v) Student folders are read by the Head Master or another adult every month. The focus is on monitoring output as much as on instructional processes. If a child is falling behind, steps are taken within a month to focus attention on the child's specific problems.

(vi) The folders are sent home every month. Parents are encouraged to read and oversee their children's work nightly. Parents who do not sign off on students' folders are contacted to be sure they are aware of, and involved in, their children's educational progress.

(vii) Calvert carries a sense of urgency through the school year. The Calvert curriculum is full, with little review time in the fall. After the first few weeks of the school year, the tempo increases significantly. By mid-year, the work is challenging, and by spring, it is difficult. Students are stretched by both the level of difficulty and the pace at which work is approached.

(viii) There is the expectation that each student will do the very best he or she can. The student's progress is the bottom line, and the school has clear ideas about the meaning of progress. Specific skills must be mastered and concepts understood. The school insists on seeing student products that demonstrate mastery of new skills. That expectation is conveyed through the monthly reports and by having the student folders checked by the Calvert administration and sent home to parents for review.

Both teachers and parents are comfortable with Calvert's high academic expectations. Prospective teachers and parents alike can examine the Calvert materials and know exactly what will be expected of them and their Calvert school children.

The Head Master at Calvert had previously been the principal at two other private schools, and has been active in national organizations. From this perspective he states that,

> More than at any other school I know, the parents who have sent their children to Calvert over the years have chosen the school for what it expects, trains, and helps the children to know and do. There is a remarkable confluence in what the school values and what the parents value, and this allows for a very efficient school.

The climate at Calvert was and remains intellectually alive, student-focused, and professional. The halls and classrooms are tidy, and the focus of all concerned (administration, parents, teachers, teaching assistants, and students) is clearly academic. That such a traditional, unbending curriculum and instructional program could succeed in an historically very-low achieving, inner-city school seemed implausible, yet Phoenix's faculty and principal voted to request the experiment. The Calvert board agreed to participate, the local foundation agreed to fund any implementation expenses, and eventually the city agreed to allow this unusual effort.

Methods

The Abell Foundation contracted with the Center for the Social Organization of Schools (CSOS) at The Johns Hopkins University to conduct a longitudinal evaluation of the implementation of the Calvert educational program at Phoenix. The evaluation design involved a multi-method methodology. All classrooms have been observed each school year, and the principal and school improvement team (SIT) have been interviewed each year. Interviews have been conducted each year with the representative of the Abell Foundation and, during most years, with members of the community. Each grade's students' folders have been examined every year.

The decision to initially implement the Calvert/Phoenix project in kindergarten and first grade only, and then to roll implementation forward one grade per year, simplified discussion of sampling and the choice of a comparison group for the examination of quantitative outcome data. The first cohort of Calvert/Phoenix first graders (1990–1991) also became the first cohort of Calvert/Phoenix second graders (1991–1992), third graders (1992–1993) and fourth graders (1993–1994). This implementation decision created an unusual opportunity to study a well matched within-school cohort. The control group for the Calvert/Phoenix evaluation has been the Phoenix students who have been in the cohorts immediately preceding the forward-rolling Calvert/Phoenix program. That is, the "Last Phoenix-Pre-Calvert" cohort is made up of students who were in Phoenix's first grade during the 1989–1990 school year and completed the eighth grade during the 1996–1997 school year. The Phoenix-Pre-Calvert (2) cohort began first grade in the fall of 1988, and completed sixth grade during the Spring of 1996, and so on. These older students from the same community, often including older brothers and sisters of Calvert/Phoenix students, became the evaluation's control group.

Wherever adequate data have been available to follow individual students over time, analyses have been limited to students who have remained at the school, either as Calvert/Phoenix or Phoenix-Pre-Calvert controls, throughout the study. Such analyses provide the maximum opportunity to determine the effects of the Calvert intervention, because they concern only students who have received the full intervention. However, other analyses, especially data from the State Performance Assessment Program, are not available at the student level, so that restricting an analytic sample to students who have received several years of the intervention is not always possible. SPAP data will include all students attending Phoenix at the time the test was administered, whether they had received four years of Calvert/ Phoenix (e.g., kindergarten through third grade), or four days. To the extent that this reality requires the program to demonstrate effects even on students who have received very little of the intervention, it becomes a conservative test of the effects of the Calvert/Phoenix program.

Input data have included background information on all students (e.g., 94+ per cent African American, 82 per cent free lunch), district and Abell grant budget information, and data on the organization of the school before the Calvert/ Phoenix program began. Process data include extensive low-inference classroom observations; comparison observations of upper-grade Phoenix classes and of same-grade Calvert classes; analyses of student portfolios; and interviews with students, parents, teachers, Phoenix and Calvert administrators, and staff of The Abell Foundation.

Several types of outcome data have been gathered. Student attendance data are gathered each year for all students attending Phoenix School. The Educational Records Bureau test (an Educational Testing Service developed, norm-referenced test frequently used by non-public schools) is administered annually to all Phoenix students in first through fourth grades. ERB testing was begun the spring of 1990, before the Calvert/Phoenix program began.

The state department of education had developed a state of the art performance appraisal system for schools. The *State Performance Assessment Program (SPAP)* is a performance-based assessment requiring extensive writing, problem solving, and occasional teamwork among students. The test is administered each year to all third graders. *SPAP* data are not released at the student level, so reports include all students at the school, whether they have had one week or four years of the Calvert/ Phoenix program. Additional data on student transfer rates and referrals to compensatory education and special education are gathered annually.

Results

Results will be presented in four sections. Implementation data from the first four years of the Calvert/Phoenix study will be followed by outcome data from those same four years. Implementation data from years five through seven will then be followed by outcome data from years five and six. A discussion of these results will end the chapter.

Calvert Implementation at Phoenix: 1990–1994

Pre-implementation

Schools' reasons for choosing specific reforms are not always aligned to solving problems that external observers see as major issues within those schools (Ross, Henry, Phillipsen, Evans, Smith and Bugge, 1997; Stringfield, Datnow and Ross, 1998). In retrospect, a very important pre-implementation development was that Phoenix School had sought out a particular solution to a specific problem. Phoenix's principal was looking for a better curriculum. In Calvert, she found a much more academically rigorous curriculum. In addition, she and her faculty found materials and an instructional and organizational model. In a school district notoriously plagued with an inability to deliver curricular support materials, the Phoenix teachers were attracted to the idea of having enough materials to last throughout the year. These were realistic expectations that Calvert has fulfilled. Further, the fact that the faculty had, in secret ballot, voted to attempt the change placed the effort on high ground when battles over change inevitably raged. In those regards, the project began on an unusually strong footing.

An achievable plan

An abiding strength of the early years of the Phoenix project was its thorough, methodical plan. At the insistence of Calvert's Head Master, Phoenix did not attempt to implement the Calvert curriculum and instructional program in all grades at once. Rather, the program was put into place the first year in kindergarten and first grade classes. The Calvert orientation was that implementing the demanding curriculum in upper grades without first preparing students for the content requirements would be an invitation to failure.

Inevitably, situations arose that were not covered in the initial plans. Those were dealt with via regularly scheduled meetings among the Phoenix principal, the Phoenix/Calvert program coordinator, the Calvert head master, and the Abell Foundation representative. In most instances, the team was able to agree on an achievable path that was universally perceived to be in the best interests of Phoenix's students. Having a structure to facilitate mid-course corrections was an integral part of the practical plan for Calvert implementation.

The second requirement imposed by Calvert was that the effort include a full-time Phoenix/Calvert coordinator. The Calvert Head Master believed that the program was so different as to require ongoing staff development, modeling of lessons, and feedback to teachers. The Abell Foundation agreed to fund the position, and a Calvert teacher volunteered to fill it. This meant that there was always support available for teachers, that the coordinator had detailed knowledge of the Calvert program, and that over time the coordinator would become very knowledgeable about the particular implementation in Phoenix school.

Implementation began in the summer of 1990. The coordinator provided two weeks of required (Abell Foundation-funded) training for the four K–1 teachers and their aides. This staff development allowed the teachers to absorb the philosophy, the curriculum, and several of the instructional requirements of the Calvert program. Throughout that first year, the coordinator visited K–1 classes, modeled lessons, provided feedback, and taught small reading groups.

In preparation for the second year, second grade Phoenix teachers and aides received two weeks of training in the Calvert program. During the school year they, too, received ongoing training, observed model lessons, were given feedback and other assistance and support. During the summers of 1992–1996, training was provided both to the teachers of the next grades scheduled for implementation, and to new teachers coming into Phoenix's earlier grades.

This gradual, rolling system had several advantages. Time was provided for each new grade's teachers to learn the system. Also, the teachers above grade one were not asked to present whole classes of second to sixth grade students with a curriculum for which students were not prepared. Rather, one cohort of students, in the seventh grade in the spring of 1997, has been the leading edge of reform at Phoenix. Finally, this rolling system allowed the teachers and leadership team to each learn to work together. Their learning benefited the early-grades' students, and their initial, inevitable missteps caused no disruptions to the majority of students and adults at Phoenix School.

Funding

A critical factor to making the plan achievable was a thoroughly worked-through funding plan. The Abell Foundation funded the full-time coordinator for the Phoenix program, the purchase of over $10,000 in books and Calvert materials each year, time for staff development, and other equipment and materials. The Abell Foundation support ranged between $50,000 and $150,000 per year through the effort's first six years.

Non-Fiscal Support

The Calvert program at Phoenix received unusually strong and diverse support over its first four years of implementation. The Abell Foundation's project manager was exceptionally diligent in her oversight of the process. She was involved in regular staff meetings, in fiscal decisions, in negotiations with the larger district, and in regular efforts to anticipate and solve problems.

Ms. Sparks, the principal, is a talented and determined person. Among other talents, Ms. Sparks demonstrated uncommon skill at working within the district's informal political machinery, producing notable media sound bites, and often winning remarkable political battles.

A third source of strong support for implementation was the Phoenix coordinator for the first four years. She had taught within the city's public system for seven years, and then at Calvert for 18 years. She proved to have substantial patience in working with students and teachers, and yet used iron resolve in dealing with persons who attempted to modify, or, as she saw it, water down, the Calvert model. Importantly, during years one through four, the Calvert coordinator at Phoenix was paid (by Abell) as a Calvert employee. When conflicts inevitably arose, her allegiance was to fidelity of implementation of the Calvert program.

The Calvert School Head Master staunchly supported the project. He oversaw much of what was implemented at Phoenix, and consistently held out for fidelity to the Calvert model. He assisted Phoenix in searching for new faculty and aides. He visited classrooms, and repeatedly made himself available for consultations. He consistently advocated nothing less than educational excellence at Phoenix, and he readily offered the position that excellence at Phoenix might require modification of some aspects of the Calvert program, such as the purchase of a more diverse set of readings. He and the assistant Head Master also assisted in checking student folders at Phoenix.

A fifth source of support came from the parents and the community. Parents were actively involved at every stage of the project. The parents were joined by community supporters in the Phoenix School Community Council and two surrounding neighborhood associations. These groups followed the project closely and have remained supportive.

Curriculum

Each aspect of the Calvert program has seen some degree of modification at Phoenix, but in years one through four, the core elements of the Calvert curriculum were put in place. The blend of phonics instruction and interesting text was installed. Student folders looked almost exactly like Calvert folders and went home on the same schedule.

Classroom instruction

Little changes in a student's academic achievement unless something changes among the student, the curriculum, and instruction. Educational research is littered with examples of interventions that never reached the students (e.g., Berman and McLaughlin, 1977; Stringfield et al., 1997). Clearly, through the first four years of implementation, the Calvert program reached the Phoenix students. Virtually all of the K–4 teachers made significant, often dramatic, changes in their teaching to provide Calvert-like instruction. The rate of using ditto sheets dropped dramatically. Students did a great deal more original writing, and experienced greatly increased levels of instruction in geography, history, and the arts. The academic pace at Phoenix was almost identical to that at Calvert. There was a clear push, without undue anxiety being communicated to students.

Several of the teachers and aides who lacked a commitment to the Calvert project were counseled to transfer out of the school or voluntarily transferred to other schools. Their replacements were drawn from a pool that included teachers applying to the city's system *and* Calvert School.

Finally, the quality of student work in many of the folders gave evidence of successful implementation. Phoenix students' products were of such quality that the Calvert Head Master expressed the belief that the majority of Phoenix's fourth grade students' folders were fully comparable to those produced by students at the highly selective Calvert school.

Outcomes: 1990–1994

Results from the first four years are presented in five areas: scores from a norm referenced test, scores from the state's performance test, attendance measures, school holding power, and disciplinary referrals.

Norm-referenced testing

The district mandated annual administration of the *Comprehensive Test of Basic Skills* (*CTBS*, CTB/Macmillan/McGraw/Hill, 1989) in grades 1–8. In addition, Calvert requested that the school administer the Educational Records Bureau (*ERB*, Educational Testing Service, 1995).

As a protection against extraneous biases from students transferring in or out, the *ERB* analysis for both experimental and controls are restricted to students who had attended Phoenix throughout the experiment. Also, while full sets of data are available, to save space, only the 4th grade ERB data are represented. Other grades produced similar data.

On the *ERB's* fourth grade reading test, the four cohorts that preceded the first Phoenix/Calvert group had produced mean national percentile rankings at the 17th, 14th, 16th, and 44th percentiles respectively.[6] These scores were consistent with the cohorts' earlier-grades' scores, which had not approached the national average during any year. By contrast, the first Phoenix/Calvert cohort produced a mean score at the 69th percentile. That lead Phoenix/Calvert group produced a nearly identical mean score at the 66th percentile when in third grade.[7]

In one sense the *ERB Writing Mechanics* test told a similar story. The last Phoenix-Pre-Calvert produced relatively stable writing scores at the 28th percentile. By contrast, the first Phoenix/Calvert cohort produced mean *ERB Writing Mechanics* scores above the 60th percentile in grade three, and the first cohort had produced similar scores in grade four.

On the *ERB Mathematics* test, the story was much the same. The Phoenix/ Calvert cohort finished fourth grade in the Spring of 1994 with an average score that placed the group mean at the 63rd percentile nationally. By contrast, the last pre-Calvert cohort at Phoenix school had finished fourth grade in the Spring of 1993, with a mean *ERB Mathematics* score at the 38th percentile.

Across three subtests, the Phoenix-Calvert students scored, on average, more than 25 percentiles higher than their pre-Calvert peers.

Student achievement measured by the State Performance Assessment Program (SPAP)[8]

SPAP was designed to be a very demanding, "raise the criterion dramatically" performance test. The test is relatively new, having been pilot-tested during the spring of 1991 and administered in all schools for the first time in 1992. While some technical problems with scoring and interpretation remain, in general, the *SPAP* is being praised as a leading example of the next generation of performance assessments. All student work on the *SPAP* is scored based on written responses to diverse tasks and questions generally considered to assess "higher order" thinking skills. The state department of education assumed that the majority of students would not score high during the initial years, but that scores will rise as schools adjusted their curricular and instructional offerings to the higher demands of the test.

The *SPAP* is administered at three grade levels: third, fifth, and eighth. In May of 1993 the first Phoenix/Calvert cohort took the third grade test. During the spring of 1994, the second Phoenix/Calvert cohort took the third grade test. SPAP data are released on a school-by-school basis, not on a student-by-student basis. Over one third of the third grade students who took the *SPAP* at Phoenix during the spring of 1994 had transferred into the school at some time between the second semesters of first and third grades. Those students had not received three full years of the Calvert program. Therefore, the *SPAP* data became a very conservative test of the effects of the intervention.

The 1994 *SPAP* provided data regarding third graders' progress in six subject areas: reading, mathematics, social studies, science, writing and language usage. The percentages of Phoenix third graders achieving at least "satisfactory" ratings were above the district average in all six areas. In writing and language usage, the Phoenix "satisfactory" rates were more than double the district averages.

Attendance

Academic success is a primary goal of schooling, but not the only one. A school should be a place to which students want to go and a place where parents want their children to be. Particularly within a specific school's catchment area, a change in attendance patterns would be a reasonable measure of students' and parents' acceptance of a specific program.

Over the first four years of the Phoenix/Calvert program, the Phoenix/Calvert students had lower absence rates than Phoenix-Pre-Calvert students. The differences varied each year, but were always enough to average at least one day per year, and one year averaged nearly five days. The overall average was over two days additional attendance per year.

School holding power

If parents perceive a school to be providing unusually valuable service, the parents might be expected to go to unusual lengths to be sure that their children continue to receive the services of that school. Research on a large, urban district has indicated that multiple moves are a solid predictor of lower student achievements (Kerbow, 1996). Among the 111 students in the two Phoenix cohorts immediately preceding the Phoenix/Calvert project (e.g., students in first and second grades in the spring of 1990), 34 students (30 per cent) were still attending Phoenix after four years of program implementation. By contrast, among the original 108 students in the first two Phoenix/Calvert cohorts (e.g., students in first grade during the 1990–1991, and 1991–1992 school years), 50 (46 per cent) were still attending Phoenix after four years. Apparently the Phoenix/Calvert parents were less willing than their Phoenix-Pre-Calvert neighbors to leave the school catchment area; or if they had to leave, they were more willing than their neighbors to make the sacrifices necessary to sustain their students in the Phoenix/Calvert program.

Disciplinary removals

The local district defines a "disciplinary removal" (DR) as occurring when a student is sent home from school from one to several days for reasons related to utterly unacceptable deportment within the school. Phoenix's principal had never been an advocate of keeping students out of school for other than the most severe problems, so the school had not had a history of high rates of DRs. During the last year before the Phoenix/Calvert began, the principal reported a total of nine DRs in grades K–4. In the four subsequent years, there were zero DRs for students enrolled in the Phoenix/Calvert program.

Implementation at Phoenix: 1994–1997

The word of Phoenix's remarkable ascent spread rapidly. The school was featured in local media, and then went national. Phoenix was featured on two national evening news programs and was described in diverse popular magazines and professional journals. The school received visits from the mayor, the state superintendent of schools, the governor, and visitors from dozens of states. Visitors came from as far away as Japan, Australia, Great Britain and Norway. For a small, inner-city school which only four years earlier had been regarded as achieving at well below their district averages, these were heady times. But in year five, things began to unravel. The unraveling was not the result of deliberately destructive action; indeed, much of it was the result of efforts to spread the positive effects seen in Phoenix's students.

Both the CSOS evaluation team and the Calvert Head Master had been deliberately cautious in interpreting early, very positive data from the Phoenix effort. The first- and second-year evaluation reports had documented substantial gains, but, by agreement among all concerned, were not released to the public. The third- and fourth-year reports indicated, if anything, more positive results. They were released, and their good news was picked up by the district's superintendent, mayor, and several local politicians. Press events were staged at Phoenix and were covered by newspapers and television media. Phoenix School, and especially Phoenix's principal, became media stars.

The Abell Foundation's interest in Phoenix had always been as a pilot study for later dissemination. After four years of careful success, the president of Abell was anxious to begin scaling up delivery of the Calvert program to the city at large. By contrast, the board of the Calvert school was sure that it didn't want staff members being distracted from the school's core mission of educating the students at Calvert. In a compromise agreement, the Abell Foundation funded continued work at Phoenix and the initiation of the Calvert program in a second school in another high-poverty area of the city.

The Phoenix/Calvert coordinator had been a 1st grade teacher at Calvert, and was feeling increasingly in danger of being out of her range as she worked with ever higher grades at Phoenix. Her rate of disagreements with Phoenix's principal had increased over the previous year, and she was eager to move.

The task of replacing the original Calvert/Phoenix facilitator posed several challenges. No teacher from Calvert volunteered, nor was the Calvert board anxious to enter into a plan that repeatedly removed highly experienced teachers from their school. A logical alternative was to draw a teacher from the ranks of Phoenix's teaching force. Eventually, the Phoenix principal, Calvert Head Master, and Abell Foundation representative settled on hiring a Phoenix second grade teacher for the coordinator position. The person chosen was well respected and had been a particularly able teacher within the Phoenix/Calvert system. However, she was less detail oriented than her predecessor. She lacked the knowledge of the specifics of the program that came with 18 years of teaching at Calvert, she lacked the natural authority of a person coming from the source of the change, and she had more grades and classes to cover (twelve classes in grades K–5 versus the initial four in K–1 and that increased to ten in K–4 for the previous coordinator). Perhaps more importantly, because Abell wished for the program to move toward self-sufficiency, the new coordinator remained an employee of the district and reported directly to the Phoenix principal.

In years one through four, when the Calvert coordinator had a disagreement with a Phoenix teacher as to the level of Calvert implementation that the leadership team deemed adequate, differences were resolved by involving a full team of Phoenix, Calvert, and Abell administrators. The effect of this scheme was a continuous push for full implementation. On more than one occasion this push had caused some contention among more senior members of the Phoenix faculty, who were not fully convinced their old methods should be abandoned.

Beginning in the fall of year five, the effect of having the facilitator report to the Phoenix principal was that the long-term Phoenix teachers could sidestep the Calvert processes by going directly to the Phoenix principal. The immediate and enduring effect was to make change, or even sustenance of previous change, optional. Several teachers whose students would have most benefited from the changes were the teachers who most successfully resisted the changes or most rapidly returned to their former, invariably less strenuous and rigorous, methods.

At the end of year five, the Abell Foundation representative and the Calvert Head Master were unhappy with the level of implementation they saw at Phoenix. Having experienced a year of non-success with confrontation at Phoenix, they sought a less direct method for returning to the previous level of implementation. With the principal from Phoenix, they argued that a single coordinator could not adequately support the implementation in grades K–6. Consequently, the person who had facilitated work at the entire school the previous year became the 5th–6th grade coordinator (with the expectation that she would eventually facilitate 5th–8th grades) and a new coordinator was hired to maintain K–4 implementation. The new primary grades coordinator was one of Phoenix's first grade teachers, and also reported directly to the Phoenix principal.

During year six, the 5th–6th grade coordinator had repeatedly experienced significant, unresolved differences of opinion with the Phoenix principal and more than one member of the Phoenix faculty on issues related to the Calvert implementation. By the middle of year six, those differences became so great that she chose to resign from Phoenix School. She subsequently became a program facilitator for a different reform in the city, and was replaced by a fourth grade Phoenix teacher, who was a graduate of Calvert.

Throughout year five, the Phoenix principal had increasingly frequent disagreements with the Calvert Head Master. Issues of hiring practices, teacher assignments, and fidelity of implementation went unresolved for months. During the summer between years five and six, the Phoenix principal and the Calvert Head Master each independently sought mediation. Coincidentally, they sought the same person's help. However, mediation efforts failed, with the Phoenix principal questioning the intentions and factual accuracy of statements made by both the Calvert Head Master and the mediator.[9]

At the recommendation of the Head Master, the board of directors of Calvert School decided that continuing Calvert's formal connection to Phoenix was no longer in their best interest and, in the winter of 1996, midway through year six of the implementation, officially ended the two schools' formal relationship. The Calvert board allowed Phoenix to continue using the Calvert materials, and formally wished Phoenix well; but clearly the board was no longer regarding the Phoenix partnership as successful.

By the end of year six (spring of 1996), the new K–4 facilitator had similarly reached the opinion that her professional interests would be better served elsewhere. She, too, left Phoenix School. During year seven (1996–1997), she was replaced by Phoenix's long-term, system-funded master teacher. Over the previous six years, very few people at Calvert, Abell, CSOS, or among the faculty of Phoenix had regarded this master teacher as even mildly enthusiastic about the Calvert program. Title aside, her appointment by the principal, without consultation with the Abell Foundation or Calvert, could hardly have been viewed as an effort to strengthen the Phoenix/Calvert program.

Having experienced one Abell-paid, Calvert-oriented coordinator for the initial four years, Phoenix experienced four district-paid facilitators in the subsequent two years, and the level of detailed knowledge of the various Calvert facilitators at

Phoenix was clearly less than it had been the first four years. Formal contact with and knowledge gain from Calvert had ceased.

The pace of instruction at Phoenix had fallen further and further behind. In years one through four, Phoenix's primary grades' classes had carefully kept pace with the Calvert lessons, so that an observer could move back and forth between the schools and see exactly the same lessons on the same days. By the winter of year seven, most primary classes at Phoenix were nearly a month behind their same-age sister-classes at Calvert.

Several classroom teachers were clearly paying less attention to students' monthly folders. When this fact, documented by several observers, was pointed out to the Phoenix principal and School Improvement Team, they denied the validity of the observations.

Compromises were made regarding student corrections of errors and the use of the first half hour of the day as a correction period became optional at Phoenix. The task of correcting folders gradually shifted from Phoenix's regular classroom teachers to the coordinators.

Another unfortunate consequence of the loss of the Phoenix-Calvert partnership was the discontinuation of regular meetings among the Phoenix principal, the Calvert Head Master, and the Abell representative. Those meetings had been valuable sources of planning and direction for the entire project, and the wealth of perspectives and resources represented at those meetings has not been, and probably could not be, replaced.

Implementation contrasts between years 1–4 and 5–6 are illuminating.

(i) *Pre-implementation*: by definition, was unchanged.

(ii) *An achievable plan*: Years one through four proceeded through a careful consideration of short- and long-term implications of actions and a broad planning framework, but years five and six simply happened. Almost all significant decisions were either delayed for months or made in a seemingly whimsical fashion without consulting all parties. Attempts to engage the full team of Calvert, Abell, and Phoenix administrators failed repeatedly, and by the end of year five, efforts to meet were discontinued. Whereas much of the first four years' implementation was built on having a stable program coordinator, the following two years saw a 200 per cent turnover in those positions.

(iii) *Financial support*: The Abell Foundation continued to provide fiscal support, at approximately the same level through years five and six. The foundation continued to support summer training, the purchasing of Calvert materials, and some personnel costs.

(iv) *Non-fiscal support*: The definition of what constituted support changed dramatically during years five and six. School changes that had been viewed as demanding but necessary during years one through four at Phoenix came to be described as intrusive and an overstepping of professional boundaries. The Phoenix principal accused both the Abell representative and the Calvert Head Master of trying to run her school. Several actions viewed as necessary technical and organizational changes by Abell and Calvert were described as political power struggles by the Phoenix principal and SIT. Ms. Sparks, Phoenix's talented and determined principal, appeared to make a calculated decision that Calvert simply could not afford to do without Phoenix, and told several groups that Calvert would not end the relationship, regardless of what transpired. Her school's remarkable rise to fame seemed to underscore her belief that Phoenix could handle its relationship with Calvert as it pleased, with no impact on student outcomes. The instability of the facilitator position(s), and the replacement of a long-term Calvert teacher with a series of increasingly compromised Phoenix teachers decreased the level of specific, detailed understanding of the Calvert program at Phoenix. The rate of change to Calvert-like instruction slowed, and in some classrooms there was more movement backward than forward.

The community was supportive of Phoenix School before the Calvert experiment, throughout years one through four, and today.

(v) *Curriculum*: In years one through four, the core elements were put in place and relentlessly guarded. In years five and six, students were asked to make fewer corrections on their work, folders regularly went home late, and the pace of instruction at Phoenix fell substantially behind the Calvert pace.

(vi) *Regular classroom instruction*: Through the first four years of implementation, the Calvert program reached the Phoenix students. Virtually all of the K–4 teachers made significant, often dramatic changes in their teaching to provide Calvert-like instruction. Years five and six saw very uneven implementation in grades five and six, and less uniform implementation of the Calvert curriculum in grades one through four.

(vii) *Summary*: The clarity and detail of the curricular and instructional program, the timeliness of materials delivery, the support of the Abell Foundation, the Calvert School, and the community, and the leadership provided by the on-site coordinators and the Phoenix principal had resulted in a strong implementation in years one through four. In years five and six, implementation suffered because of a lack of directional unity among Phoenix and Calvert administrators and the challenges faced by four new coordinators. However, in some regular classrooms, implementation of the Calvert program remained solid, even in years five and six.

Results: 1995–1996

Presentation of results will parallel those for the years 1990–1994.

Norm-referenced testing

In the Spring of 1994, Phoenix School's first-through-fourth grade *ERB* scores were typically well above national averages. Two years later (in the spring of 1996), the story had changed. The extent of the change depended on the specific sub-test, but the general direction was downward. On the *ERB Reading* test, the fourth grade mean was at the 44th percentile, and the 5th grade was at the 46th. These scores represented substantial, longitudinal declines among the same students.[10] The lead Phoenix/Calvert cohort completed sixth grade in the spring of 1996, and this group's mean *ERB Reading* score remained slightly above the national average, at the 53rd percentile. The pattern is one of moderate declines over two years.

The *Writing Mechanics* tests in grades four, five and six indicate very substantial drops in writing achievement. Troublingly, the same students' mean score change from two years earlier (for students in fourth through sixth grades in 1996) in *ERB Writing Mechanics* was a very substantial 15.9 NCEs. Equally disturbing, where two years earlier the lead Phoenix/Calvert cohort had scored more than 20 NCEs above the last pre-Calvert cohort, the Phoenix/Calvert group's 1996 mean was essentially identical to that of the pre-Calvert cohort. In writing, a hallmark of the Calvert program, the two year declines had been remarkable. Mathematics told a similar story.

In the two school years between the 1994 and 1996 administrations of the *SPAP*, Phoenix School had invested substantial amounts of time in "teaching to the test". In spite of this effort, third grade 1996 *SPAP* scores were, on average, essentially unchanged from 1994. The first two Calvert/Phoenix cohorts to take the fifth grade *SPAP* test scored at essentially the same levels as had the last two pre-Calvert groups (1993 and 1994).

Attendance levels among Phoenix/Calvert students were down slightly from 1994 (93.7 per cent) in 1995 (92.8 per cent) and 1996 (93.0 per cent). It remained the case that a greater percentage of Phoenix/Calvert students were remaining in the school long term, than were pre-Calvert students (53 per cent vs. 33 per cent).

Discussion

Phoenix School has spent the last seven years in a remarkable school restructuring project. The faculty and administration voted overwhelmingly to import a whole new curriculum, an attached new instructional-delivery system, and a new organization/school culture. For the first four years, Phoenix was remarkably successful at making the transformation, and student achievements rose impressively. In years five through seven, use of the imported curriculum continued, though level of implementation declined significantly, and the school's organizational system/school culture largely reverted to Phoenix's "old ways". Attendance and reading scores dropped slightly, with writing and math scores on a norm referenced test falling dramatically.

What sense is one to make of this roller-coaster ride? A few reflections follow:

(i) *Inner-city students are capable of achieving.* The problem of low achievement among high-poverty, inner-city children is not the children themselves. As was the case in the *Special Strategies Studies* (Stringfield et. al., 1997), Phoenix Schools' first four years of reform provided compelling evidence that the children can perform at and above current national average levels.

(ii) *A more structured, more content-oriented curriculum is almost certainly necessary, but clearly not sufficient.* Almost no one at Phoenix ever suggests going back to the district's regular curriculum. However, as years five and six demonstrate, a better curriculum without high standards of instructional and organizational conduct is not enough. Senge's (1990) *The Fifth Discipline* is the cornerstone text on "organizational learning and organizational processes". It begins with an example of technological advances in air travel. Phoenix implemented a "technologically superior" curricular and instructional package. The superior technology yielded valuable results only when the school also incorporated a complex set of organizational processes. When the human processes began reverting to old ways, student achievements began to slip. This is not to argue for the primacy of culture or climate over an educational "technology", or the reverse. Rather, Phoenix/Calvert demonstrates the need for a better curricular and instructional program (a "technology") *and* a more open, learning-oriented climate.

(iii) *"Change is resource hungry".* This Fullan and Miles (1992) quote was acted out at Phoenix. The school received extensive, seven-year fiscal support from a private foundation, and could not have implemented Calvert with any less money. Even more important than money had been the support from staff of the Abell foundation and from Calvert School. Ironically, the fiscal supports have remained, yet it is *the highly-skilled human supports/resources that appear to have been sorely missed* during the last three years at Phoenix.

(iv) *Implementation is hard; institutionalization is harder.* Many people at Phoenix thought that after four years, they knew the Calvert program, and could continue without Calvert support. Yet four years of hard work had not prepared their faculty and administration to continue the program without ongoing support and collaboration. The road to institutionalized school reform is very long.

(v) *The solution is not simple, and teamwork is essential.* The Calvert effort involved importing a highly-articulated curriculum, two weeks of summer staff development for each staff member, ongoing, in-class modeling of lessons, opportunities to practice, feedback, regular checks on student performance, and four years of effort from a sophisticated, diverse team of problem-solving people. Teachers came to believe that all children can learn. They believed not because they were taught it in a workshop, but because they *saw* all their children learning. Teachers came to believe that civility in the halls among these inner-city students was possible, not because someone from outside declared it, but because they *saw* civility coming down the hall, one grade per year. The technology of Calvert, plus professional development, created an environment in which the school climate improved dramatically.

(vi) *The most intellectually interesting aspect of Phoenix's years five through seven has been that, in a formal sense, the Calvert "technology" remains in place.* New teachers have been trained each summer, and there are full-time facilitators. The Calvert curriculum remains in place, and is being followed, albeit at a slower pace. What has decayed at Phoenix is the culture or climate. The belief that every hour of every day is precious has evaporated. The belief in, and even interest in, the teachability of every student in every content area has diminished. The very substantial effort required to insist that students update and correct their folder work has slowly but surely been replaced by a much less labor intensive effort to have classroom aides and facilitators make final corrections in students' folders so that the folders are impressive for visitors. *The decay in the underlying school climate and culture has resulted in a degrading of the clearly superior technology.* In Appendix 10.1 a climate instrument is provided that would have accurately differentiated Calvert, and Phoenix during its first four years of Calvert implementation, from Phoenix today.

(vii) *"It ain't over 'till it's over".* The Yogi Berra quote is as true in school reform as in baseball. During the 1996–1997, a group of Phoenix teachers have banded together in an effort to reinvigorate the Calvert process. They have seen what is possible, and they are disturbed by their current directions. They have a much more substantial base of teacher and student skills to build from than Phoenix had seven years ago. The principal has seen her school through a remarkable rise and fall and wants to rise further. She may lead that effort or she may retire next year. The entire group of teachers may band together. The Phoenix experiment could rise from it's ashes, couldn't it?

Appendix 10.1: The Phoenix Academic Climate Differential

After detailed observation in diverse classrooms, careful examination of students' work, and interviews with teachers and administrators, complete the following:

GOALS: (Response to item 1): __________

1. The curriculum and accompanying instructional delivery in classrooms is academically challenging for all students:

1	2	3	4	5	6	7	8	9
Not at all demanding				Typical				Clearly demanding for all

GOAL CONGRUITY: (Sum of responses to items 2–4): ________

2. Working as a team, the school's administration is fully aware of the specific goals of the curriculum:

1	2	3	4	5	6	7	8	9
None are versed In Specifics				Some are moderately aware				All are well versed in the Specifics of their curriculum

3. The goals of the curriculum are congruent with the observed goals of the administrative team:

1	2	3	4	5	6	7	8	9
No Alignment				Moderate				Clearly Aligned

4. The goals of the curriculum are clearly congruent with the observed goals of the teachers:

1	2	3	4	5	6	7	8	9
No Alignment				Moderate				Clearly Aligned

BELIEF IN CURRENT CURRICULUM AND INSTRUCTIONAL PROGRAM:
(Sum of responses to items 5–7): ________

5. The observed extent to which the administration, considered as a team, believes that the current curricular and instructional offerings can offer "state of the art" academic challenges to all students:

1	2	3	4	5	6	7	8	9
Zero				Moderate				Total

6. The observed extent to which the faculty, considered as a team, believes that the current curricular and instructional offerings can provide "state of the art" academic challenges to all students:

1	2	3	4	5	6	7	8	9
Zero				Moderate				Total

7. The extent to which the faculty members see the school administration's actions as supportive of very high levels of student achievement:

1	2	3	4	5	6	7	8	9
Not at all				Moderate				Total

ADULT-ADULT CLIMATE: (Sum of items 8–11): __________

8. Extent to which the administration, considered as a team, knows all teachers, their curricular and instructional strengths and limitations, values their contributions, and works to provide faculty with the activities and tools necessary to improve their skills:

1	2	3	4	5	6	7	8	9
Zero				Moderate				Very extensive

9. The extent to which teachers perceive that the administration is aware of their strengths, limitations, and day-to-day needs, and is working to address them:

1	2	3	4	5	6	7	8	9
Zero				Moderate				Very extensive

10. The extent to which faculty and administration engage parents and other child caretakers in the academic lives of the students:

1	2	3	4	5	6	7	8	9
Zero				Moderate				Very extensive

11. The extent to which parents and other child-caretakers perceive that the faculty and administration involve them and other parents in the academic lives of their children:

1	2	3	4	5	6	7	8	9
Zero				Moderate				Very extensive

ADDRESSING STUDENTS' PROBLEMS: (Sum of items 12 and 13): ___________

12. When a student or group of students makes the same academic mistake more than once, the assumption on the part of the teacher(s), administration, and school-home partnership is that this is a shared problem that can, must, and will be solved, involving as many human resources as necessary. There is virtually no student-academic problem that can not, must not, and finally will not be solved by this team. The school's academic climate is one of shared problem-solving, not blaming or defeatism:

1	2	3	4	5	6	7	8	9
Rarely to never in evidence				Sometimes in evidence				Clearly, strongly

13. When a student or group of students create a social problem in a classroom or the school, the assumption on the part of the teacher(s), administration, and school-home partnership is that this is a shared problem that can, must, and will be worked out, involving as many human resources as necessary. There is virtually no student-social problem that can not, must not, and finally will not be solved by this team. The school's social climate is one of shared problem-solving, not blaming or defeatism:

1	2	3	4	5	6	7	8	9
Rarely to never in evidence				Sometimes in evidence				Clearly, strongly

Notes

1 Preparation of this chapter was supported by grants from the Abell Foundation of Baltimore, Maryland, and by a grant from the Office of Educational Research and Improvement, US Department of Education, to the Center for Research on the Education of Students Places at Risk at Johns Hopkins and Howard Universities (Grant No. $117D-40005). However, any opinions expressed by the author is his own, and do not represent the policies or positions of the funding groups or agencies.

2 A pseudonym. In addition, a few non-critical details regarding the school have been changed, in an effort to ensure the school's anonymity.

3 Since 1994, the name of Chapter 1 federal compensatory education funding has been changed to Title 1.
4 Pseudonym.
5 More recently, the service has been used my missionaries, entertainers, athletes, and US families opting for home schooling.
6 All mean scores presented in this chapter were computed using scale scores which, after computations, were converted to percentiles for ease of reading and interpretation.
7 The 2nd cohort of Phoenix/Calvert students were in third grade at the end of the project's fourth year, and their mean *ERB Reading* score was at the 68th percentile.
8 As with the school name, this is a pseudonym, chosen to help preserve the anonymity of the school.
9 It remains the opinion of the author that both the Head Master and the would-be mediator acted in good faith.
10 As in 4th year analyses, all *ERB* analyses are restricted to students who had participated at the school throughout.

References

BERMAN, P. and MCLAUGHLIN, M. (1977) 'Federal programs supporting educational change. Vol. VII, Factors affecting implementation and continuation', Santa Monica, CA: Rand.

CRANDALL, D. et al. (1983) *People, Policies and Practices: Examining the Chain of School Improvement*, Andover, MA: The Network, Inc.

CTB/MACMILLAN/MCGRAW HILL (1989) *The Comprehensive Test of Basic Skills*, Monterey, CA: CTB/Macmillan/McGraw-Hill.

EDUCATIONAL TESTING SERVICE (1994) *Comprehensive Testing Program III*, Princeton: Educational Testing Service.

FULLAN, M. and MILES, M. (1992) 'Getting reform right: What works and what doesn't', *Phi Delta Kappan*, **73**, 10, pp. 744–752.

HIRSCH, E.D., JR. (1996) *The Schools We Need*, New York: Doubleday.

KENNEDY, M. (1978) 'Findings from the follow through planned variation study', *Educational Researcher*, **7**, 6, pp. 3–11.

KERBOW, D. (1996) 'Patterns of urban student mobility and local school reform', *Journal of Education for Students Placed at Risk*, **1**, 2, pp. 149–72.

ROSS, S., HENRY, D., PHILLIPSEN, L., EVANS, K., SMITH, L. and BUGGE, T. (1997) 'Matching restructuring programs to schools: Selection, negotiation, and preparation', *School Effectiveness and School Improvement*, **8**, 1, pp. 45–71.

SENGE, P.M. (1990) *The Fifth Discipline*, New York: Doubleday.

STRINGFIELD, S., DATNOW, A. and ROSS, S. (1998) 'Scaling up school restructuring in multicultural, multilingual contexts: Early observations from Sunland County', Santa Cruz, CA: Technical Report no. 2, Center for Research on Education, Diversity and Excellence, UCSC.

STRINGFIELD, S., MILLSAP, M., HERMAN, R., YODER, N., BRIGHAM, N., NESSELRODT, P., SCHAFFER, E., KARWEIT, N., LEVIN, M. and STEVENS, R. (1997) *Special Strategies Studies Final Report*, Washington, DC: US Department of Education.

TALLMADGE, G.K. and WOOD, C.T. (1981) *User's Guide to the ESEA Title I Evaluation and Reporting System*, Mountain View, CA: RMC Research Corporation.

Chapter 11

Three Creative Ways to Measure School Climate and Next Steps

H. Jerome Freiberg

Introduction[1]

You have read throughout the book multiple ways to measure climate in schools. This final chapter will explore three additional climate measures that have proven to be very useful in responding to student concerns as pupils make the transitions from one level of schooling to the next and the impact ambient noise has on behavior and learning. Additionally, as the concluding chapter of *School Climate: Measuring, Improving and Sustaining Healthy Learning Environments*, a "Next Steps" will be presented to assist in establishing a framework for implementing the ideas and instruments presented in the book.

School climate is an ever changing factor in the lives of the people who work and learn in schools. Much like the air we breathe, school climate is ignored until it becomes foul. It can become a positive influence on the health of the learning environment or a significant barrier to learning. Included in this chapter are three, seldom used climate measures: (i) Leading Concerns of Elementary Age Students Entering Middle School and Middle School Students Entering High School; (ii) Entrance and Exit Interviews of Students attending and graduating High School; and (iii) Ambient Noise and Its Effect on Student Behavior in Hallways and the Cafeteria.

This book has shown the elements that make up the climate of school are highly complex, ranging from the quality of interactions in the teachers' lounge to the noise levels in hallways, and cafeterias, from the physical structure of the building to the physical comfort levels (heating, cooling and lighting) of the individuals, to how safe students and teachers feel in their school and surroundings. Community perceptions about the school and even the size of the school and the opportunities for students and teachers to interact with each other in small groups both formally and informally adds to the health of the learning environment. The support staff from cafeteria workers, to bus drivers, to custodians, to office staff, add layers to multiple climate dimensions. Any one factor will not in itself determine a school's climate and its influence on the learning of students, however, it is the interaction of school and classroom climate factors that create a fabric of support that enable members of the school community to teach and learn at their optimum levels. While climate is mostly an affective or feeling element of learning it has clear implications for achievement and academic well being.

The Need for Feedback

The quality of teaching and learning is a reflection of many complex factors but without continuous and varied sources of feedback, improvement efforts are eroded by a lack of history of accomplishments and a sense of direction. In practice, few climate measures tap students as a source of feedback. However, by third grade, most students could tell you if they like or hate school, which teachers are caring and if they are learning. Most third graders have spent more than 5,000 hours in classrooms (Pre–K through 3rd grade). They represent a critical basis upon which to measure the health of a school and the effects of school reform efforts. In addition to other more traditional voices in the school (teachers, and administrators) students can give an unique perspective. Feedback about individual and organizational health of a school learning community is a necessary component for school reform and improvement efforts.

The movement toward small unit organization of large schools and other reform efforts are hindered by a lack of knowledge about school and classroom-based efforts and the perceptions of others who are key partners in the learning environment (students, parents, and community). As a result, the enterprise of educators to improve or sustain education may become lost in a sea of activity. Measuring the influence of change-directed actions on the climate in which teaching and learning occurs, should be a key component in improving and sustaining educational excellence.

The Impact of Changing School Levels

Change from one school level to the next can be an unnecessarily frightening experience for many youngsters. Perceptions have a direct effect on the climate of the school. In a series of questions that were developed for students in West Virginia, and since replicated with thousands of students in several states and other countries, elementary (grades 5 or 6) and middle school students (grade 8) were asked to identify their greatest concerns in moving from their current school to the next level. Table 11.1 shows the survey questions and Table 11.2 reports the results of findings from school districts in Houston, Texas, Chicago, Illinois and Norfolk, Virginia. A total of 338 5th and 6th grade and 324 8th grade students are reflected in these results. The concerns are very similar for both groups of students. The findings were presented to teachers and administrators during summer staff development workshops. Actions plans were developed based on the data. For example, instead of asking students to present before the entire class (concern number 4 on the survey) the first day of school, students introduced themselves to each other in small 2–3 member groups. As students felt comfortable, they presented before the

Table 11.1 What students worry about
On an answer sheet, fill in the circle that represents the extent to which you agree with each of the following statements.

Not worried about this 1	**Hardly worried about this** 2	**Worried about this** 3	**Very worried about this** 4

1. Being different from others	16. Getting to class on time
2. Drugs	17. Keeping up with assignments
3. Failure	18. Making friends
4. Giving a presentation in front of others	19. Not having an adult who listens
5. Being picked on	20. Moving from classroom to classroom
6. Being made fun of	21. Length of class periods
7. Being sent to the principal	22. Not knowing what is expected
8. Getting lost	23. New rules and routines
9. Hard class work	24. Textbooks
10. Getting along with other students	25. New teachers
11. Homework assignments	26. Size of the building
12. Unkind people	27. Taking tests
13. Lockers	28. Club activities
14. Getting on the wrong bus	29. Opportunities for after-school activity
15. Lunchroom	30. Physical education program

*Table 11.2 Top-ranked concerns of students surveyed in Chicago, Houston, and Norfolk**

Students Entering Middle School N = *338*	Worried/ Very worried	*Students Entering High School* N = *324*	Worried/ Very worried
1. Being sent to the principal	51.77%	1. Failure	51.22%
2. Failure	50.19%	2. Keeping up with assignments	50.00%
3. Drugs	43.53%	2. Taking tests	50.00%
3. Taking tests	43.53%	3. Giving a presentation in front of others	43.90%
4. Giving a presentation in front of others	39.06%	4. Hard class work	42.68%

* Rankings were determined by the percentages of students who responded with worried or very worried to the items on the Student Concerns Survey.

entire class or groups of four to six members. Follow-up discussions indicate that both students and teachers thought the strategy was very effective in alleviating this concern. Strategies were also developed for the other student concerns. Creative interest area name tags were used so students could walk around and identify common interests with their peers. Many teacher concerns were also addressed in the process. The administrative team spent time in each homeroom classroom talking about the support that was available to each student (survey rankings concerns numbers 1, 2 and 3) as well as school-wide expectations. In one school, the administrators showed students their high school year book pictures to give a human side to the administrator. Several principals taught at least one class a week to keep in touch with the realities of classroom instruction. Teachers worked on study and test-taking skills during homeroom and content area classes (survey rankings concerns numbers 2, 3 and 1). Planner assignment/project books were given to each student to support better time-management skills with the goal of reducing the failure rates through better organization and greater responsibility for and awareness of assignments. In one high school and middle school, students made assignments books using computers (concerns numbers 2, 1 and 5). Tutoring sessions were also started after school by the honor society students and teachers. Students could gain extra credit for attending the sessions.

The advantages to this feedback process are enormous. We invest huge amounts of effort and money in the teachers, the textbooks, the equipment, and furnishings for our schools. Feedback would begin to let us know the extent to which this learning environment and its curricular content is being received and integrated into the life of the student. It would also bring the students into seeing themselves as citizens rather than tourists in their schools. (See Freiberg, *Educational Leadership* September, 1996). Students realize that they have an opportunity to participate in shaping the educational process. The cost would be very small in relation to the valuable information obtained (Rogers and Freiberg, 1994).

Entrance and Exit Interviews

Combined with the student concerns survey, video tapes of focus groups of students selected randomly were conducted from entering students and those graduating. The principal of an inner-city high school in Chicago held focus group interviews at the end of the school year. She was interested in determining student views on the level of support they received from teachers and administrators. The students indicated they felt less teacher support in helping them when they were having difficulty in a subject. A school climate survey conducted during the same time period with approximately 600 students from 9th–12th grades found a statistically significant decline in student perceptions of teacher support from the same climate survey given the previous school year. The information was presented to the faculty and administration during their August before-school staff development workshop. They created several action plans to improve their academic support for students at the school.

Some high schools also video taped students who had dropped out of school. The video process brings a human face to the numbers. The tapes are played during summer or before-school inservices for the faculty. In many instances teachers were amazed at the "thank you's", the student stories about a teacher or group of teachers who made the difference in their lives and the tears that flowed from their eyes. Some students made concrete suggestions about course schedules, homework and social events in the schools. The teachers asked for the video tapes each year.

The graduating students were asked four questions:

(i) What do you like about your school?
(ii) What was your most memorable experience in high school?
(iii) What area would you like to have improved in your school?
(iv) What is one message you would like to give your teachers?

The entering students from middle school were asked the following questions:

(i) What do you like about your current school?
(ii) What is one concern you have about going to high school?
(iii) What is something you will do to improve your success in high school?
(iv) What is one message you would like to give your teachers?

The middle school students liked the smallness of their schools and were concerned about getting lost and the size of the high schools. They wanted their teachers to "be friendly rather than mean". One student said, "I had problems in middle school but I want a chance to start over". The teachers of freshman classes developed a series of strategies that focused on students getting to know each other and themselves the first days and weeks of school.

Student feedback should be a cornerstone of school improvement efforts. The opportunities given students to reflect on their learning experiences and the need for all school participants to make changes based on needs of the learner will only enhance teaching and learning opportunities. There are some elements of climate that are more overt than others. The level of noise in common areas of the school — hallways, and particularly the cafeteria can have an unsettling effect on pupils and create levels of stress that influence student behavior in subtle but important ways.

The Cafeteria from Hell

The climate of a school can be set by what happens in the common areas, (e.g., playground, hallways and the infamous cafeteria). Every teacher and student has a story about their cafeteria. As one middle school teacher told me during a meeting on school climate, "Our cafeteria is from hell". In an elementary school with five hundred students in pre-kindergarten through sixth grade, the teachers said that student behavior and discipline had improved in the classroom but every morning after breakfast there were five fights outside the cafeteria. This was a cafeteria I had to visit. The teachers had requested more controlling discipline strategies to stop the fights.

The cafeteria was like many I have seen over the years. It had a combination folding tables and chairs, seated about 300 students and had an entry area where students received their breakfast card from an aid. They proceeded to the serving area and then found a seat after some jostling. The four-year olds and twelve-year olds came for breakfast continuously from 7:00 until 7:30 a.m. A majority of the students were eligible (based on family income levels) for free or reduced breakfast and lunch. What struck me immediately was the noise levels — they were excruciatingly high. The machines in the cafeteria were all running, an aid was on the Public Address (PA) system telling Billy or Sarah to "find a seat and sit down". The cafeteria workers seemed to be playing the *1812 Overture* with the stainless steel pots and pans. Students were emptying their trays by banging them inside a metal trash can. Adults were shouting across the room for specific students to be quiet. Students were scrambling to find seats with their friends and few adults acted as if they were glad the students came. The students talked over this din and, after 30 minutes in the cafeteria, I was ready to fight.

Students react to noise in different ways and some students respond to high noise levels by becoming aggressive. At times student behavior is a healthy response to an unhealthy situation. What also struck me was the lack of positive eye contact between adults and children. The tone of the aids and other cafeteria workers was less than positive. I observed no smiles, even a good morning or a friendly face. When I said "good morning" to an older child he looked at me as if I had called him a bad name.

I met with the faculty that afternoon and provided them with an "Ambient Noise Checklist" (see Table 11.3). I explained the relationship between noise levels and stress. I did not have empirical evidence from the school but it was my observation that many students become aggressive with elevated stress levels from the noise (Freiberg, 1999). Also, the general lack of caring contact with adults had to

Table 11.3 Cafeteria ambient noise checklist

If you hear . . .

- Announcements/public address system
- Adults talking to students across the room
- Banging of trays/clattering of silverware
- Machine noise
- Banging of pots and pans in the kitchen

Then . . .

- Do not use public address system.
- Provide lessons in table manners.
- Organize lunch time (assign tables, limit time, appoint cafeteria managers).
- Create rules with the students.
- Play calm, relaxing music.
- Model the behavior you expect from students.
- Eat lunch with the students once or twice a week.
- Expand the overall lunch times for the school and shorten the actual lunch time of the students. This will allow lines to move faster and students to find seating more easily.
- Make the teacher the cafeteria manager for his or her class for a week, or for however long it takes to establish a good climate. The teacher then trains six students as cafeteria managers.
- Appoint the principal or another authorized person to be always on duty in the cafeteria.
- Allow classes who behave well for a week to go on a picnic.

be contributing to the fights and other "discipline" problems. I asked the faculty, "Would you want to have breakfast in your cafeteria?" The response was laughter and a resounding "no!" "Then why" I asked, "would you want your students to eat under these conditions?" The faculty and administration used the Ambient Noise list and made a series of changes. The aids were provided training in relating positively to children. A teacher greeted the students at the front of the serving line. The cafeteria workers eliminated the banging of pots and pans. A sponge stick to clean the plates replaced the banging in the metal trash cans. Students were assigned regular tables each day and could talk with any student on either side or directly across from them. This eliminated the cross-table shouting matches. The PA system was placed in moth balls. Adults went to children and spoke directly to them. The results were dramatic. The cafeteria became a pleasant place to eat with the noise levels that of a restaurant rather than a raceway. The cafeteria workers were amazed at the peacefulness of their work environment. The Chief Cook explained, after 25 years at the school this was the most pleasant time she had experienced. And not surprisingly, within two weeks, the five fights that had occurred every day, stopped.

The Ambient Noise Checklist also proved effective in a high school in Chicago. Upon visiting the school I noticed the hallways were very noisy without any students. The school, which is in a high crime area has security staff — all with walkie talkies or as I called them "squawk boxes". In the classes I could here about the latest problem from these "squawk boxes". They were clearly an educational distraction, noisy and created a climate of anxiety. I shared this observation with the principal. To my pleasant surprise a return visit found quiet in the halls and no external distractions from the "squawk boxes". All the security people had communication head sets that allowed them to talk and listen without disrupting the learning environment.

Now, these three measures of climate may not be earth shattering in the scope of national standards and school reform efforts. I believe however, that lasting change comes from the little things in classrooms and schools. Ways to allow for feedback from students and teachers and other shareholders in the educational community requires an openness to change and an intellectual interest in improving the conditions for teaching and learning.

Next Steps

Change takes vision and "vision is the ability to see what is unseen, realize what has yet to be, and act upon one's beliefs in the face of uncertainty" (Rogers and Freiberg, 1994, p. 363). A starting point in the change process is to assess where you are now and where you hope to be in the future and measure the dissonance between the two points. To accomplish this, *10 Variables for Change* are provided in Table 11.4. Accompanying each variable are indicators that help define the variable. The variables and indicators for change are designed to guide you in planning the use of the climate measures presented throughout the book.

Table 11.4 10 variables for change

Variable 1 — Define the goals
It has been noted that change for change sake is futile. Said another way — change without direction is chaos.

Indicators: (i) Describe in writing the ideal situation given maximum change.
(ii) Describe the situation which exists at present.
(iii) Measure the dissonance between the two.

Variable 2 — The size of the unit to be changed
The resources needed to change a school system of 5,000 students is vastly different than those for 50,000 students. A pilot program with 50 students in one school may fail when the attempt is made to expand the program throughout the school or in other schools.

Indicators: (i) Number of administrators in the system.
(ii) Number of faculty in system.
(iii) Number of students in system.
(iv) Degree of compactness of system (physical distance between people, buildings or centers of operation).

Variable 3 — The degree of entrenchment of the unit to be changed
Systems which have been entrenched for long periods of time take greater resources to change. Once the change begins it increases at a rapid rate.

Indicators: (i) The time the system has operated under a non-change philosophy.
(ii) The number of people satisfied with present conditions.
(iii) The number of new or experimental programs operating in the system.
(iv) The ease or difficulty of developing a new program.
(v) The general support of new ideas.
(vi) The amount of paper work required before a new program can be implemented.

Variable 4 — Key people and basic support groups or "How to survive the politics"
A critical component to change is identifying the key people. Many people and groups are negative to change unless their support is solicited. The usual case is the key people in the system or interested groups are asked to react after the fact. This tends to create a defensive position.

Indicators: (i) Identify the budget decision-makers.
(ii) Identify the people who may object to change.
(iii) Identify the people who may support change. (e.g., students, colleagues, parents, legislators (yes — if they are well informed) union or professional organizations, colleges.)

Variable 5 — Credibility
This variable seems to have the greatest effect on the success or failure of lasting change. Too often people attempt to change a situation before they have gained credibility within the existing structure.

Indicators: (i) Number of times veteran staff members ask to work with you.
(ii) The number of helping questions asked of you each day.
(iii) Your relative position in social work groups in the cafeteria, etc.
(iv) Number of social interactions with colleagues.
(v) Important committees to which you are elected by your colleagues.

Variable 6 — Patience and sensitivity to basic needs of people
Change initially seems to threaten people's basic need for security. A change agent must be sensitive to those needs and basic concerns.

Indicators: (i) Those changes which are threatening to the self are more easily assimilated when external threats are at a minimum. Change should be more supportive than threatening.

Table 11.4 (Continued)

(ii) Change which requires a reorganization of the perception of oneself is threatening and tends to be resisted (Rogers, 1969).
(iii) Based on Maslow's Hierarchy of Human Needs — the security needs of an individual must be met before significant change can occur (Maslow, 1970).
(iv) People need different types of interaction related to tasks and relationships. Some people require high tasks and low relationship interactions while others may require low tasks and high relationships. (See other possible combinations from the chart below (Blanchard and Hersey, 1969)).

tR	tr
Tr	TR

T High Task
t Low Task
R High Relationship
r Low Relationship

Variable 7 — Knowledge of judo
Postman and Weingarten (1971) discuss in an era of rapid change, managing the change process in *The Soft Revolution*. They discuss ways an individual may use the weight of the institution against itself to create change.

Indicators: (i) Follow absurd rules and regulations to their fullest.
(ii) Don't desecrate in any way an important cultural symbol.
(iii) Don't be too symbol-minded yourself.

Variable 8 — Resistance phenomenon — Marshmallow effect and trickle up — Flood down
Coping with the resistance factors of change can be a tedious and frustrating process. The "Marshmallow effect" occurs when a memo is sent or a verbal suggestion is made and the system absorbs it without any feedback. After a few attempts, most people follow the routine and forget further suggestions. Once individuals succumb to the system, they are susceptible to the "Flood Down — Trickle Up" syndrome. Administrative requests and demands flood down along the chain of command while feedback from the ranks becomes highly structural and formalized.

Indicators: (i) Response time (or lag) to your written memos.
(ii) The number of your suggestions implemented by the system.
(iii) The amount of griping done by your colleagues about the system.

Variable 9 — Change readiness
The first attempt at a relatively conservative change may fail only to be followed by a successful radical change. The ability of a system to change may be directly related to the number of attempts.

Indicators: (i) Is there verbal support from the top or bottom of the system for change?
(ii) Is there an elected or moral mandate for change?
(iii) Do people around you agree with your stated position?

Variable 10 — Lasting change is a slow process
Change may be compared to a good wine. It needs time to ferment.

Indicators: (i) Do you have at least two-three years to allow the change to occur?
(ii) Do you have the overriding need to be identified as the change agent (change should outlasts its agents)?
(iii) Will the change be recognized by people in the system as a positive factor?

The *10 Variables for Change* model indicates that the key to maintaining and improving school climate would be to involve all members of educational community in both the planning and implementation process. The climate measures provided in this book should act as catalysts in either introducing, improving or sustaining healthy learning environments. The issues of credibility, size of the unit, change readiness and the lasting change effect need to be considered as you move from measuring the climate to making necessary changes to either improve or sustain the climate.

Determining the vehicles to improve school climate which could be used as the catalyst for change could range from a school retreat with all members invited to an on-site course on school climate provided by a local college, to a total school reform effort designed to bring all members of the school community together. The selection of a vehicle for changing or sustaining the school's climate should be derived from a shared vision and include those that rarely participate in schools decision-making process (e.g., students, cafeteria workers, parents, business and community leaders).

There are no marching bands or great honors for people who prevent problems, only the great satisfaction that something worth doing has been done. Making a positive difference in lives of others will sustain us all through the next millennium.

Conclusions

The conclusion of a book can be seen as an ending or as a beginning. I hope as you have turned these last pages, you can see yourself at the beginning of an expedition that will lead to a lifetime of exploration and sharing with others.

A journey is much like a river, beginning with individual droplets of water that link with each other, and feed into streams, that eventually become great rivers and oceans. Without these small droplets, the rivers would run dry and the oceans vanish. We are much like droplets of water, the paths taken both individually and collectively will influence others and change the future.

Educational change, like a river, will take time to reshape the landscape. Meaningful change seems to become less daunting when we look at one child, one classroom, and one school at a time. As with droplets of rain, it is the linking together than brings about a significant reshaping (excerpted from Rogers and Freiberg, 1994).

I trust your journey through the pages of this book, with its themes of measuring, improving and sustaining healthy learning environments, reflects a starting point. At its best, life is a changing process, never determined in advance. It is my hope you will join with others to form a river of change, the beneficiaries of which are those who want and need to learn in caring communities with caring people. This change should not be prescribed by others but rather designed by yourself. Not all journeys are trouble-free. There are times when we pass through the shadows to get into the light. The process alone makes us a bit wiser. Gaining wisdom however, comes not from time or age, but from living the challenges of life, learning from mistakes, and building on experiences. The disequilibrium created through new experiences, is in the truest sense, learning (excerpted from Rogers and Freiberg, 1994).

There are many ways to measure change in the climate of a school but without some sense of what was, it will be very difficult to conclude what is and what should be. Each measure in this chapter and this book becomes a tool for *measuring, improving and sustaining healthy learning environments*. Moving forward requires some sign posts along the way and measuring climate must be one of the beacons of educational reform. Knowledge is power and knowledge about the interactions between individuals and in groups within a learning environment, becomes the greatest power of all.

Note

1 The first section of this chapter is abstracted from Freiberg, H.J. (1998) 'Measuring, school climate: Let me count the ways', *Educational Leadership*. **56**, 1, pp. 22–6. © 1998 H. Jerome Freiberg.

References

Blanchard, K. and Hersey, P. (1969) *Management of Organizational Behavior: Utilizing Human Resources*, Englewood Cliffs, N.J.: Prentice Hall.

Freiberg, H.J. (1996) 'From tourists to citizens in the classroom', *Educational Leadership*, **51**, 1, pp. 32–7.

Freiberg, H.J. (1998) 'Measuring, school climate: Let me count the ways', *Educational Leadership*, **56**, 1, pp. 22–6.

Freiberg, H.J. (ed.) (1999) *Beyond Behaviorism: Changing the Classroom Management Paradigm*, Needham Heights: Allyn and Bacon.

Maslow, A. (1970) *Motivation and Personality*, 2nd edn., New York: Harper and Row.

Postman, N. and Weingarten, A. (1971) *The Soft Revolution*, New York: Dell Publishing Co.

Rogers, C.R. (1969) *Freedom to Learn*, Columbus, Ohio: Charles E. Merrill Publishing Co.

Rogers, C.R. and Freiberg, H.J. (1994) *Freedom to Learn*, 3rd edn., Columbus: Merrill.

Notes on Contributors

Miriam Ben-Peretz is Professor Emeritus in the Faculty of Education at the University of Haifa, former chair of the Department of Teacher Education and Dean of the Faculty of Education at the University of Haifa and the President of Tel-Hai College. At present head of the Center for Jewish Education in Israel and the Diaspora at the University of Haifa and chair of the Research Authority at MOFET Institute. Her main research interests are: curriculum theory and practice, teacher education and educational policy. She has published extensively in books, encyclopedias and journals including: *The Teacher Curriculum Encounter: Freeing Teachers from the Tyrany of Texts* (The State University of New York Press 1990), *Learning from Experience: Memory and the Teacher's Account of Teaching* (The State University of New York Press, 1995), 'The quest for Utopia: Social ideologies and the curriculum' *American Journal of Education* (1997) **105**, 4, 437–445, and as coeditor with Sally Brown and Robert Moon, *The International Encyclopedic Dictionary of Education* (Routledge – forthcoming).

Sharon Conley received her PhD from the University of Michigan. She is a professor in the Educational Leadership and Organizations program in the Department of Education at the University of California, Santa Barbara. Her writing and research interests are in the general areas of organizational behavior in education and the managerial work environments of teachers. She is the author of numerous articles on teacher participation in decision making, teacher work conditions, teacher evaluation, and teacher compensation. Her recent articles include 'What matters to whom: Predictors of teacher satisfaction in a career development plan' (with Eugenia Bas Isaac and Jody Brandon) published in *Journal of Personnel Evaluation in Education* in 1998 and 'Teacher compensation and career development,' (with Allan Odden) published in *Educational Evaluation and Policy Analysis* in 1995.

Bert P.M. Creemers is professor of Education and director of GION, the Groningen Institute for Educational Research of the University of Groningen in the Netherlands. His current research interests concentrate on research and evaluation of educational effectiveness and improvement. His recent publications are about effective teaching practices and the cost-effectiveness of improvement efforts in schools. He is also involved in internationally comparative research projects in the field of educational effectiveness.

John A. Feldman is the director of Curriculum and Instruction for the Cranford, New Jersey Public Schools. As a former high school principal, he has had a long time interest in the climate of secondary schools. Dr Feldman is a graduate of Montclair State University, holds Master degrees from Syracuse and Rutgers Universities and a doctorate in educational administration from Rutgers University. The Organizational Health Inventory was developed as part of his doctoral thesis.

Barry J. Fraser is professor and director of the Science and Mathematics Education Centre at Curtin University of Technology in Perth, Australia. He is co-editor of the 72-chapter *International Handbook of Science Education* published by Kluwer in 1998, and editor-in-chief of the new Kluwer journal *Learning Environments Research: An International Journal.* He is a fellow of the American Association for the Advancement of Science, International Academy of Education, Academy of the Social Sciences in Australia, and Australian College of Education.

H. Jerome Freiberg is a John and Rebecca Moores University Scholar, Professor of Education in the College of Education, at the University of Houston, editor of the *Journal of Classroom Interaction* and international director and founder of the Consistency Management & Cooperative Discipline Program. Dr. Freiberg has received the University of Houston's Teaching Excellence Award, the College of Education Award for Teaching Excellence and the College of Education Senior Research Excellence Award. Two recent books include, *Universal Teaching Strategies* (1996) 2nd edition with Amy Driscoll and the revised 3rd edition of *Freedom to Learn* (1994), by the psychologist Carl Rogers. Forthcoming books include: *Beyond Behaviorism: Changing the Classroom Management Paradigm*, Needham Heights: Allyn & Bacon; and *Perceiving Behaving, Becoming: Lessons Learned*, Association of Supervision and Curriculum Development.

Archie George is currently director of Program Review and Assessment at the University of Idaho in Moscow, Idaho. Prior to assuming this position, he was assistant director of Institutional Research, also at the University of Idaho. A native Idahoan, Dr. George received a Bachelor's degree from Gonzaga University in Spokane, Washington, and a PhD from the University of Texas at Austin. Current research interests include studying the relationships between program implementation and student learning, organizational change, and higher education enrollment modeling.

Gene Hall is a professor of educational leadership at the University of Northern Colorado. He received his PhD in science education, from Syracuse University in 1968. From 1968 to 1986 he was a research program director and ultimately director, of the national Research & Development Center for Teacher Education, at The University of Texas at Austin. From 1986 to 1988 he was a professor of educational leadership at the University of Florida. He moved to the University of Northern Colorado in 1988, where he served as the dean of the College of

Education for five years. Throughout his career, his research and consulting has centered around various aspects and elements of the change process in organizational settings. He has been the lead architect of the Concerns Based Adoption Model (CBAM), which places heavy emphasis on understanding the personal side of the change process.

Wayne K. Hoy is the Novice Fawcett Chair in Educational Administration at The Ohio State University. He received his doctorate from The Pennsylvania State University in 1965. His primary research interests are theory and research in administration, the sociology of organizations, and the social psychology of administration. Professor Hoy has written more than a hundred articles, books, chapters, and papers. His most recent books are *Administrators Solving the Problems of Practice* (Allyn & Bacon, 1995) with C.J. Tarter; *Educational Administration: Theory, Research, and Practice* (McGraw-Hill, 1996) with Cecil Miskel; and *Quality Middle Schools: Open and Healthy* (Corwin Press, 1998) with Dennis Sabo.

Haggai Kupermintz is a lecturer and project director at the Stanford University School of Education. His interests are educational and psychological measurement. social science research methodology, and the structure of cognitive abilities. His research integrates diverse methodologies and attempts to establish links between psychometric models and cognitive processes in performance. Recent publications include 'The Bell Curve: Corrected for skew', *Education Policy Analysis Archives*, (1996) **4**(20), [Online: http://olam.ed.asu.edu/epaa/v4n20.html], and with R.E. Snow 'Enhancing the validity and usefulness of large-scale educational assessments: III. NELS:88 mathematics achievement to twelfth grade'. *American Educational Research Journal*, **34**, 124–150.

James Meza, Jr. is professor and chair of the Department of Educational Leadership, Counseling, and Foundations at the University of New Orleans. He is also director of the University of New Orleans Center for the Accelerated Schools Project. Dr. Meza's research interests are in the areas of school restructuring and school improvement. He is the former executive director of the Louisiana State Board of Elementary and Secondary Education and chairperson of the Academic and Faculty Affairs Committee of the Southern University System Board of Supervisors. His current publications during 1997 include 'Middle Level Practices', *NASSP Bulletin*, **82**, 99–103; 'Changing roles: Coaching models for restructuring schools', *NASSP Bulletin*, **81**, 80–90; and 'The accelerated schools movement: Expansion and support through accelerated schools centers', *National Forum of Teacher Education Journal*, **7**, (1), 3–13.

Donna E. Muncey is a cultural anthropologist and a research faculty member at St. Mary's College in Maryland. She has studied school reform as social change in the United States, Spain, and Costa Rica. Her other research interests include social differentiation, social organization, and cultural continuity and change. She is the co-author of *Reform and Resistance in Schools and Classrooms. An Ethnographic View of the Coalition of Essential Schools* (Yale University Press, 1996). More recently, she and Sharon Conley have prepared two articles on aspects of teaming and school reform (both are forthcoming, one in the *Journal of Personnel Evaluation in Education* and the other in *Theory Into Practice*) and she is the co-author (with Joyce Payne and Noel S. White) of 'Making curriculum and instructional reform happen: A case study' published in the *Peabody Journal of Education* **74**(1), 1999.

Gerry J. Reezigt is a researcher at GION, the Groningen Institute for Educational Research of the University of Groningen in the Netherlands. Her research activities concentrate on adaptive instruction in elementary schools and its effects on student outcomes, the effectiveness of grade retention, models for effective early childhood education and their effects on school careers of disadvantaged children, and the effectiveness of new models of teaching.

Kathryn S. Sanchez is the assistant superintendent for Research and Accountability in the Houston Independent School District. She received her doctorate in Educational Administration in Higher Education from the University of Houston. Dr. Sanchez recently co-authored the article, 'Community involvement jump-starts a districtwide character education program,' in the *Journal of Staff Development*, and 'Beating the odds: A support program for at-risk students,' in *ERS Spectrum*. Her research interests include program evaluation, school administration, and district-level accountability.

Shifra Schonmann is a senior lecturer at the University of Haifa, Faculty of Education. She is the head of the development and administration of Educational Systems and directs the Laboratory for Research in Theatre/Drama Education. The continuing focus of her work and research is on theatre/drama education, curriculum planning, and teacher training. She has published numerous articles on these issues, as well as the book *Theatre of the Classroom*. She formerly served as chief supervisor of Theatre Education in Israel and as co-writer of several curricula. She acts as chairperson for the National Committee for Youth and Children's theatre, and is currently engaged in extensive research in theatre education, children's theatre festivals and workshops on war and peace, the Bible as theatrical text, and health education as theatre.

T.A. Stein is assistant professor in the Center for Educational Studies at the Plattsburgh campus of the State University of New York. He currently teaches graduate courses in research design and methodology, curriculum theory, and educational pscyhology. In the past he was responsible for teaching an undergraduate, school-based curriculum and instruction course in the elementary teacher education program. He has also directed a federally funded grant project, 'Building Educational Communities' which provided 55 teachers across three rural counties in upstate New York with the training and support needed to create interdisciplinary curricula that integrated telecommunications technology, and which in many instances, involved international connections among teachers and students. His research interests revolve around two main areas: (1) examining the connections of democratic education to political theories of democracy and psychological theories of moral development, and (2) examining the effects of the Consistency Management and Cooperative Discipline Program on student academic achievement and school climate with co-authored publications in the second area.

Carla J. Stevens is the manager of Assessment and Accountability in the Houston Independent School District's Department of Research and Accountability. Ms. Stevens' publications include two articles on alternative certification programs for teachers published in *Education and Urban Society*, and two articles regarding the misuses of program evaluation in public education published in *New Directions for Program Evaluation*. Her research interests include evaluation of programs for at-risk youth, assessment of student progress, and accountability issues.

Sam Stringfield is a principal research scientist at the Johns Hopkins University Center for Social Organization of Schools (CSOS). He serves as co-director of the Systemic and Policy Studies section of the Center for Research on Education of Students Placed At Risk (CRESPAR). Stringfield is also co-director of the Program on Integrated Reform at the University of California at Santa Cruz Center for Research on Education, Diversity and Excellence (CREDE). He is a founding co-editor of the *Journal of Education for Students Placed At Risk (JESPAR)*. Stringfield has authored over 80 articles, chapters, and books. His two most recent projects concern designs for improving programs within schools (*The Special Strategies Studies*, Stringfield et al., 1997) and for improving whole schools (*Bold Plans for School Restructuring: The New American Schools Designs*, Stringfield, Ross, & Smith, 1996). Prior to coming to Johns Hopkins, Stringfield worked as a teacher, a program evaluator, a Tulane University faculty member, and as coordinator of the Denver office of Northwest Regional Educational Laboratory. As a Kellogg Fellow, Stringfield studied the politics and economics of school improvement in the US, Asia, Africa, and Europe. Stringfield has served as the chairman of the School Effectiveness and Improvement special interest group and is currently on the annual meeting committee of the American Educational Research Association. He was 1997 program chair and 1999 program co-chair of the International Congress for School Effectiveness and Improvement (ICSEI).

Charles Teddlie is professor of Educational Research Methodology at Louisiana State University. He received his PhD in social psychology from the University of North Carolina, Chapel Hill in 1979 and thereafter served on the faculties of the University of New Orleans, the University of Newcastle-upon-Tyne (U.K.), and LSU. He also served as assistant superintendent for Research and Development at the Louisiana Department of Education. He has published more than 70 chapters and articles and is the co-author or co-editor of six books, including *Schools Make a Difference: Lessons Learned From a 10-year Study of School Effects* (1993),

Forty Years After the Brown Decision: Social and Cultural Implications of School Desegregation (1997), and *The International Handbook of School Effectiveness Research* (in press). He has lectured on school effectiveness research and educational research methodology in the United Kingdom, the Republic of Ireland, the Netherlands, Norway, Russia, the Ukraine, and Belarus.

Index